A BIOGRAPHY OF PAULINE JOHNSON

BETTY KELLER

DOUGLAS & McINTYRE
Vancouver / Toronto

Douglas & McIntyre
1615 Venables Street
Vancouver, British Columbia

Canadian Cataloguing in Publication Data

Keller, Betty.
    Pauline, a biography of Pauline Johnson

    Bibliography: p.
    ISBN 0-88894-322-9

    1. Johnson, E. Pauline (Emily Pauline),
1862-1913 - Biography. 2. Poets, Canadian
(English) - 19th century - Biography.
    I. Title.
PS8469.0392Z73   C811'.4   C81-091266-X
PR9199.3.J64Z73

Jacket design by Nancy Legue

Printed and bound in Canada by John Deyell Company

Acknowledgements

During the five-year period in which I researched and prepared this manuscript, a great many people came to my rescue with their expertise, their suggestions and their knowledge. To them all I am sincerely grateful. Among them were:

Dr. Marlene Hunter of West Vancouver; Lilia D'Acres of Lions' Bay; Judith Robinson of London, England; Florence Pratt of North Vancouver; Irene Burkholder of Burnaby; Kitty Maracle of North Vancouver; Tom Shorthouse of Vancouver; Eric Makovski of Victoria; Hilda Keenleyside of London, Ontario, and the Tony Arkells of Vancouver;

David Mattison of the Sound and Moving Images Division of the British Columbia Archives; Linda Eley of the Brantford Public Library; Charlotte Stewart, Director of Research Collections at Mills Memorial Library, McMaster University; Suzanne Dodson and the staff of the Government Publications and Microfilms Division, University of British Columbia Library; Ann Yandel, Head of Special Collections, U.B.C. Library; Anne McDermaid, Archivist of the Douglas Library, Queen's University; Edith G. Firth, Head of the Canadian History Department, Metropolitan Toronto Library; Wilbur N. Lepp, Local History Librarian, Saskatoon Public Library; Katherine Greenfield, Head of Special Collections, Hamilton Public Library; Marie Pook, Regional Collections, the D. B. Weldon Library, University of Western Ontario; Elizabeth Spicer, London Public Library;

Anthony J. Kostreba, Head of Periodicals, Library of Congress;

Mary E. Cowles, Specials Collections Librarian, Oberlin (Ohio) College Library; Lee Ash, Consultant to the American Museum of Natural History; Mary Webb, Kewanee (Illinois) Public Library, and the staff of the Newspapers Division of The British Library, London;

William R. Robbins, Director of the Brant County Museum, Katherine Bridge and Bryan Young of the British Columbia Archives; Trevor J. D. Powell of the Saskatchewan Archives Board; Barry Hyman of the Provincial Archives of Manitoba; Phyllis Blakely of the Public Archives of Nova Scotia; Marianne MacKenzie of the Peterborough Centennial Museum; the staff of the City of Vancouver Archives; Catherine Hennessey of the Prince Edward Island Heritage Foundation; Teri Rohlwing of the David C. Cook Publishing Company, and John Ryder of the Bodley Head.

I want to thank my sons, Christopher and Perry, for the many times they assisted uncomplainingly with research. And finally, I would like Cherie Smith to know how much I have valued her encouragement and her prodding since this project first began.

Contents

Introduction

This is the story of an extraordinarily successful platform recitalist and comedienne who was queen of Canada's entertainment circuit for a decade and a half, a woman who had them rolling in the aisles in High River, Alberta, and weeping in the salons of Hanover Square, London. Sometimes she was funny, sometimes she was dramatic, and there were times when she made her audience's hair stand on end; yet she was always elegant, and could charm the most unruly backwoods audience into adoring submission. And every poem and monologue and playlet that she ever performed came from her own pen.

This was Emily Pauline Johnson, or Tekahionwake, the Mohawk Princess, as she was billed on the recital circuit, the woman who is known today only as that Indian poetess who wrote "The Song My Paddle Sings." Ironically, she became a recitalist to earn the money to publish her first book of poems, and the recital platform became her home for the next sixteen years. She could not forsake it because her recitals popularized her poetry, but she always considered herself a poet.

After her death in 1913 her poems slipped from popularity, then temporarily regained some of their former status during the 1920s when a wave of reverence for nationalistic symbols swept Canada. New editions of her collected works were published and her lyrics appeared in anthologies and school texts. In 1931, before this new popularity began to wane, Mrs. W. Garland (Ann) Foster prepared a biography which she called *The Mohawk Princess: Being Some Account of the Life of Teka-hion-wake (E. Pauline Johnson)*. It was an interesting choice for a title because it listed three falsehoods about the lady before the reader got past the cover of the book. Tekahion-wake was a borrowed name, the lady was less than half Mohawk, and she was not a princess. However, the author was not entirely responsible for these misrepresentations since her primary sources for the book were Pauline's last partner-manager, J. Walter McRaye, and her sister Eva, both of whom had a stake in maintaining the prevailing public image of the dead poetess-entertainer. Eva, who had burned all Pauline's personal papers to keep the image intact, told the biographer only those stories that showed Pauline in a complimentary light; McRaye told outright lies.

Mrs. Foster's biography was the kind of fairy tale that readers of the Depression years needed, and Pauline's romantic image was soon firmly established in Canadian hearts even as the first harsh criticisms of her poetry were spreading over the pages of the country's literary journals. Unfortunately, for the next forty years, though her poems had vanished from school anthologies and Canadian literature surveys, biographers in search of "Canadian Women of Note" regurgitated the facts of her life as presented by Mrs. Foster.

But Emily Pauline Johnson was not the saccharine and virtuous Indian maiden poetess that Mrs. Foster's book depicts. She was an aggressive, manipulative, talented, and utterly charming part-Mohawk woman who travelled from town to town entertaining, proclaiming her Indian-ness, and drumming up sales for her books of poems and stories. It was not the life she had been reared to expect. She had been waiting for marriage to some genteel Ontario gentleman, but when none had proposed by the time she reached her thirtieth birthday, she launched the career that brought her fame.

Although she suffered from debilitating streptococcal diseases all her life, it was breast cancer that claimed her when she was only fifty-one. By that time she had become completely estranged from her family and had developed such an aversion to her only sister that she tried to prevent her sitting by her deathbed. Yet Pauline Johnson had so thoroughly captured the hearts of her public that the city of Vancouver gave her a civic funeral. Thousands wept as her funeral cortège passed by.

Only a woman of enormous optimism, vitality and magnetism could have carved out the career she did, withstood the difficult travelling conditions, drawn enthusiastic audiences from coast to coast, and kept them coming to hear her year after year when all she had to offer was a repetition of the same stories and poems she had given them before. That they continued to come for sixteen years was less a tribute to her poetic genius than an appreciation of her talents as one of the turn of the century's finest entertainers.

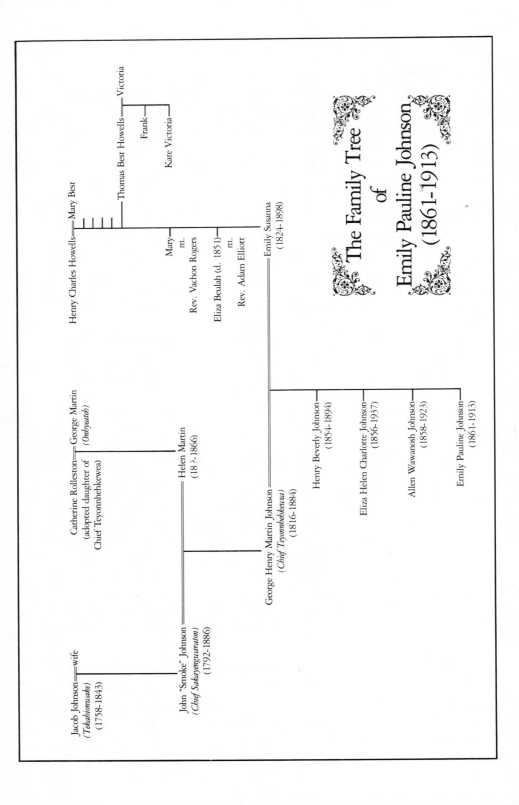

The Family Tree
of
Emily Pauline Johnson
(1861-1913)

Jacob Johnson ══ wife
(*Tekahionwake*)
(1758-1843)

Henry Charles Howells ══ Mary Best

Catherine Rolleston ══ George Martin
(adopted daughter of   (*Onwyateh*)
Chief Teyonnhehkewea)

Thomas Best Howells ══ Victoria

Frank

Kate Victoria

Mary
m.
Rev. Vachon Rogers

Eliza Beulah (d. 1851)
m.
Rev. Adam Elliott

John "Smoke" Johnson
(*Chief Sakayenguaraton*)
(1792-1886)

Helen Martin
(18 ?-1866)

George Henry Martin Johnson ══ Emily Susanna
(*Chief Teyonnhehkewea*)   (1824-1898)
(1816-1884)

Henry Beverly Johnson
(1854-1894)

Eliza Helen Charlotte Johnson
(1856-1937)

Allen Wawanosh Johnson
(1858-1923)

Emily Pauline Johnson
(1861-1913)

Chapter One

Heritage

BY CANADIAN LAW Pauline Johnson was an Indian. But her legal status was far less decisive in shaping her life and her career than her conviction that she was an Indian. Though there was more white than Indian blood flowing in her veins, romantically she looked to the past of her father's people for inspiration and found it in their legendary battles, their heroic deeds, and their great council fires. She ridiculed those who thought they saw the influence of her English forebears in her writing and in her person. She wrote:

> There are those who think they pay me a compliment in saying that I am just like a white woman. My aim, my joy, my pride is to sing the glories of my own people. Ours was the race that gave the world its measure of heroism, its standard of physical prowess. Ours was the race that taught the world that avarice veiled by any name is crime. Ours were the people of the blue air and the green woods, and ours the faith that taught men to live without greed and die without fear. Ours were the fighting men that, man to man—yes, one to three—could meet and win against the world. But for our few numbers, our simple faith that others were as true as we to keep their honour bright and hold as bond inviolate their plighted word, we should have owned America to-day.[1]

The Indian nation from which she claimed descent was the Mohawk nation, one of the six members of the Iroquois Confederacy which had been organized by Hiawatha (Taoungwatha), a man renowned not for his exploits in battle but for his wisdom and his abilities as a statesman. Legend says that he lived in the fifteenth century when the Iroquois people warred on one another and on the neighbouring Hurons so constantly that none of them prospered. Sometimes when two of these nations had recognized a common cause they formed alliances, but these disintegrated as soon as the danger had passed. Battle was their only guarantee of independence.

Hiawatha, however, proposed a federation where each nation would retain its own council to manage its local affairs, while matters common to all would be controlled by a permanent federal council or senate. The federation would be open to all Indian nations so that as it grew there would be fewer and fewer excuses for war.

Hiawatha first took his dream to his own people, the Onondagas, but it was opposed by their chief Atotarho. Chief Dekanawidah of the Mohawk people, however, saw the wisdom in this confederation and encouraged his people to become the first member-nation. Next to join were the Oneida and Cayuga nations. Then envoys from these three nations persuaded Atotarho to allow the Onondagas to join by promising that theirs would be the leading nation in the Confederacy, their chief town would be the administrative capital, and their senators would number fourteen compared with ten for each of the other nations. They would also guard the Confederacy's wampum belts, the long bands woven from strings of wampum beads in patterns that recorded the history of the tribes. The Onondagas then persuaded the two-branched Seneca nation to be the fifth member. The Tuscaroras became the sixth member in 1712, and after that time the federation was also known as the Six Nations Confederacy.

The chiefs who sat as senators were called Pine Tree Chiefs in honour of the emblem of the Confederacy. When one died, a member of the same family succeeded him. Inheritance followed the female line; therefore, the successor might be any male descendant of the late chief's mother or grandmother—that is, his brother, his cousin, or his nephew—but never his son. The family council chose this successor, the chief matron being given the deciding vote.

This decision was then sent to the federal Senate for ratification, and the new chief inherited the name of his predecessor,[2] though he still kept his personal names.

The Mohawk nation had been settled in the valley that bears its name for several centuries when the first white men came there to farm in the early seventeenth century. The contact was peaceful, for though the Iroquois had been great warriors, they were now primarily hunters and farmers. They saw little threat in the white man's encroachments, for there seemed to be plenty of land for all. They were eager to learn better farming methods from their new neighbours, and the white men were happy to receive the Indians' advice about the land.

The Iroquois people had been idol-worshippers until this time, but they were persuaded to accept Christianity by the missionaries of the New England Society. The Mohawk nation was almost wholly converted and when their new chapel was built at the beginning of the eighteenth century, they were rewarded by the gift of a silver communion service from Queen Anne.

The tide of white settlement into the Mohawk Valley eventually brought a young Irishman whose name would in time be handed down to Pauline. William Johnson came to the new world as an apprentice to his wealthy landholding uncle but soon acquired a vast estate of his own on the northern bank of the river. He became deeply involved in the Mohawks' affairs, even partially adopting their life style, and they in turn honoured him with a chieftaincy and the title Warraghiyagey which meant "the man in charge of affairs." After his first wife died, he married a Mohawk girl, Molly Brant, and assumed responsibility for the education of her brother, the future chief Joseph Brant or Thayendanegea, who was then in his early teens.

William Johnson became Sir William when he led the Mohawk Valley militia to a tidy victory over the French in one of the skirmishes of the continuing border war. As further proof of his government's gratitude, in 1755 he was appointed superintendent of the Six Nations Iroquois. The Indians welcomed this appointment; they trusted him completely and invited him to all their celebrations and ceremonies. At the settlement of Niagara, he attended a mass baptismal rite where a young boy with the Indian name of Tekahionwake or Double Wampum was among the children being baptized. The boy's parents had chosen the Christian name Jacob for him, but the baptism was being held up because they could not settle on a surname. Johnson stepped forward and volunteered his own name, and the child was baptized Jacob Johnson, the first member of a new family line. The boy would become Pauline's great-grandfather.

The Mohawks' complete trust in the judgement of William Johnson, however, ultimately led to the disintegration of the Six Nations Confederacy because it drew them into an alliance with the British. And they quickly learned that if they were for the British, they had to be against Britain's enemies: first the French and then, after the Boston Tea Party, the Americans. Although officially neutral, the Iroquois actually stood side by side with the British during the fighting. Within the Mohawk Valley, the settlers took the Indians' participation in the war as a signal to drive them out of their traditional lands, and the Mohawks retaliated with raids on farms and townsites. In the course of one of these raids on a Dutch settlement near Philadelphia, they took captive a teen-aged girl named Catherine Rolleston. She was to become Pauline's great-grandmother.

Taken to a Mohawk village, Catherine Rolleston was adopted into the family of Chief Teyonnhehkewea or Double Life, who was the official custodian of the Queen Anne communion service. When she arrived at marriageable age, she was engaged to a young Mohawk named George Martin, or Onhyeateh. This engagement was arranged in the usual manner of the Mohawks by the parents of the bride and the groom, but it was remarkable in one respect: the groom—perhaps at the bride's insistence—journeyed all the way to New York City to buy a ring, a narrow gold band with a square translucent stone, which would in time become a family heirloom.

When the Americans won their independence in 1782, the Iroquois people discovered they had lost their ancient lands. The British, however, eager to keep them as allies, offered as compensation a strip of land twelve miles wide extending from the source to the mouth of the Grand River, comprising nearly 570,000 acres,[3] and a second tract on the Bay of Quinte. This would have been ample for all the Iroquois people, but in the years of delay between the end of hostilities and the granting of the land, many of them made their peace with the new American government and elected to stay in their old homeland. In the end, only sixteen hundred Indians came to the Grand River Reserve and they were adequately settled in a small corner of it. Joseph Brant, now the recognized leader of the immigrants, then transferred large tracts of land to homeless white farmers who had fought beside him against the Americans. In this way he raised funds for his people and assured them of friendly white neighbours. Throughout the next century, the reserve lands dwindled still more as the Six Nations gave land back to the government in exchange for funds to be held in trust and paid annually to the members of the Six Nations. In 1829, for example, one square mile was ceded as a site for the town of Brantford, and in 1853 all of the Indians moved to the south side of the river to allow more white settlement on the north side.

Among the 450 Mohawks who came to the Grand River settlement[4] were George and Catherine Rolleston Martin and their young family. Like other Mohawk women, Catherine marched along the trail with all her household possessions on her back and her children at her heels, since by Iroquois law the wife owned all the family goods inside the house and the husband owned everything outside it. By the same laws, the children became members of their mother's clan. In Catherine's bundle was a unique possession. As the adoptive daughter of Teyonnhehkewea, she had been entrusted with the safety of the Queen Anne communion service. Her task was not an easy one. The American soldiers escorting the Indians to the border were neither remarkably honest nor remarkably friendly; once when she lagged behind, a soldier prodded her bundle with his bayonet, scratching one of the communion pieces. When the Indians arrived in Canada, the communion service was split between those going to the Bay of Quinte and those who were settling on the Grand River. The scratched piece went to the Bay of Quinte.

Jacob Johnson was another of those who came to the Grand River. Now grown to manhood, he married, and on 14 December 1792 he became the father of a boy whom he named John after the only son of his own namesake, Sir William Johnson. As a boy, the Mohawk John Johnson followed Joseph Brant into battle, and at twenty took his place beside the British troops in the War of 1812. He took part in the battles of Queenston Heights, Stoney Creek and Lundy's Lane, and gained a reputation as a leader when under cover of night he and some companions set fire to the city of Buffalo. The British were impressed with him as a fearless warrior, but among his own people he was far better known as an orator. He loved the music and drama of words, and could hold his listeners spellbound with his eloquent logic and his mellifluous voice.

The British were anxious to have an intermediary within the Iroquois Senate and recognized in Johnson the ideal candidate. They forced the Senate to award him a chieftaincy, though by Iroquois law he was not eligible since he was not descended from one of the families that held a chieftaincy. The young man was given the new post of speaker of the Senate and the title Sakayengwaraton. Since this word can be roughly translated as "Smoke," he became known as John Smoke Johnson, but the title really meant "the haze that rises from the ground on an autumn morning and vanishes as the day advances." The name could not be inherited by his descendants, however, since it was not one of the names in the list of senators in the first Senate.

Johnson was not of a "royal" family, but his wife was. He had married Helen Martin, the eldest daughter of Catherine Martin. Although her mother was a white woman, Helen Martin spoke not a word of English and even denied her white ancestry.

Pauline's father, George Henry Martin Johnson, was the second of the five children of John Smoke Johnson and Helen Martin Johnson.[5] Born on 7 October 1816, he grew up like all the boys on the reserve to be an expert hunter and canoeist, but he was never interested in physical pursuits for their own sake. He was a romantic who thrived on adventure and pageantry, high-flown words, heroic deeds, lavish ceremonies, and the symbols of power and importance. The world beyond the reserve fascinated him and he pressed his father for stories of moonlit forays behind the American lines. From his grandfather Jacob Johnson, he begged for stories of the War of Independence and the Napoleonic Wars. He longed to be "a man in charge of affairs" like his forebear, Sir William Johnson.

George Johnson had an excellent ear for languages, and even as a child became fluent in the languages of the neighbouring tribes, the Onondagas and the Oneidas. His father taught him to speak English, but since John Smoke Johnson could neither read nor write the language, he sent his son to school in the white village of Brantford. George's schooling came to an end when the Rebellion of 1837 broke out. Looking for adventure, he rode off to Kingston to serve as a despatch rider under Sir Alan McNab.

He served honourably though not heroically and returned to the reserve where he caught the eye of a newly arrived missionary. The Reverend Adam Elliott, who was looking for an interpreter, took young George to live in the Tuscarora parsonage. George's job was to translate Elliott's sermons into the Indian languages and serve as his interpreter when he travelled on the reserve. It was the perfect appointment for the young man because within the church he found the drama and ceremony he craved, and his duties allowed him to feel like "a man in charge of affairs."

In his new position, George became very serious and rather self-important. There were still many pagans among the Indians who had settled on the banks of the Grand, and he decided it was his duty to see that they were Christianized. In one village, a group of Delaware Indians who had joined the Iroquois nations in their flight north were rumoured to be worshipping a wooden idol. Johnson, having investigated and found the story true, burst into the Delawares' meeting place and smashed the idol with an axe. The Delawares were so stunned by this self-appointed avenger that they let him go unharmed with their idol's head tucked under his arm.[6]

It was in the Elliott household that George Johnson met Emily Howells, who would become his wife and the mother of Pauline. The Reverend Elliott's wife was the former Eliza Howells from Bristol, England. She and Emily were two of the eight children of a Quaker father, who had run a divinity school, and an Anglican mother. Although forced out of the Society of Friends for marrying a non-Quaker, Howells had continued to follow the strict beliefs of the Quakers and had raised his children in that faith.

When his wife died, he remarried and in 1832 took his entire family to America, settling in Putnam, Ohio. There he worked for the emancipation of the slaves. His new wife cared little for her stepchildren, regarding them only as servants for her own growing brood. One by one they escaped from the family home to make their way elsewhere. The last member of her father's first family, Emily Susanna Howells became her stepmother's workhorse and the nursemaid to her stepsisters and brothers.

As a small child, Emily had been "high-tempered," but as a good Quaker she had completely suppressed this tendency. However, by the time she reached adulthood she was prone to alternating depressions and extreme elation,[7] the classic symptoms of a submanic-depressive personality. In her periods of depression she searched for the defects that lurked beneath the surface of her character and conducted campaigns to root them out. At the same time, she was hypersensitive to the criticism of others, always afraid that her faults could be seen by all, though in fact to others she appeared to be a perfectly self-possessed young woman with exquisite manners. She achieved this façade through exceptional self-control.

Emily seems to have felt responsible for her mother's death in some way, probably because she was sent off to boarding school almost immediately after her mother died, and was taken directly from there to the ship bound for America, without seeing her home again or her mother's grave. When she was nine years of age, she tore the frontispiece from a book and kept it as a reminder of her guilt. It was a picture of a girl on her knees beside a marble tomb with a caption reading, "Oh, if she'd but come again, I think I'd vex her so no more!" On the reverse, Emily had written, "Ah, my dear mother, I was too young to vex you much, only four years old when you died."[8] Until the day she died, she kept this page in her handkerchief drawer as if the recorded facts of her mother's death would exonerate her.

Emily's belief in her own guilt was constantly confirmed during her terrible bouts of depression and by her day-to-day existence as a servant in her stepmother's house, a treatment which she saw as punishment for her sins. To counteract the guilt, she became fanatically religious, though this obsession gradually turned into a compulsion for cleanliness and order, not just in physical terms but in the mind and the soul as well. Her goal was to become, as she called it, "aristocratic,"[9] which to her meant avoiding all unclean thoughts such as anger, deceit, envy and, most importantly, any thoughts about sex. She did not even allow herself to think about marriage because it might lead to thoughts of sex.

When Emily was twenty-one, her sister Eliza Elliott invited her to live with her and her family in the Tuscarora parsonage. Since Eliza had four children, Emily's position there would be roughly the same as it had been in her stepmother's home, but she was quick to accept the offer. She knew she could count on Eliza to treat her as an aristocrat. At the parsonage she met the twenty-nine-year-old George Johnson and warmed to him immediately. In spite of his years in the white world, George was strangely innocent where white women were concerned and he was quite willing to interpret Emily's aloofness exactly as she wished it to be interpreted. From the first, he regarded her as a chaste maiden in a high tower and himself as a gallant knight worshipping from afar.

Not long after Emily's arrival, George fell ill with typhoid fever. His death would have been an inestimable loss to the Reverend Elliott, not only because of his abilities an an interpreter and assistant but also because of the warm friendship existing between the two, and Elliott offered Emily a new silk gown if she would nurse him back to health. She refused the offer of the gown but agreed to nurse the patient. In the course of George's convalescence, the two fell in love and decided to marry.

The Elliotts were in favour of the marriage, but Helen Johnson was adamantly opposed. She had repudiated her own white blood and she had no intention of admitting another white strain into the family, especially in the form of this chilly young woman. In the manner of her people, therefore, she set about arranging a marriage with the parents of a Mohawk girl. George, caught between his duty to his mother and his promise to Emily, compromised by refusing the Indian girl and postponing his marriage to Emily. They would wait for his mother's approval; but the years went by without diminishing her opposition. George carried out his courtship with meticulous propriety, writing letters to Emily daily and hiding them coyly in a hollow tree nearby. Emily hid her replies in the same place, even though they both still lived under the same parsonage roof. Not one improper word or gesture ever passed between them. Kissing was out of the question.

George Johnson's choice of a white woman as his bride should not have surprised his family. He had lived in the white world for nearly twenty years, had adopted white men's clothes and with them white men's values. In selecting Emily he was simply patterning his future life on that of his friend and mentor, the Reverend Elliott. Emily represented the perfect wife as far as Victorian white society was concerned: she was strong-willed and morally upright, but she was also dutiful and subservient to her menfolk. She was artistically accomplished and thoroughly versed in all the social graces, but she had also been trained in household management and the care of children. And to cap it all, she was very pretty.

Emily accepted George because he was almost everything that her Christian middle-class background had led her to expect in a husband: he was gallant, handsome, deeply religious, assertive, intelligent and socially at ease. And he was capable of providing a respectable home and income for his wife and family. In fact, Emily could find nothing wrong with George except his worship of Napoleon. After he had learned to read English, George pored over everything that had ever been written about this man, small in stature but possessing the power to turn Europe upside down. And even though France was the enemy of the British government, George had developed an almost comic adulation of the little corporal. He collected pictures and books about him, wore similar items of dress, and even imitated his mannerisms. Emily regarded this worship of "old Boney" with gentle amusement; it was a small fault in such an exemplary man. She herself preferred Lord Nelson.

Emily's only real problem in marrying George was his race. Within her social class, and to a lesser extent in the lower classes of society as well, Indians were considered unacceptable as mates. Hudson's Bay factors and fur traders sometimes married Indian women, but they were far from civilization, and society made allowances for men in these circumstances. But women in upper middle-class Canada never married natives; it simply was not done. For a woman who was as highly susceptible to criticism and social censure as Emily was, ignoring the inevitable stigma took courage. Two factors probably influenced her decision. First, as a Quaker Emily could not allow herself to discriminate against a member of another race; to have rejected George's suit would have amounted to a lack of Christian charity. Her father had constantly admonished her to pity and pray for the Negroes and the poor Indians, and her son Allen would later tease her that she "had pitied one poor Indian so much that she had married him."[10] Her Christian precepts, therefore, demanded that she treat George's proposal as she would treat that of any other man.

The second factor influencing her acceptance was Helen Johnson's opposition, since it implied that Emily Howells was not good enough for the Mohawks; and though Emily found many faults in herself and suffered anxiety and remorse for her shortcomings, she knew her pedigree was not to be disdained. Within her small frame there was an iron will and so she set herself to outlast Helen Johnson.

In the meantime, the chieftaincy, which carried the title of

Teyonnhehkewea, became vacant. It had been held by Helen Johnson's brother Henry Martin, and Helen as chief matron of her family now had the deciding vote in the selection of her brother's successor. She chose her second son, George. The nomination was ratified by the Senate and George was installed in office, but almost immediately an objection arose because several years earlier George had been appointed to the post of interpreter for the Canadian government. The job had quickly developed into something akin to chief executive officer for the government on the reserve. He was, in fact, often referred to as the "Warden" of the reserve. The Iroquois Senate questioned whether it was consistent with the laws of the Confederacy that a salaried official of the Canadian government should also be a member of the Senate and find himself in a potential conflict of interest. There was no precedent to follow, but it was the majority's view that George Johnson must be disqualified. Helen Johnson was outraged. It was perfectly reasonable, she argued, to deprive a man of office for something he had done, but it was quite out of the question to do it for something that he might do in the future. She flatly refused to nominate another candidate. She knew she held the winning hand in this, for without Teyonnhehkewea, the Mohawks would lose one of their seats in the Senate. After four hundred years, it was unthinkable that this seat should be vacant. The Senate relented.

George was now entitled to don the costume of a Mohawk chief: clinging buckskin leggings and jacket, both of them fringed and embroidered with countless quills and moosehair stitchery, soft moccasins, and in his hair an eagle's plume. Though he loved the elegance of white men's clothes, the romance of a chieftain's costume was irresistible; he could no more abandon one role than the other and from this point on he would straddle both worlds, looking upon himself as a spokesman for the Mohawk people while leading a white man's life.

In 1849 Emily and George resolved to wait no longer to marry, though Helen Johnson still refused to give her blessing. But while the wedding arrangements were being made, it was discovered that Eliza Elliott had developed consumption. Emily laid her plans aside once more in order to take care of her sister and her children. Eliza died in the fall of 1850; the following year her three youngest children contracted scarlet fever and one by one they too died. Another year passed before Emily and George could begin making plans again.[11]

The marriage of Emily Susanna Howells and George Henry Martin Johnson finally took place in St. Mark's Church in Barriefield, Ontario, on 27 August 1853, but not before some unexpected last-minute opposition from Emily's relatives. After the death of Eliza and her children, Emily's presence at the parsonage was no longer necessary and she moved to Kingston to the home of her sister Mary. She had always been aware that Mary's husband, the Reverend Vachon Rogers, was opposed to interracial marriages, but she hoped to convince him of George's superlative qualities so that he would consent to perform the marriage service. However, when Rogers realized that Emily really intended to marry her Indian, he ordered her out of the house. For good measure, he told her that if she married her red man, her children would never associate with his.[12] Emily made her way to the home of a friend, Jane Harvey, who arranged the ceremony in Barriefield.

Emily wore a simple dress of grey merino and a white bonnet. George came like a peacock in a fitted suit of fashionable maroon broadcloth with a silk velvet collar, a white silk stock, white gloves and a black silk topper. It was another marvellous opportunity for a fancy costume.

The bride was now twenty-nine years old; the groom was thirty-seven. In accordance with Canadian law, by this marriage Emily became an Indian and all her children would be classified as Indians.

The wedding created a storm in Upper Canada's closely knit upper middle class, and Emily Howells became something of a freak. Curious crowds gathered outside the church as if they were waiting for a circus parade. Carriageloads followed the couple to the Toronto railway station as they began the return journey to Brantford. And newspaper announcements expressed incredulity.

Emily was ill during the five-day return journey from Barriefield, but her symptoms vanished quickly at the sight of the flowers and gifts and the crowd of well-wishers waiting at the parsonage. George had bought her a silver tea service; her brother-in-law Adam gave her initialled silver spoons, pearl-handled knives and forks, and satin for a dress; and the people of the Huron Nation brought a set of place mats made of doeskin with the tribal designs of the Six Nations worked in porcupine quills. The only disappointment was Helen Johnson's continued refusal to acknowledge her son's marriage. Not until the first grandchild was born the following year did she relent. Then she came to present Emily with a tiny moccasin which had been her own first child's baby shoe. [13]

The long years of her mother-in-law's opposition to the marriage, the Reverend Rogers's refusal to conduct the ceremony, the circus atmosphere surrounding the wedding, and the innuendos in the newspapers had all conspired to make Emily enormously sensitive about her marriage. Now, instead of looking for faults in herself, she analyzed everyone's reactions to her and her beloved George. Writing to her husband from Kingston where she was visiting friends, the Dupuys, in the winter of 1854-55, she said, "All my friends are delighted to see me. They say I look as well as ever and it is just like old times. I do not see that I am treated with the least disrespect because I am the wife of an Indian chief. . . ." [14]

In all of this, George must have suffered as much from the slurs of society as from Emily's reaction to them, but he was so devoted to her that he resolved to give her everything she would have had if she had married a white man. With his savings and the money he had earned from an investment, he bought two hundred acres close to the Tuscarora parsonage on reserve land vacated earlier that year by the Mohawks. It lay between the river and the road to Brantford, somewhat remote from the major portion of the Indian settlement. The site he chose for the house was on the edge of a low bluff so that it would overlook a large stand of black walnut trees and the river's floodlands. The largest of these trees he ordered cut and sawn into beams for the new house. However, construction progressed very slowly, and it was not ready for occupancy until after Emily had given birth to two children. Henry Beverly was born in July 1854 and his sister Helen Charlotte Eliza was born in September 1856. The boy was sometimes called Henry and sometimes called Beverly, but the girl was never called by any of her given names; instead she answered to Evelyn or more often Eva, after Harriet Beecher Stowe's heroine.

The Johnsons moved to Chiefswood, their new house, in December 1856. [15] The house that Pauline was to call home was built of three-inch-thick boards and finished on the outside in roughcast (stucco). It was square except for two entrance porches on opposite sides of the building and a summer kitchen added to a third side. On each of the two main floors there were four rooms; above them was a roomy attic with skylights. Each room had a spacious fireplace. Visitors often remarked on the twin entrances to the house, one of them facing the river and one facing the road, and it soon became accepted that this signified that both Indian and white guests were equally welcome in the Johnson house.

Across the lane, which bisected the property and provided access to the river from the main road, there was a cow barn; and opposite it, somewhat nearer the house, was a horse barn. The grounds were landscaped with shrubbery and vines and there was a well-tended vegetable garden. And in the midst of it all, a lordly peacock preened and spread his tail.

All the rooms of the Johnson house were elegantly wallpapered, and the parlour windows were curtained in deep red fabric which picked up the colour of the roses in the black velour carpet. The furniture was mostly handcrafted walnut, carved with designs which matched those on the lintels and trim of the house. The parlour was dominated by a large square rosewood piano, the focal point of the Johnsons' family life.

In this elegant house two more Johnson children were born. Allen Wawanosh arrived in 1858 and three years later, on Sunday, 10 March 1861, the youngest and most famous of the Johnsons was born. Her parents named her Emily Pauline.

Chapter Two

Chiefswood

THE YOUNGEST CHILD of George and Emily Johnson was named Emily after her mother, and Pauline in honour of the only sister of Emperor Napoleon of France, whose life was the object of George Johnson's consuming interest. He had in fact tried to name each of his children in turn for his hero, even announcing to the officiating minister at the baptism of his eldest son, Henry Beverly, that the name was to be "Napoleon Bonaparte." Luckily, his wife's signals were understood by the minister, but Johnson persisted in calling the boy "Boney" until he was well into his teens. For his eldest daughter, he had favoured Josephine in honour of the Empress but was over-ruled, and though he named Allen for a visiting Chippewa chief, he nicknamed him "Kleber" after a Napoleonic general whom he thought especially admirable. But with Pauline's christening, he felt his hero had been paid due homage at last. To make his point clearer, however, he always called her Pauline, reducing her first name to a preliminary initial. Her friends and siblings called her Paul or Polly.

She was a brown-skinned, grey-eyed baby with golden brown hair that waved loosely around her face, tightening into curls when the weather was damp. But though she was a "good" baby, her health was always more precarious than that of her older brothers and sister, and she was subject to heavy colds and bronchitis. Emily Johnson worried and fretted over the child, for she had watched her beloved sister Eliza and her niece Mary Margaret both die of consumption. The winter she turned four, Pauline had such constant earaches that the pain left her exhausted. Her father, recovering from injuries suffered early in the year, was in no mood to listen to her whining and angrily told her to be quiet. Pauline was instantly silent even though her mother rushed to her defence, saying that she was just a baby. Family legend has it that she never cried out in pain again.[1]

There is some evidence that early in her childhood she had at least one attack of erysipelas, an ailment that also afflicted her father. This is a highly contagious infection which, because of the lax hygienic precautions of those days, spread rapidly from one family member to another. Until the discovery of sulfa drugs, doctors simply sent the patient to bed in the hope that he would recover. For both Pauline and her father, the disease was to have serious consequences in later years.

Because of her frequent illnesses, Pauline spent most of her early years close to her mother's skirts and consequently tended to absorb and reflect her mother's moods. Emily was constantly examining her children for traces of her own moodiness and her own childhood bad temper and when she found them (as she did in Pauline) she attacked with determination, insisting that the children see their faults and conquer them. There must be moderation and control in all things, she told them.

As a result of Emily's campaign to perfect her children they all became hypersensitive about their failings. Emily preferred to call their anxiety "shyness" and taught them to hide it by assuming a dignity far beyond their years. At the same time, she added to their problem by passing on to them her own fear of being considered "plebeian."[2] From the time they were babies, she trained them to discourage social intimacies. Before she was three, Pauline had been taught to shake hands with men and boys; only elderly friends of her father were allowed to pick her up or kiss her. To the little boys of family friends who tried to kiss her, her mother announced, "My little girl does not care to kiss gentlemen!"[3] Although Emily smiled when she said this, the children understood that she was perfectly serious. Kissing games, even among family members, were forbidden in the Johnson household, though such games were a highlight of every party held in Upper Canada at that time.

Emily only intended to discourage her children's intimacy with the opposite sex, but she was never specific about the danger they were in because she could not bring up the subject of sex. Instead she warned them about being considered "plebeian" and they understood this to mean that they should not be intimate with *anyone* outside the family, either male or female. As a result, they appeared coldly reserved to outsiders. Their white peers called them "stuck-up"; the children of the reserve called them "proudy."[4]

By the time she was eight, Pauline had one injunction pounded into her brain: any boy who tried to kiss her was offering an insult by the freedom he was taking. About that summer, Pauline wrote:

> Some jolly schoolboys and girls from the city came to spend the holidays with their aunt, a neighbour of ours. One day, while we were all romping together, a laughing-eyed boy of nine or ten suddenly developed a teasing tendency. "I'll kiss all you girls and make you cry!" he shouted, waving his arms like a windmill, and rushing toward the biggest girl, who took to her heels, screaming with laughter and calling back: "Georgie, peorgie, pudding and pie, kiss the girls and make them cry." Of course he caught her, kissing her a half-dozen times; then he chased and captured several others, and finally made a rush for where I stood, my little back fortified against a tree trunk, my face sullen and sulky. "Run, he'll catch you!" shouted the others, but I never stirred, only stood and glowered at him, and with all the indignation my eight years could muster, I shouted at him. "Don't you dare insult me, sir!" The "sir" was added to chill him and it did. He left me alone.[5]

Control was so important to Emily Johnson that she made a point of never losing her temper with her children. Pauline remembered seeing her annoyed, sometimes irritated, but never at any time angry. Emily expected her children to obey her, but she never struck them to enforce her will or to punish them. She preferred to send the offenders to their beds without dinner. On one occasion, when Eva and Allen were to be sent to bed without a lamp as punishment, the two gathered a jarful of fireflies and, amid much giggling, smuggled it upstairs. Emily's punishments were not on the whole immediately effective, especially when the tiny Pauline stationed herself outside the bedroom door of the one being punished, visiting through the keyhole and making comforting promises that she would buy the culprit some sweets next time she went to Brantford. But in the long run, Emily's disapproval accomplished her ends; the young Johnsons grew up subdued and self-disciplined.

In later years Pauline wrote admiringly of her mother's perfect control of her emotions and the example she set for her children, but this constant repression of anger added an extra element of tension to family relationships. It was largely responsible for the later inability of the brothers and sisters to resolve their differences. None of them except Eva would admit to being angry or having a grievance. Eva, who lacked the subtlety of the others, never seemed to understand that by venting her anger she was transgressing the family law of control.

Emily demanded meticulous observance of the rules of etiquette and made a point of setting an example for her children at all times. She never appeared among her family in the morning until every detail of her appearance was correct "even to her collar, cuffs and brooch."[6] She expected her family to pay the same attention to grooming. Each afternoon before tea was served, she and her daughters changed their gowns, whether or not they had company. Etiquette and Emily's obsession with cleanliness and order required this ritual.

The young Pauline and her brothers and sister were taught always to take the slice of cake or the apple or orange nearest them on the plate. "It would have been an unforgiveable breach of etiquette for us to reach beyond the adjacent slices to secure a brown crust if we wanted it,"[7] Pauline later wrote. As an infant she was taught to use her cutlery and napkin correctly and from then on was expected to handle them as an adult would. Once when she was given a plate of bread and butter in the Elliott kitchen by Adam Elliott's second wife Charlotte, she carried the dish to the dining room, enjoying Charlotte's consternation when she said, "Mother never lets me eat in the kitchen!"

The children were admonished never to waste food. "If you want to throw your pocket money away, do so," said Emily Johnson, "even your ribbons if you would prefer to go without them; but food must never be wasted while others are hungry."[8] Throughout her life Pauline dutifully ate every scrap placed before her, though the habit sometimes created a problem during her travels when she found herself at gourmet banquets.

Emily was (to use Pauline's expression) a "teeth crank" who refused to allow her children to indulge in sweets, even limiting the

Christmas and Queen's birthday indulgence to five "sugar-sticks," one for each child and the fifth to be divided between them the following day "to ease the dissipation."[9] Saved from the candy habit, the young Pauline, when not yet ready for primary school, turned down a gift of candy in favour of a book of verses, and took pride in later years in never having spent her school pocket money on "sweets." However, when a reporter questioned her about the candy-versus-book of poetry anecdote and asked if this meant that she did not like candy, she replied that she adored it, but that she had always loved poetry more.

Emily once told Pauline that in all her married years, her husband had never uttered a word to her that could not have been said to the finest lady or gentleman. Indeed, no coarse or vulgar word was ever heard at Chiefswood. Emily made it a family rule that no topic should be brought up in private that could not be discussed with all the members of the family. Since she was arbiter of family topics, she effectively controlled private conversations as well, and the Johnson children grew up with strange gaps in their knowledge of human functions.

Emily hated idleness in herself and in her children. Although there were always servants at Chiefswood—never less than three: an Indian nursemaid, a white cook, and a stableman—she set her children daily chores to instill in them the habit of industriousness. The boys were required to bring in firewood, Eva cleaned the lamps, and Pauline swept the stairs. Forty years later Pauline wrote:

> How endless those stairs were! I can count them yet—nineteen horrors, with mahogany coloured velvet carpet, so difficult to dust, a strip of linen in the centre, so gloriously easy to slide over, and broad, polished brass rods, perfect demons for holding the "fluff" from the velvet. With my dustpan and whisk broom, I would toil half way down the endless flight, then sit amidships with woe-begone face, and wonder why Milly the Nurse, or Jane the cook, or even mother herself, could not do this labor. Then I would hear a voice calling, "Come, chicken, mama knows you have only half finished; work away like a little woman; school will begin in ten minutes." Then I would get to my stiff little legs again, and reattack those stairs that stretched down behind me with infinite length. I must admit that I have thoroughly hated dusting down stairs ever since, but I know the work

rendered me more capable in after years, more considerate of servants, for mother's excuse in making us do the work was, "It is something whereby you can help Milly and Jane."[10]

On the other hand, Eva Johnson felt that their upbringing had taught them too thoroughly to despise domestic and manual labour; she recalled that they were seldom required to do any chores.

Pauline accepted her mother's discipline easily because she was not by nature a rebellious child. She was never bad tempered even when she reflected her mother's moods of depression and restlessness, and when she did become depressed the family put it down to her delicate health or "the consumptive temperament." Pauline described it as "dreaming" or sometimes as "having grey days."

But most of the time she was merry and then the family doted on her. She became the peacemaker. Hating to see her sister and her beloved brothers quarrelling, and aware of her mother's displeasure, she would come running to interpose herself between the combatants in an effort to make peace.

She was talkative. She would follow her father, her brothers and her sister, but especially her mother, talking nonstop. She asked questions, she made up rhymes, and she philosophized. And when there was no one to talk to, she talked to herself.

She was gregarious. She loved visits from special family friends such as visiting Indian superintendent Col. Jasper T. Gilkison and his young daughter Augusta. The superintendent would laugh when she called him Mr. Kitten because she could not pronounce his name, and he would swing her onto his shoulder and carry her off for a romp in the garden. And she adored the visits of her mother's brother Thomas Best Howells and his wife and family from Paris, Ontario. For many years she was "best friends" with their daughter Kate Victoria, who was nearly her own age, and their games often included Kate's brother Frank as well.

In spite of this, life was lonely at Chiefswood for the youngest Johnson. Allen, three years older, was a robust and healthy child, off on his own adventures for the most part. The two older children were busy with their education and had little time for entertaining the baby of the family. Many of her days were spent dreaming and "making poems." Even before she could read or write her name, she sang her poems to her mother who sometimes wrote them down for her. After she had learned to write, the poems came faster. "My verses sang themselves in my head until I had to write them down," she said.[11]

She spent hours with a small black dog named Chip which her father had brought home from a Tuscarora family. She "taught" the dog English by reading her brother Allen's primers to it, and actually taught herself to read at the same time. She dressed the dog in doll's clothes and hauled it around the house in a little wagon, chattering to it incessantly.

She played in the sun for hours with a kitten called Sooty, and rode the black pony, Marengo, which her father had named after a Napoleonic victory. In summer there was croquet on the lawn with the family and friends, and "foot" ball played with the wooden head of the Delaware idol. It was not until the rough treatment caused the nose to break off that the head was finally given the status of a historical relic and displayed on a shelf in Chief Johnson's study. And sometimes up in the attic in winter, Pauline played with the bleached skulls that the family had found washed up on the banks of the Grand River. They had come from an old Indian burial ground which the river had invaded. Later, when the Johnsons left Chiefswood, the skulls were left behind, and Pauline wondered with amusement what the new tenants had thought when they found them.

Pauline was conscious of the isolation of her life even when young. One day when she was about five, she told her mother irritably that she did not have a single friend in the whole world. Emily put down her work and told her to run from the house to the barn gate six times. "And take the dog with you!" she said. The child ran back and forth while her mother counted the runs, and the dog barked as he ran at her heels. Finally the little girl sank breathless and laughing at her mother's feet, and the crisis was temporarily over. Emily firmly believed in action to take one's mind off trouble; discussing the problem might expose some unpleasantness.

Pauline never made friends with the children of the reserve. To begin with, most of them lived across the river from Chiefswood and there was no easily available crossing. In the second place, Pauline's health would not have allowed her to participate in the activities of the reserve children. Having no real children's games, from an early age they imitated their parents' activities: hunting, fishing and canoeing. And finally, there was always the possibility of unacceptable behaviour among the Indian children.

Although Pauline's bond with her mother was very strong, the real focus of her affections was her father. She believed him flawless. She idolized him for his undeniably handsome features, for his integrity and his gallantry, and because she saw him as a leader of men. As she grew older, he became her ideal Indian, the man against whom she would measure all other men. And because she believed him infallible, she trusted his judgement and his values in all things, so that in measuring her own worth she used his standards of womanhood.

His heroes became her heroes. Although her mother had made it quite clear that she was not fond of "old Bonaparte," Pauline loved the pictures of Napoleon that her father hung on the walls of the parlour and the study. She sat on his knee to be told of Napoleon's invasion of Russia, of the battles of Austerlitz and Marengo and Trafalgar, just as he had sat on his grandfather Jacob Johnson's knee to hear the same stories. And when her father dressed up like Napoleon to have his picture taken, Pauline was thoroughly impressed.

He stood her in front of the autographed portrait of Count von Bismarck and explained how a German friend had sent a portrait of her own father in his full chief's regalia to Bismarck, and how the count had sent this picture in return. He told her of the time he had appeared at a theatre in New York in costume with two large medals pinned on his chest. The theatregoers were goggle-eyed and, concluding that he must be at least the Czar of All the Russias, had rushed the box where he sat with two of Emily's American nieces. The three of them had to be rescued by theatre attendants, and their carriage brought round to the side door of the theatre so that they could make their escape.

He told her stories of Hiawatha and of the great Shawnee chief, Tecumseh, who had tried to create a pan-Indian alliance in the Midwest to stop the encroachment of the whites. He read part of Richardson's novel *Wacousta* to her and called it "the greatest book of its kind ever written." From it she learned the story of Pontiac's attempt to capture Fort Detroit under the cover of a lacrosse match and of the peace eventually concluded by the family namesake, Sir William Johnson.

But the story her father told best concerned the first "long-distance" performance of Alexander Graham Bell's telephone. The inventor had invited her father and a number of other guests to dine at the Bell home and participate in an experiment. During the dinner he explained to his guests how he had stapled wire to fences and trees for two and a half miles, all the way to the office of Walter Griffin, the Great Western Telegraph operator in Brantford, who was to accept their calls that evening. In the experiment Griffin had no trouble hearing all the guests clearly, so when George Johnson was asked to speak into the phone, someone suggested he speak in Mohawk.

"Sage gasha," Johnson said into the phone.

"Can't hear you," Griffin answered.

"Sage gasha," Johnson said again.

"Something's wrong here," said Griffin.

Johnson replied in Mohawk again.

"What's that? Oh, I say, professor, you might have invited me! How many bottles have you opened?"

For Pauline, much of her father's glamorous image was established by his reputation in the world beyond the reserve. She was tremendously proud of his ability to move between the two cultures, tuned to the requirements of both. On the reserve, his closest friends were Simcoe Kerr, who was the grandson of Joseph Brant, and Chief George Buck, the leading chief of the Onondagas of the Grand River Reserve. These three carried an enormous weight of opinion among the people of the Six Nations, but George Johnson was a man to be reckoned with in the white world, too. Many of Brantford's most influential citizens were his close friends and he was often sought out as a liaison between whites and Indians on ceremonial occasions. When Pauline was only seven, she watched her father ride into the clearing in front of the Mohawk Church as escort to Arthur, Duke of Connaught, who was to be made a chief of the Six Nations people. As the third and most favoured son of Queen Victoria, the duke was on a goodwill tour of Canada. It was Chief Johnson's privilege to help him dismount and to lead him inside the church to inspect the communion service and the Mohawk Bible. And it was Chief Johnson who interpreted for him when he later knelt on a red blanket in front of the church to be given the title of Kavakoudge, or Sun-Flying-Eastward. And though Pauline was very excited to see the queen's own son right there on the reserve, the focal point of her attention was always her father.

The duke's visit was not the only occasion when royalty came to the reserve. On 25 August 1874 the governor general of Canada, Lord Dufferin, and his Lady came to inspect the reserve and stopped at Chiefswood. And in 1879 the Marquis of Lorne (later Duke of Argyll) and his wife Princess Louise (a daughter of Queen Victoria) also called at the house. For the young Pauline, unaware of the machinations of Ottawa, these visits corroborated her belief in her father's importance. But in fact the bureaucrats were merely following their usual practice of displaying to royalty only those Indians who would help maintain the fiction of a happy, prosperous indigenous people.

Next to her parents, the greatest influence on Pauline's young life was her grandfather, John Smoke Johnson. He was already sixty-nine years old when she was born, but he was to live another twenty-five years, lucid to the last. He had held the post of speaker of the Senate since 1842 and had gained the nickname the Mohawk Warbler for the poetry and music of his language in debate. He had a vast knowledge of Mohawk history and ceremony and was the only one left on the reserve who could read the wampum belts and understand every word of the complicated Book of Rites, the compilation of the Six Nations official ceremonies. He could also recall with relish his long-ago exploits on the battlefield.

Once, Pauline asked him, "Grampa, did you ever kill a man?"

The old man sighed and shook his head. "Not many, my dear, not many. Only seven at the most!"[12]

Pauline thrilled to the bloody tales he told her, and most of the Indian poems and legends she later wrote were derived from them. But to the end of her life she spoke with regret of the wealth of stories that had died with him, stories she had not taken the time to hear.

The Johnson family life was not, however, all idyllic. On Saturday, 21 January 1865, as Emily was lighting the lamps, George Johnson staggered into the parlour, covered in blood.

"Well, Emily," he said, "I got myself hurt at last!"

He fell to the floor unconscious. Emily's terrified cry brought the servants and children, but within moments she had regained control of the situation. She ordered the children to their rooms and sent the stableman to Brantford for a doctor. Four-year-old Pauline tried to cling to her mother, but was packed off to her room by the nursemaid.

As the government's representative, George Johnson had been trying to stop timber buyers from selling rotgut whisky to the Indians in exchange for their timber. It had been only a matter of time before the buyers retaliated. On this night two men had attacked Johnson as he walked through the village of Middleport. One of them, a man named Mills, carried a lead ball fastened to the end of a piece of heavy elastic, and had used it to beat Johnson about the head, breaking both jaws and causing severe concussion and bruising.

When the doctor came, the servants carried Johnson upstairs to his bedroom while the children watched fearfully from their bedroom doorways. For four days he lay delirious and raving. Another nineteen days passed before the jawbone fractures set and, during all this time, Emily sat constantly at his bedside. The children were allowed to tiptoe to the bedside from time to time to reassure themselves that papa was still alive. Eleven-year-old Beverly begged his mother's permission to go out and shoot the man who had done this to his father, but Emily sternly forbade it. Shortly afterwards Mills was caught and sentenced to five years in the Kingston Penitentiary, but his companion escaped the law. George Johnson's face was permanently scarred from the attack and he suffered from bouts of neuralgia for the remainder of his life.

When she was seven Pauline's formal education began in the upstairs schoolroom where the family's English governess had been teaching her older brothers and sister. The eldest, Beverly, had already been sent off to Hellmuth College in London, Ontario, and the second child, Eva, would follow him to Hellmuth Ladies College in a year's time. Pauline's only written comment on the two years she spent in the care of this governess was to the effect that the woman had filled her with verbs which she had hated.

After the governess left the family, Pauline and her brother Allen were taught for a while by their mother, and then enrolled at the school on the reserve. This was an unsatisfactory experiment. The Johnson children's education to this point had emphasized literature, history and languages, while the reserve children had been coping with the standard reading, 'riting and 'rithmetic, so that the Johnsons were too far advanced in some areas and totally lost in others. In addition, being wary of intimacies, they were afraid to make friends. The Mohawk children felt they were being patronized, while the Johnsons looked on their own behaviour as being correct for aristocrats.

Two years later, Allen was accepted by the Brantford Collegiate and consequently both children were withdrawn from the reserve school, as the family felt Pauline should not attend there alone. No other school was available, and the governess with the hated verbs had already left the family, so Pauline was allowed to study under her mother's supervision for the next three years—her eleventh to fourteenth years.

At Chiefswood there was no lack of reading material. The Johnsons had an enormous library, and Pauline once told an interviewer that she had read every line that Scott and Longfellow had written by the time she was twelve. Whether or not this was literally true, she definitely had acquired an exceptional background in literature before she was in her mid-teens. She had by then read extensively from the works of Browning, Tennyson, Byron, Keats and Milton. She would lie across her bed for hours, a book of poetry in her hands. Whenever her brother Allen's education parallelled her own, she would read aloud with him, mostly from Shakespeare's plays and sonnets, and sometimes they would act out scenes from the plays for the family's approval. When all the Johnsons gathered in the evening to discuss what each had done that day, Pauline was given the opportunity to discuss her day's studies with the others. Then she would sit curled up with a book for the rest of the evening, oblivious to the passage of time. It was not uncommon for the whole family to be still reading or talking in the parlour at eleven o'clock at night.

Pauline's health had improved considerably by the time she was eleven and she was allowed to go farther from home to explore the reserve. She was fascinated by the Grand River which bisected the reserve and flowed right past the Johnson's front door. In those days

> the Grand was a river of free and winding beauty, so shallow in parts one could almost touch the pebbles with one's hand by leaning out of the boat; there were many rapids, swirling, leaping, dancing; the

banks were blue with wild irises; busy chipmunks scurried and played among the trees; now and again one caught the yellow flash of a canary, or the longer sweep of a bluebird's wings. [13]

On this beautiful river, Pauline was now taught to paddle a canoe by her brothers, who were as skilled as any of their Mohawk neighbours. She soon knew every shallow and rapid on the river and paddled her single-blade canoe "Wildcat" as if she had been born on the water. She also became adept at archery and snowshoeing, but, for the rest of her life, canoeing was to be her special love and the means by which she increased her stamina.

She was not the only girl in that period who took up canoeing, though it was not as popular then as it would be in the late 1880s and '90s when it became a society sport with international meets and races. However, it was already considered a social grace when Pauline was young.

Life would have been an idyll for Pauline in this period except for her father's continuing difficulties. In October 1873, eight years after he had been badly wounded by the man Mills, George Johnson was attacked on a lonely road late at night by six white men wielding clubs. They knocked him to the ground, broke six of his ribs with a blow from a club, then shot him and left him for dead. Fortunately, the bullet only grazed his body and, when his attackers had gone, he got up and staggered along the road for several miles to a farmhouse where he could get help. It was noon the next day before he returned to Chiefswood, and a doctor was summoned to bind his broken ribs. Weeks passed before he left his bed, and several months went by before he took up his duties on the reserve.

Until the first attack on him in 1865, Chief Johnson had been in robust health, but the injuries he suffered then sapped his strength. This second attack marked the beginning of the long slide downhill that would end in his death eleven years later. His bouts of neuralgia increased and he suffered other illnesses, probably strep infections, which further weakened him. But though he was deteriorating physically, he had become more determined to destroy the timber robbers and bootleggers who preyed on the Indian people, and he was helped by the public reaction to this latest attack on his life. Both whites and Indians gave their support, and at last he was able to curb some of the lawlessness.

Pauline had been too young to understand the first attack on her father, but she was fully capable of understanding the second one. Yet she did not consider it a racial incident. Her later writings make it clear that she looked upon it as a conflict between a good man and bad men, not as white men versus an Indian. And even though her hero-father lost this battle, her admiration for him increased because he had been defending the Right.

When she was fourteen Pauline was sent to the Brantford Collegiate. At the same age, her brother Beverly and her sister Eva had been sent to the prestigious Hellmuth Colleges, but this choice was apparently not offered to Allen or to Pauline. It is not clear from her writings or those of her sister why the younger ones were not given this opportunity, but since Pauline was the favourite child it certainly was not intended as a slight. Nor was it the result of financial difficulties, for the family income had remained stable. It is more likely that Brantford was chosen because of Pauline's earlier health problems and her special place in the family.

Hellmuth Ladies College in London, Ontario, was a high-class finishing school with an excellent curriculum and rules that were strict enough to satisfy even Emily Johnson. Eva Johnson had thrived in this carefully controlled environment and looked upon her years at Hellmuth as the happiest of her life, but she was a far different person from her sister. Pauline always rose reluctantly in the morning and was the last to put down her book and go to bed at night. Only constant pressure from Emily had trained her to pick up her belongings, and she found it impossible to stop chattering when she felt she had something to say. The rules of etiquette had governed the Johnson household, but Pauline had never allowed them to interfere with her comfort and Emily had always been a little less strict where Pauline was concerned.

These circumstances made the more relaxed atmosphere of Brantford Collegiate a better choice for Pauline than Hellmuth. Emily took her to be enrolled and installed her in a boarding house run by the Johnsons' friend David Curtis, Brantford's elderly customs inspector, and his three unmarried daughters. The five other boarders were all young men, some of them articling lawyers, some of them clerks, but Emily did not appear worried about leaving her daughter in their company. However, before returning to Chiefswood, she gave Pauline some last-minute advice: "Never under any circumstances allow a gentleman to take liberties with you; never allow him to lay a finger on your hand. It is only ill-bred girls that allow boys to touch them. It is not aristocratic."[14]

Pauline knew "as little as a baby" about sexual matters and had not the slightest understanding of the "evils" her mother was trying to protect her from. But thanks to her mother's warning, she was frozen with terror in case someone touched her. "Consequently I was a very lonely, isolated girl of fourteen, away from home for the first time, for I carried this creed with me as far as women were concerned as well as men, and even women don't care for a chilling, haughty, reserved young miss, who is continually on the look-out to snub them for approaching intimacy."[15]

In her classes she had little difficulty with English or history, but her previous reading had made her precocious and impatient with the standard curriculum. In her copy of *The Fifth Book of Reading Lessons,* which she used in 1877, she prefaced the title of the poem "Ode to Duty" with "Darn the . . ." and the poem "Labour" became "Labour is Devilish." At the back of the book she wrote out stanzas of poems she enjoyed. They included:

> I weep the more because I weep in vain.
> Weep I cannot, but my heart bleeds.

> *

> Bright visions rise of joys long past
> When on this much loved spot was seen
> Faces with smiles—too sweet to last,
> Now faded like a beauteous dream.

> *

> What though in lonely grief I sigh
> For friends beloved no longer nigh
> Submissive still would I reply
> "Thy will be done."[16]

Pauline had known only one death, that of her grandmother Johnson who had died when Pauline was five. Apart from her father's troubles, there had been no serious upheavals or tribulations in her young life. The emphasis on loss and grief in these favoured poems, therefore, seems only to reflect her love of drama and was possibly a romanticization of death and despair in place of the forbidden subject of love.

Unlike her sister and her brothers, she had no aptitude for mathematics, and this subject caused her endless distress. Two and two would never quite make four for Pauline, especially when it came to her finances. Eva and her brothers, unable to understand this ineptitude on Pauline's part, called her irresponsible.

Pauline's greatest pleasure at the collegiate was the opportunity to perform in plays and pageants. She had acted in home entertainments, but her family had been a fairly uncritical audience. The school provided her with a real stage and a real audience for the first time, and from the applause she realized she had a genuine talent for acting. She promptly made up her mind to become an actress; her parents made up their minds that she would most definitely not become one. In their opinion the theatre was an entirely unsuitable place for a young lady. Although she was disappointed, Pauline never fought this decision, but she never entirely relinquished the idea either. The family did nothing to discourage her from taking part in amateur theatricals; in fact, they encouraged her. On one particular weekend, family friends from Brantford, a mother and two daughters, visited Chiefswood where they were entertained after tea with a war dance. This was followed by a dramatic recitation on the life of Pocahontas, with Pauline playing the Indian maiden and her cousin Frank Howells playing Captain Smith. Possibly her family hoped she would tire of theatre if she had enough exposure to it.

The process of adapting to life in Brantford seems to have been uneventful. At first the other girls considered her "stuck-up" and prudish, but Pauline was labouring not only under her mother's orders concerning intimacy but also her rule on acceptable language. Her final dictum on that had been, "Never allow the girls to talk of vulgar things in your presence!"[17] Fortunately, Pauline, being naturally gregarious and enthusiastic, overcame the restrictions Emily had placed on her and by her second year was one of the more popular girls in the school.

Whereas the children on the reserve had looked on the Johnson children as not quite Indian, the students at the Brantford Collegiate saw her as wholly Indian, though they were puzzled that she did so many things just like a white girl. Pauline had never questioned what race she belonged to. She had always considered herself Indian, but it was not until she entered school in Brantford that she felt she had to proclaim the fact of her Indian-ness. This was the beginning of a campaign she would carry on for the remainder of her life.

She had become a beautiful young woman by this time. However, her appearance belied her Indian ancestry. Her eyes were grey-green like her mother's, and though her curly hair was often described during her professional life as black—perhaps because reviewers preferred their Indians to have jet-black hair—it had now darkened from its original golden brown to dark bronze, the colour it was to remain. Her complexion was not very dark; it was described once as "lightly tanned"[18] and another time as "pale olive."[19] In fact, it would have been difficult to recognize her Indian blood simply by looking at her. A Winnipeg newspaper later offended her by saying that she looked like a Neapolitan beauty.[20] Only her nose suggested her Indian ancestry, and she used to make a point of posing in profile for photographs in order to emphasize it.

She left the Brantford Collegiate in June 1877 when she was sixteen years of age. She had come to the end of her formal education and, though an American newspaper columnist once sneered that "she talks like a Vassar graduate only with a trifle more naivete," she always referred to herself as an uneducated woman. In terms of years in the classroom this was true, though her education had been augmented by her wide reading and the influence of her father and grandfather. As a result, she shone brilliantly in social situations, never at a loss for words or topics of conversation even when she found herself dining with the aristocracy or politicians or famous writers and poets. But her lack of formal education seriously restricted her scope as a writer. She never graduated beyond learning by rote, never acquired the technique of inquiry or research, and never felt free to create except within the limits of acceptable patterns and models.

Her first steps towards a career in writing occurred after she returned to Chiefswood from the collegiate, long before she had any intention of developing a career. She had been "making poems" from the time she could talk, but the time and the opportunity for concentrated periods of writing had not been available as long as she was a student. Having finished school, she devoted the next two years to writing poetry, though only scraps of it have survived. Some early short pieces have turned up in the autograph albums that schoolgirls used to pass among their friends. In one, Pauline wrote:

Pine trees sobbing a wierd unrest,
In saddened strains.
Crows flying slowly into the West,
As daylight wanes;
Breezes that die in a stifled breath,
O, happy breezes embraced by death.[21]

Fifteen years later she reworked and expanded this fragment into the poem "The Firs."

In 1879 she wrote her first full-length poem. It was dedicated to her friend Jean Morton, a Brantford girl whom she had met at the collegiate. Pretty and petite, with dark brown hair and brown eyes, she had become Pauline's inseparable companion, and whenever the two of them joined a group to go canoeing or skating, they became the centre of attention. Pauline's poem "My Jeanie" was typical of the highly sentimental verses that girls of this period presented to one another:

When thou art near
The sweetest joys still sweeter seem
The brightest hopes more bright appear
And life is all one happy dream
When thou art near.

Pauline had become interested in boys when she was at the collegiate, but all her contacts with them had been at group events: picnics, canoeing, social evenings, church suppers. She regarded these youths as companions and treated them as she did her brothers, playing little tricks on them, making jokes, and competing with them in sports. On one occasion, she embroidered a tobacco pouch for Douglas Reville, who took it as a sign of her favour until he found out that she had presented a similar gift to half a dozen other young men. There was little pairing among these young people, though it was not unthinkable for a youth to steal a brief kiss from his latest "crush" when no one was looking. These middle-class young men, however, were only too aware that any serious interest in a young lady would have to wait a very long time. They were expected to have achieved social position and financial security before they married. Many of them, even after waiting till their mid-twenties to become engaged, would have to wait another eight or ten years for marriage simply because they had not proved themselves successful in their prospective father-in-law's eyes. A case in point was Jean Morton's marriage to Douglas Reville; they became engaged in 1884 but did not marry until 1893, after he became editor of the *Brantford Courier*.

Therefore, even after they left school, Pauline's girl friends did not look for imminent marriage. They toyed with romance, had "crushes" on this or that young man, and brief flirtations at houseparties and country fairs. Their hearts were broken regularly when their chosen young man turned his eyes on another girl, but there was always another young man to take his place. Most of the girls' close relationships were with female friends on whom they lavished affection and handmade gifts.

In the Johnson household, there was no talk of "beaux, fellows, or spooning,"[22] and Emily directed all conversation about men away from "sentimentality" as she called it. And even though all her children except Pauline had reached marriageable age, she would not allow any talk of love or marriage because she believed that it would inspire the wrong kind of speculation. Emily did not disapprove of marriage for her children, but she believed that marriage should simply happen. There was a definite inevitability to the process, so the way to prepare for it was to stay pure and keep one's thoughts elevated.

One of the few times that Pauline saw her mother really annoyed was when the family doctor came to pay a social call. Knowing that Emily had no intention of discussing marriage with her daughters, he launched into the topic himself. "Mother interrupted quite fretfully, 'Doctor, you never step into this house but you begin that foolish topic. You seem never to talk of anything but love and marriage, love and marriage.'"[23]

Young men coming to the house to court Pauline were treated to musical entertainment, chess, checkers, croquet or a stroll around the grounds. Pauline was never restricted in where she could go with a young man, only in her behaviour while with him. She could go horseback riding or canoeing with him, as long as she never allowed him to touch her hand. For the young men, it was rather like being told they had leprosy.

Though Chiefswood and the beautiful Grand River still held their old magic for Pauline, her two years at the collegiate had fully developed the gregarious streak in her that she had inherited from her father. The family home now seemed too isolated and lonely, and she began an almost aimless life of visiting friends and relatives, returning to Chiefswood now and then to write and to welcome friends who had come on return visits. In 1881, for example, she spent July with friends at Camp Knock-About in Muskoka, early August brought to Chiefswood a friend of her brothers from London, Ontario, and the last two weeks were spent with friends in Goderich. For two weeks in September she visited a former school friend, Charlotte (Lottie) Jones, in London, and two weeks in October were spent with relatives in Wingham. Then there were day trips to Hamilton to visit her brothers who were both employed there, and overnight shopping and theatre trips to Toronto with her mother.

It was the pattern of existence typical of the daughters of the well-to-do who were simply putting in time waiting for marriage. In cities like New York and London and even Toronto, women were talking of women's suffrage and the right of women to enter the professions, but in places like Brantford such ideas were considered quite mad. There it was still accepted that a woman's duty was to marry; only if that failed to happen should a woman consider a career. But while waiting for marriage there was little to occupy their hands or their minds. Therefore, when they were not visiting one another they were writing letters to plan the next visit or to discuss boys. Even Pauline, who faithfully obeyed her mother's order not to discuss beaux and love affairs at home, wrote about them to her friends instead. In a letter to Lottie Jones from Wingham in 1881, she wrote: "There is a bank here and a young fellow therein that Wingham seems to have decided I shall make an impression on, so perhaps the next letter you get from me I shall have the inevitable spasm. . . ." She complains of feeling blue on leaving London after her visit with Lottie and says she "took a 'last fond lingering look' down the river where St. George [Jellette] and I had such a lovely little trip in the 'La Belle Pauline' which he sacrificed for $25." A year later Lottie returned from a trip to Winnipeg and reported that she had passed one of

Pauline's former gentlemen admirers on the street there. Pauline replied:

> It is a good thing you did not scream out my name when he passed as he might have fainted and then there would follow a romance. But you saw the "Saint" or rather the sinner—for the hard-hearted wretch wrote me a note before he went and in the worst cold blooded manner wished me adieu. I nearly died and got thin on the spot. I have lost ten pounds this summer and all through that dreadful boy I know.

Fortunately, her suffering was eased by regular letters from another gentleman named David who had just sent her his photograph.

At Chiefswood, however, there were more serious problems to occupy the Johnsons. On 24 April 1878, George Johnson had been assaulted for the third time. He had been walking home from the Council House when a troublemaking Indian named Joshua Turkey alias Williams leaped from the bushes and attacked him. Although his injuries this time were confined to bruises and lacerations, the incident had a deep psychological effect on him, so that recuperation took much longer than the injuries seemed to warrant. His family hovered around worriedly, consoled only by the fact that all the Johnson men were long-lived. They waited for him to resume his old way of life, but he never did. His step was slower after that time and he took little part in Senate affairs. Often he was too unwell to carry out his government duties or accompany Superintendent Gilkison as interpreter and liaison.

Eva had become engaged, and then sometime during 1879 the engagement came to an end, either through the death of her fiancé or as the result of a quarrel. In either case, Eva considered him dead. Since love and marriage could not be discussed within the family, she was left alone in her grief and covered her wounds by becoming coldly rigid in her principles and unresponsive to the needs of any of the other members of the family.

In 1882 Kate and Frank Howells's mother, Victoria, died. Pauline had spent a great deal of time with the Howells family in nearby Paris where Aunt Victoria had welcomed her so warmly that Pauline had felt she was the "best, dearest friend that a girl ever had." She wrote to Lottie: "For me to go to Paris and see the dear old home occupied by strangers—to know that the days of perfect joy I spent within its halls can never return—to see little 'Chick' [Kate] in her black dresses—to see that lonely hallowed grave—is simply torture and then to think of Frank—homeless." Pauline did not realize as she wrote these words that they foreshadowed her own future.

Tragedy came to the Johnson family in February 1884. On Tuesday, 12 February, Chief Johnson attended a reception for the newly appointed bishop, the Very Reverend Baldwin, at Grace Church in Brantford. It was raining when he emerged from the meeting, so that as he rode home he was drenched to the skin and went to bed with the first signs of a cold coming on. In the next two days his cold became worse, and by Friday the symptoms of another attack of erysipelas had begun to appear. On Saturday Emily sent for Dr. Phillips of Brantford who did what he could to make him more comfortable, but on Monday when his condition was worse, the specialist Dr. Digby was called in. There was nothing he could do. The red patches had spread over Chief Johnson's face, neck and chest, and his fever was raging out of control.

Outside the house, a crowd of Indians waited each day for news, then on the evening of Tuesday, 19 February, they slowly dispersed. Minutes later, the death cry began echoing up and down the river. Chief George Henry Martin Johnson, Teyonnhehkewea, was dead.

On Friday the chief's remains were brought to Brantford by train and taken to the Grand Trunk terminal where an immense crowd awaited the train's arrival. A hush fell as the casket, covered by the Union Jack and piled high with crosses and wreaths of lilies and immortelles, was carried through the crowd to the hearse by His Honour Judge Jones, Lieutenant-Colonel Gilkison, lawyer Allen Cleghorne, and Chiefs John Buck, William Wedge and Samuel Sayers. From the depot, a long procession followed the hearse to the Mohawk Church. There the service of the Anglican Church was conducted by the Reverend Archdeacon Nelles, assisted by the Reverends Anthony, Barefoot, Casswell and McKenzie.

But though the funeral service had been conducted by white men, it was the Indian people who buried him. At the graveside an old chief began to sing a Mohawk hymn, and all the Indians joined in the chorus. Then Chief Buck, the fire-keeper of the Council, addressed the mourners in the Onondaga language, reminding them of the virtues of the man they were burying. Beside Chief Buck, a young man interpreted for the white people. At the end of the speeches they lowered Chief Johnson into his grave.

The Johnson children stood side by side, aloof from the crowd, none of them yielding to the emotions they felt. At Chiefswood, with a nurse in attendance, Emily Johnson lay in bed too ill and broken to attend the funeral. Then, just as she had done when they were courting, she began to write little letters to the man she loved, as if he would once more collect them from some trysting place in the woods.

On 17 May, three months after his death, she received a parcel containing a painting of Lord Nelson dying, surrounded by his wounded men. Her husband had ordered it for her before he died. She wrote:

> I often think what fun the poor fellow [George] may have had laughing at me while we may have been looking at those wretched dying and bleeding men. He bought Lord Nelson for me as he knew I had not much love for "old Bonaparte. . . ."

Chapter Three

Brantford

THE DEATH OF Chief Johnson forced the family to take stock of their financial position. His government income had ceased, and that income was absolutely necessary for the upkeep of Chiefswood because it had never been developed as a producing farm. The chief had sold off some of the original two hundred acres, but he had cultivated only enough of the remainder for his family's needs. Since neither of his sons had shown any interest in the land, it would have been pointless to develop it further. There was no prospect of Emily's making it pay its own way and her own income would not begin to support the place. The annuity that her thoughtful husband had provided was barely adequate for her own needs.

In building Chiefswood, Chief Johnson had envisioned it being passed on to his children and then his grandchildren, but at the time of his death, none of his children had married, though the eldest was now thirty years old. Beverly was in Montreal working as the head cashier in the Canadian head office of New York Life, earning a good salary but with no prospects of marriage. Allen at twenty-six worked in an insurance office in Hamilton. A popular man-about-town, he showed no signs of settling down with a wife. Eva had renounced marriage. No one had yet asked for Pauline's hand. Chiefswood was not about to ring with the laughter of another generation of Johnsons.

Emily was not ready to make a decision; for a year she brooded in her room at Chiefswood and refused to face the problem. Eva, undaunted by the situation, plunged with determination into a job in the office of the Indian superintendent in Brantford. It was as if she had only been waiting for the moment when she could put her organizational talents to work.

For Pauline, Chief Johnson's death came at a time when she had done nothing to qualify for a position in the literary field and she had no other talents to offer an employer. During the last six years only one of her poems had been published. In January 1884, less than a month before her father's death, "To Jean" had been published in the New York magazine *Gems of Poetry.* Pauline had hoped to see it published by Douglas Reville of the *Courier,* but Reville had decided it was good enough for a wider audience. *Gems of Poetry* promptly accepted it. Three more of her poems were published in the same magazine later that year, but unfortunately it ceased publication in 1885.

Another minor success came in the summer of 1885 when the Johnsons had just ended their period of mourning. It happened that the burial ground of the Seneca orator Red Jacket had become endangered by highway construction and the remains had to be reinterred in a new cemetery. The Mohawks of Brant County, though estranged from their former allies in the United States, for this occasion appointed seventeen members from the reserve to attend the ceremony. Pauline and Eva Johnson were two of those appointed. Pauline prepared a poem to honour Red Jacket, but she did not read it at the ceremony; it later appeared in a booklet published to commemorate the occasion, and she was warmly thanked by the Council of the Senecas.

In the spring of 1885 the difficulty of maintaining Chiefswood came to a head. Since the three women could not afford to operate the place, and neither Beverly nor Allen was willing to come home to take over its management, Chiefswood would have to be leased out. On 15 April 1885 the estate was rented to a farmer named William Peddie for $250 a year, to be paid in two equal installments. His lease was to run for eight years.

The idyll was over. With Chief Johnson's death, the life had been taken out of Chiefswood. The house had been the chief's creation, the structure intended to contain his own vision of the good life. His dramatic personality had dictated the pattern of all their lives. There would be no more evenings of family theatricals or singing around the piano. There would no longer be the rumble of men's voices from the chief's study, the endless conferences on Mohawk affairs. No more royal carriages would draw up to the door.

For Pauline, the year since his death had been a waiting time; she had found it impossible to plan for the future in this empty house. There would be an element of release in leaving Chiefswood's contrived life style and entering the workaday world of Brantford. Even so, it was a painful departure. Eva busied herself supervising the packing and the removal of the furniture while Emily, deeply depressed, sat until the last possible moment in the bedroom she had shared with her husband. When Eva called her to come downstairs to catch the train, she came quickly, climbing into the carriage without a word. She never looked back.

For a few months the three women lived in a house at the corner of Chatham and West streets, then moved to a duplex on Napoleon Street (it later became Dufferin Avenue). For Emily, the street name was another constant reminder of George. With a white picket fence to protect its tiny front garden from passersby, No. 7 Napoleon was considered a "little old fashioned house,"[1] even in 1885. It was made of brick with gingerbread trim; its windows were rounded at the top with matching rounded, hinged shutters which could be closed at night. Little of Chiefswood's heavy maple furniture could be accommodated here, but the rosewood piano once more took the place of honour in the new parlour and over it was spread the red blanket on which the Duke of Connaught had knelt in 1869. On the parlour mantle sat the combination tomahawk-peace pipe that had been given to Chief Johnson by the Cayugas, and the scalping knife he had made for himself out of a deer's foot. Under the parlour table sat the head of the Delawares' idol, grinning malevolently. On the wall was mounted a carved powder horn which had been taken from a Kentuckian by John Smoke Johnson in 1812.

Pauline and her mother settled down to keep house, and Emily's spirits gradually lifted. Eva marched forth each day to the office of the Indian superintendent, and Allen visited regularly from Hamilton. Beverly's visits, however, grew fewer and fewer as his work took him to Halifax and New York and Philadelphia.

Pauline's social life became much more restricted. She made fewer visits to friends in London and Goderich because there was no money for that kind of indulgence and she did not have the facilities to provide return visits. There had been times in the past when she had felt that Chiefswood did not measure up to the homes of her wealthier friends such as Lottie Jones; No. 7 Napoleon was considerably less imposing than Chiefswood.

But though the lack of money was restricting in many ways, it also opened up a new area of contacts. Pauline spent more time with Brantford friends like Jean Morton and the social set to which Jean belonged. She took frequent trips to Hamilton to visit her brother and together they attended the theatre and recitals. Pauline's favourite plays were those starring the red-haired Belgian actress, Mademoiselle Rhea. Her command of English was negligible, which led to some hilarious moments on stage, but the public loved her because she was bewitchingly beautiful and because her costumes were so elegant. She was, in fact, billed as the most exquisitely dressed actress on the North American stage. Many of the clothes she wore onstage were quite inappropriate for the roles she was playing, but this did not seem to bother her audiences. They were looking for glamour, not authenticity.

One night, after a performance of *The Widow* in November 1885, Allen and some of his friends took Pauline backstage to meet Mlle Rhea. She greeted them still wearing her famous "Queen of Holland dress," a heavy gold satin gown with a bird of paradise embroidered over the skirt and a four-yard-long train of black satin embroidered with gold roses. It had been the queen's coronation gown. Pauline, as fascinated by the woman as the gown, was swept into the glamour and drama of the actress's world, and Mlle Rhea, recognizing Pauline's genuine admiration, invited her to tea the following day. The friendship that developed between them was carried on via discreet visits backstage and afternoon teas at the star's hotel. Pauline was extremely proud of the friendship, in spite of her mother's view of actresses, and she willingly accepted the mademoiselle's advice and her suggestion that Pauline join the Hamilton Dramatic Society, an organization of amateur actors. Pauline remembered with pleasure the performances of her school days and was happy to be onstage again, even though the standard of the Hamilton group's presentations was far from professional. At the same time, this lack of professionalism reassured her family that she was not in the process of making a career of the stage.

Pauline had returned to her writing once the family was settled on Napoleon Street, and after the failure of *Gems of Poetry* she located a new market. This was the journal *The Week,* which began publishing in Toronto the first week in December 1883. Almost immediately it developed a wide circulation and became influential in guiding the reading tastes of the young Dominion. For writers it became a prestige market. Among the poets it published were Archibald Lampman, Bliss Carman, Duncan Campbell Scott, Charles G. D. Roberts, and the "lady poets" Agnes "Fidelis" Machar and Mrs. "Seranus" Hamilton. For the first three months the journal was edited by Roberts, but because he was an ardent nationalist, he soon quarrelled with the journal's owner, Goldwin Smith, who believed that Canada's destiny lay with the United States. When their differences intruded on the editorial policy of the journal, Roberts resigned and went back to his teaching career in Nova Scotia, from where he passed judgement on the Canadian literary scene for the next thirteen years.

When Pauline's poem "The Sea Queen" was printed in *The Week* on 16 April 1885, Roberts had long since left the editor's desk, but he still maintained a healthy interest in everything in that journal's pages. He was very impressed with the poem and promptly began a correspondence with Pauline which lasted for the next twenty-five years. *The Week* also published "A Cry from an Indian Wife" in its 18 June edition, but this work received a mixed reaction from readers. A week after it appeared, the journal published a gentleman reader's poem written with identical meter and rhyme scheme. Condescendingly, the writer explained to Pauline, whom he addressed as "the dark daughter of the forest," that she would just have to understand that men must work and women must weep no matter what race they came from. Pauline, realizing that he had failed to get the point of her poem, made no public reply. *The Week* published six more of her poems in the next two years.

In the spring of 1886 the city of Brantford commissioned the sculptor Percy Wood to prepare a statue of Chief Joseph Brant to stand in Victoria Square. In the manner of the time, two ceremonies were scheduled: one to lay the cornerstone of the monument and one to unveil it when it had been set in place. The cornerstone-laying ceremony was held on 11 August. The day was exceptionally hot, but the ceremony was well attended by both Indians and whites. One of the most interested of the spectators was "Grandpapa" Johnson who was now in his ninety-fourth year. He had been given a chair close to the cornerstone and watched intently as the collection of memorial objects was placed inside the hollow stone and then capped, and he listened to the speeches of the dignitaries, his head cocked on one side, carefully measuring their words. He was totally unaware that he was the object of most of the crowd's interest. Everyone knew that the old man was the only person there who had actually known Brant.

At last the audience was asked to be very quiet, and the old man was assisted to stand on a chair. Then in a low voice he told of his first meeting with Brant long ago and how he had followed him into battle. He remembered him well though he had been only fifteen when Brant died. The old man's speech was eloquent and when he climbed down from the chair, the people felt that somehow they had touched Brant himself.

Two weeks later on Thursday, 26 August, John Smoke Johnson died in his sleep. He was buried in the Mohawk cemetery beside his wife who had died twenty years earlier.

Shortly after John Smoke Johnson's death, Pauline assumed her great-grandfather Jacob Johnson's Indian name as her own in order to draw attention to the Indian heritage of which she was so proud. From then on, she signed all her poems "E. Pauline Johnson" and "Tekahionwake." In an interview she explained that if her great-grandfather had not been Christianized, her name would have been Miss Tekahionwake anyway, but this was stretching the facts. Tekahionwake had been his only name before he was Christianized and was not transferable to his heirs. Her adoption of the name, however, offended no one because it was not an official inheritable title, and it pleased those who felt that her poetic talents brought honour to the name.

By October Percy Wood had completed the Brant monument and the date for the unveiling was set for the thirteenth and the fourteenth of the month. It was to be a gala occasion involving every merchant and businessman in town, and every farmer and Indian beyond it. The *Brantford Expositor* prepared a special souvenir edition, Brant memorial medals were struck, the printers turned out *The Life of Brant* and *Brant's Memoirs* by the thousands, merchants began a brisk trade in Indian "relics," and all the shops flew "Brant flags" just below the Union Jack.

On the thirteenth a parade led by the Dufferin Rifles Band marched through the city's streets to Victoria Park. At least half of those who marched after them were Indian chiefs and warriors from all over the United States and Canada who had come to pay their respects. The ceremony itself was impressive. The assembled bands and choirs united for the first two verses of the 100th Psalm; then the Reverend William Cochrane led the crowd in prayer. Finally, Lieutenant Governor Robinson was handed the cord that would unveil the statue of Brant, while twelve chiefs were given the cords that would unveil the accompanying groups of figures and the bas reliefs. At a signal, they all pulled and the curtains fell to enthusiastic applause . The monument was a fine tribute to the great warrior and a credit to the town.

Afterwards the lieutenant governor delivered his speech, followed by the Mendelssohn Society singing "The Brant Memorial Song." For Pauline, standing at the front of the crowd below the platform, the waiting seemed interminable. Then at last William Foster Cockshutt, the aspiring politician and owner of Cockshutt Plough Limited and Brantford Roofing, rose importantly to his feet, cleared his throat and said:

> The lines I am about to speak are from the pen of Miss E. Pauline Johnson; they are creditable alike to the young Indian poetess and the race for whom she speaks, and serve to prove that our Six Nations are capable of fine literary culture and fully able to handle the pen as well as the sword. The spirit of loyalty and fidelity to Queen, country, and nation that pervade the ode are worthy of emulation by all of us. They contain a fitting tribute to Brant and his contemporaries who fought so nobly and sacrificed so much to prove their allegiance to the British flag.

He then outlined Pauline's heritage and concluded, "This ode is offered to the public as a souvenir of this day."[2]

Amid the applause, Pauline mounted to the platform, assisted by her old friend "Mr. Kitten," Lieutenant-Colonel Gilkison, and was given a seat next to Cockshutt who proceeded to read her poem, "Ode to Brant." The crowd was delighted and the applause swelled when she rose at the end of the reading to present the first copy of the poem to the lieutenant governor's wife. In return she received a large bouquet of flowers. Her poem had been a great success and no one in Brantford could now be unaware that Pauline Johnson was a poet.

A few people outside Brantford were unaware, however. The *Toronto World* told its readers: "Miss Pauline Johnson, a pleasant looking Indian maiden, was presented to Mrs. Robinson. She is the writer of some good verse that has appeared in *The Week* and other papers. A memorial ode entitled "Brant" composed by her was read and enthusiastically applauded."[3]

Pauline, with her usual humour, wrote in reply:

> Alas, how damning praise can be.
> This man so scared of spoiling me
> Shook all the honey from his pen,
> Dipped it in bile and scribbled them.
> "No compliment on her I'll laden,
> She's but a pleasant-looking maiden!"

She kept this piece of doggerel to herself.

The *Globe,* however, sent a reporter to interview her for its "Women's World" page. In a long article published on 14 October 1886, "Garth Grafton," who claimed to have "had the pleasure of her acquaintance for some time," told readers that:

> She's tall and slender and dark with grey eyes, beautifully clean cut features, black hair, a very sweet smile, and a clear musical pleasant voice.[4] I've always thought her beautiful and many agree with me. She certainly has the highest attribute of beauty, the rare fine gift of expression. She is charmingly bright in conversation and has a vivacity of tone that is almost French.

Most of the article concerns Pauline's explanation of Indian customs and traditions, but it concludes:

> Miss Johnson's literary work is familiar to all readers of *The Week* in Canada and to no small public on the other side [the United States]. Her poems have a dreamy quality that is very charming and while she has given us no sustained work as yet, we may doubtless expect it e'er long. She writes best of her own people whom she dearly loves.[5]

The *Globe* also published a poem addressed to Pauline, referring to her as "Scarce noticed, lightly valued, settled down in this small

corner of a province vast / Her day in decadence of race is sadly cast."
The *Hamilton Spectator* took umbrage at this. Said their reporter:

> The friends of the charming young lady who is the subject of the poem
> will feel like challenging the accuracy of those statements. She cannot
> but be noticed wherever she appears. She is highly valued. If she has
> settled down at all it cannot be in more than one small corner and it
> would be hard to convince those who saw the young lady in a recent
> dramatic performance in Hamilton that many of her days are sadly
> cast. If Miss Johnson's day is sadly cast at the present we have no doubt
> that the potent cause of that mysterious misfortune is the poet who has
> presumed to tune his lyre in her praise.[6]

Pauline thoroughly enjoyed all this attention. "Ode to Brant"
had received far more public comment than she expected, and she had
won twenty-three column inches of publicity for herself in the
newspapers. As Brantford's newest personality, she was petted and
pampered by all the hostesses in town and received far more invitations than she could possibly accept. For a while her social life left
little time for writing.

But when all the fuss died down, she resumed her life as before.
Her fame had not brought her a rash of marriage proposals nor had it
established a base for a career. For the next five years—her twenty-
sixth to her thirty-first—she remained out of the spotlight. A charming young woman with some slight renown as a poet, she lived in an
old-fashioned house on Napoleon Street with her bustling sister Eva
and her widowed mother.

At her husband's death Emily had put on mourning and she
continued to wear it until she died. She occupied her time in the
intervening years keeping house for her daughters. She seldom
socialized or entertained and confined her outings to church on
Sunday. On the anniversaries of her wedding day, she visited
George's grave, gathered bits of dry grass, and fashioned crosses out of
them to remind her of "things that happened long ago." In the
summer of 1890, after her graveyard visit, she wrote wistfully: "This
afternoon, dearest George, I went to see your grave. It is a long walk
for me but I must try and go there once a year as long as I can. . . . Not
many years and I shall sit by your side for I am getting old."

She was sixty-six when she wrote this note and had another eight years to wait for death.

While her thoughts all dwelled on joining her husband, her consolation was Pauline. In her she saw all the traits that she had found so admirable in him. They had the same instinct for drama, the same flair for costume and ceremony. Like the father, the daughter had a magnetic personality and could charm anyone she turned her smile upon. She had more than her share of his crusading spirit and determination and, like him, when she made up her mind on any issue she could not be moved. But the final bond between Emily and her daughter was a talent that the chief had not shared: Pauline's ability to express herself in verse. Emily had never been very articulate, but she had always been deeply moved by beauty, and she felt that Pauline's poems were the expression of her own emotions. So as the years went by, Pauline's poems blinded Emily to her daughter's faults, to the friends she chose, and to her thoughtlessness.

Eva never openly acknowledged her mother's preference for Pauline; rather, in the hope of sharing some of her mother's affection, she fussed over Pauline too, insisting that Pauline devote her energies to writing while she herself went off each day to work in the Indian superintendent's office. But Eva was not uncritical of Pauline and later she bitterly attacked her for failing to fully appreciate her mother. Pauline retaliated with hostility.

Pauline's poetry gradually made new contacts for her and won recognition from people in the arts. But some of the people she pursued failed to be impressed. When she sent some of her poems and her photograph to John Greenleaf Whittier at Christmas 1890, he wrote back:

My dear Miss Johnson:

I have received with great pleasure thy poems so kindly sent me. They have strength as well as beauty, and study and patient brooding over thy work will enable thee to write still better. It is fitting that one of their own race should sing the songs of the Mohawk and Iroquois, in the English tongue. There is a splendid opportunity before thee. And I am very glad to see the fine and thoughtful face of the young poet, for which I truly thank thee.

My good friend General Armstrong of Hampton, Va., visited me not long ago with some of his Indian pupils who sang charmingly. One of them a lovely young girl was about to be married to one of the young men of her nation, who was with her.

With renewed thanks and all good wishes I am thy aged friend,

John G. Whittier.
Danvers, Mass., 4/3/1891[7]

For Whittier, Pauline ranked with General Armstrong's singers, and though she was pleased to quote his line about strength and beauty, she never used the whole letter in later publicity. His advice about study and patient brooding was unnecessary; she had little else to occupy her time.

In this five-year period she appears to have had no sense of urgency, no anxiety that life was passing her by. She continued to take part in performances by the Hamilton Dramatic Society each winter, and in summer she went canoeing with her friends in the Brantford Canoe Club. She saw less of her women friends after they married since she had little in common with them. Besides, she found that married women confided things to each other that were not proper for the ears of an unmarried woman. People drifted in and out of her life, many of them considerably younger than she was, attracted to her because of her minor fame.

She still fully expected to marry. There seemed no reason why she should not. She even made a bet with her friend Jean Morton that she would marry first, and it must have seemed a fairly safe bet considering Douglas Reville's slow progress in acquiring the money for a home. It was agreed that whoever married first would receive a piece of statuary from the other. It was Jean who received a white porcelain statue of a Greek slave girl after Pauline returned from London in 1894.

Pauline had grown more beautiful. At a picnic beside the Grand in the summer of 1980, she lay

stretched at full length, her brown hands clasped under her head, looking at me with that sidelong, Indian glance I know so well, thin lips puckered into a slow smile, grey eyes narrowed by half shut lids. She even lies upon the ground with more grace and ease than any other woman, no touch of self-consciousness in the stretch and curve of her lithe body, the arms and throat sun-kissed to the colour of bronze, the lines of her young face deep cut already, keen as a hawk, still as an old Redskin.[8]

Photographs confirm this description. She had become a gracious and elegant woman, her manners and deportment were impeccable, and her developing ability as a poet was considered to be perfectly acceptable for a lady of her class. She was the ideal wife for the up-and-coming city councillor or solicitor or bank manager. However, men of this description never came calling. Instead a succession of brash young men sought out her company.

Peggy Webling was a twenty-year-old English girl who came to Brantford in 1890 to live at her uncle's farm. In her memoirs she described an event that took place that summer after she had become friends with Pauline.

> At one place there was only a rough fence between the circus grounds and the banks of the river. There we found Pauline Johnson with a very good-looking young Canadian, both sitting against her upturned canoe, enjoying the fun from a distance.
>
> "Hello! are you 'hooking in,' Paul?" we cried; to "hook in" being slang for managing to see a show without paying.
>
> "No! Guess if I wanted to be on the other side of the fence I'd borrow a dollar from one of you," said Pauline.
>
> Then Pauline presented her companion to us, and we all talked until the greatest event of the Fair took place, a parachute descent from a balloon, never seen in Brantford before. There was a wild stampede from the grounds in the vain hope of seeing the parachute land.[9]

The good-looking Canadian's name was Alfred Watt, and he married Peggy's sister Josephine six months later. He was not the only bright young fellow to seek out Pauline. She was, after all, an admirable companion: witty, charming, beautiful, and not averse to paddling the canoe if a fellow did not know how. She enjoyed the attentions of most of them, but some she found too boring to tolerate. She took Frank Russell canoeing on Lake Joseph one evening and conversation drifted to the topic of the racial spirit to be found in traditional songs and dances. Growing bored, Pauline suddenly leaned over the side of the canoe with her face almost at the surface of the water, and gave a bloodcurdling war whoop. She almost lost her paddling partner overboard.

None of these young men interested her for long. They were gadflies and summer moths; they were not suitors. Pauline's standard for a husband was very simple but was almost impossible for any man to meet. The man she married had to measure up to her father in looks, intelligence, manliness, charm and courage, but since her evaluation of her father's qualities lacked any degree of objectivity, and since this evaluation had become more and more exaggerated in the years since his death, his equal was hard to find. Strangely enough, she never seems to have seriously considered a partner from among her father's people. This may have had more to do with the changing economy and political outlook on the reserve than with her own choosiness. The Mohawks had little time for the half-Indian/half-white life that Johnson had led; they were fighting desperately to hold their lands against the encroachment of white settlers, to find alternates to the dwindling timber supply, and to maintain a decent standard of living. Their attitude to Queen and Country was undergoing a drastic change in the face of inequities and injustice. The young men of the Grand River Reserve had little time for poetry and poetesses.

Unfortunately, Pauline was not entirely eligible to be the wife of one of the white men of her social class. It was the reverse of the problem her mother had experienced in marrying her father. The matrons of Brantford found her utterly charming, but none was anxious to accept a half-breed daughter-in-law no matter what her other qualifications were. And it was not as if they could hope to downplay her Indian ancestry so that people would forget it in time. Pauline proclaimed it loud and clear, crediting everything in which she excelled to her Indian blood. The irony was that she was more white than Indian, and only the Canadian law which says a woman's Indian status derives from the status of her father or her husband supported her claim to being Indian.

In her five years of "study and patient brooding," Pauline continued to write poetry. Two of her short poems were accepted for the poetry anthology *Songs of the Great Dominion,* compiled by William Douw Lighthall in 1889. These were "In the Shadows" and "At the Ferry," both of them inspired by the Grand River. "In the Shadows" had been published in *The Week* on 17 September 1885, and "At the Ferry" was published there a year later. In addition, "In the Shadows" had been accepted by the London magazine *Athenaeum*, but not before it had been turned down by eleven American magazines, among them *Century* and *Harper's*. At *Harper's*, the editor, W. D. Howells, scrawled his opinion on the poem's margin. "It will never go," he wrote. "It has no backbone!" Pauline was indignant:

> Now no one would expect that a little watercolour of a sunset would have any backbone. With a big painting in oils it would be different. That poem was a little watercolour picture. At any rate, W. D. Howells had no right to criticize it, especially as it was in manuscript. . . . He is not a poet—he is a novelist—and no one but a poet should judge poetry. . . .[10]

Howells was, of course, the widely respected author of the campaign biography of Abraham Lincoln, as well as a novelist and critic. However, the real root of Pauline's anger was not the fact that he did not have the credentials to dismiss her poem, but that he was one of her mother's American cousins and many people believed she came by her writing ability through that side of her pedigree. She would have been even less pleased if she had known that during his term as U.S. consul in Venice (1861-65), Howells had displayed pictures of the Johnson family to the Venetians, presumably as examples of the North American savage.

After "In the Shadows" was published in the *Athenaeum*, Pauline sent Howells a copy of the issue with a heavy circle drawn around the poem. He did not reply.

In 1891 Pauline was thirty years old and she was beginning to suspect that she would not marry. She was not the only spinster in her circle of friends, but most of the others had definite prospects. Pauline had none. She must, therefore, find some way to support herself before her mother died or face the bleak prospect of a life as a dependant of her brothers and sister.

She knew of only one respectable career for which she was suited, but it had so far yielded little money. Of the thirteen poems she had sold since 1884, not one had returned more than three dollars, in spite of the fact that she was becoming a minor figure in the literary world. Unfortunately, Pauline was no businesswoman. She had no idea how to command higher prices for her work or how to parlay her writing into a livelihood. However, in 1891 she took her first positive step towards launching a career; she began experimenting with new writing forms, having found that there was a good market for articles in the quality literary magazines published in New York and Boston. But a full year passed before one of her submissions was accepted.

Pauline would probably have settled on a career of writing poems and articles for the rest of her life if a former school friend, Frank Yeigh, had not read a copy of *Songs of the Great Dominion*. Yeigh came from an old Brantford family and his father had been a reporter for the *Brantford Expositor;* the young Yeigh had also begun his career there before going on to Toronto when his father took a job with the *Toronto Globe* in the mid-eighties. His aspirations led him away from newspaper work, however, and by the spring of 1892 he was private secretary to the Honourable A. S. Hardy, premier of Ontario, though he was still dabbling in free-lance journalism and doing some lecturing as well. He was part of Toronto's smart professional writers' set, well connected in society, and extremely commercially minded. At thirty-two he was engaged to marry Kate Westlake, the editor of *Fireside Weekly*. She had a considerable reputation as an enterprising newspaperwoman and had written an "instant novel" based on the execution of Chief Sitting Bull in South Dakota in 1890. She had sold it to Bedell Publishing of Pittsburg for five hundred dollars, easily the equivalent of ten thousand today.

In this achievement-packed atmosphere, Frank Yeigh looked for ways to enhance his image. He had always been a joiner and whatever he joined he soon led, beginning with the presidency of the Ontario Shorthand Writers Society in 1886, then moving through a series of community-oriented organizations to become a director of the YMCA in 1890. A year later he won the presidency of the Young Men's Liberal Club of Ontario by promising to reform and reinvigorate the club. In the fall of 1891 he devised a flamboyant nationalist program intended to publicize the club's new "Canadianism" policy. For the opening event he borrowed the idea of "the literary evening" which was then so popular in Quebec, and invited an audience provided by the Young Men's Liberal Club.

In selecting the authors for his program, Yeigh turned to *Songs of the Great Dominion.* When he had first read the anthology, he was pleased to find Pauline's poems in it because he had known her well in his Brantford school days. He had also seen her perform on stage. She was not as widely known as most of the other authors in *Songs,* but he placed her at the top of his list, if only because her personal attractiveness would be an asset. In the first week of January 1892, he wrote to her and outlined his plan. Pauline was delighted to be asked, but she wrote back with practical attention to priorities: "I have nothing to wear!" Considering her income at the time, her complaint probably had an element of truth in it.

In 1926 Frank Yeigh wrote an article for the *Ottawa Journal* describing Pauline's first public appearance. According to his story he told her: "Fix yourself up in Indian togs!" and she did. But Yeigh is the only one who remembers seeing her in the "striking Indian costume she made up for the occasion and wore at hundreds of recitals in after years." Pauline's biographer, Mrs. W. Garland Foster, describes how Eva helped Pauline to make a "simple white dress" for the recital, but Eva herself makes it clear that Pauline wore an old dress made of grey silk. All the newspaper reviews of the recital refer to a simple white gown. Probably Pauline wore a very pale grey silk gown that she had owned for some time.

On Saturday, 16 January 1892, Pauline travelled to Toronto and checked into the Rossin Hotel where the Johnsons always stayed when in the city. She was alone; her mother seldom left home any more, and neither Eva nor Allen had time to attend.

That evening, the room was already overflowing a half hour before the recital was to begin in the Gallery of Art at the Academy of Music, and the young gentlemen of the Liberal Club were kept busy fetching more chairs for the late arrivals. Yeigh, the novice impresario, stopped worrying that no one would come and began to worry that his recitalists would not live up to the publicity that he had been putting out.

The evening began with a poem by Agnes Machar who wrote under the pen name "Fidelis"; her poem was read by the Reverend D. J. Macdonnell. The audience responded warmly; they had all read Machar's poems in the *Globe* and *The Week.* Then followed "General Bain on Sandy Beach," a prose selection, and a poem entitled "Mother," both by Wilfred W. Campbell. The applause was polite.

Then William Douw Lighthall read the chapter called "Nation-Making" from his book *The Young Seigneur,* but by this time the audience was squirming. (The *Toronto Globe* commented the next day that "some of the evening's selections were longer than had been expected.")

Pauline, fourth on the program, had been waiting patiently in the wings, alternating between bouts of absolute confidence and desperate stage fright. "I could feel the cut-steel bead fringe of my dress striking against my knees. When I reached the platform, I clasped my hands behind my back and kept my eyes on the corner of the room while I recited."[11]

To the audience she appeared perfectly calm. She had chosen to recite "A Cry from an Indian Wife," the poem she had based on the Riel Rebellion of 1885. Her voice, though not a large one, was clear and full of expression and she had no difficulty capturing her audience. When she came to the final lines, the hall was terrifyingly still.

> O! coward self I hesitate no more;
> Go forth, and win the glories of the war.
> Go forth, nor bend to greed of white men's hands,
> By right, by birth we Indians own these lands,
> Though starved, crushed, plundered, lies our nation low . . .
> Perhaps the white man's God has willed it so.

She finished and the room remained absolutely silent. She bobbed her head to indicate the end of the poem and turned to leave the stage. Then she stopped; the audience had broken into wild applause. She turned back, hesitated, then bowed and walked off. From backstage she could hear shouts of "Encore! Encore!" Yeigh met her in the wings, smiling with excitement and relief. She had transformed his evening of disaster into the most important cultural event of the season. He tucked her hand under his arm and led her back onto the stage. When the applause died down, he assured the audience that she would recite for them again that evening.

"As Red Men Die," the poem she read for her encore, was based on a legend told to her by her grandfather. It concerned one of her forebears who had chosen death on a bed of live coals instead of life as a slave. A tale of barbaric simplicity and melodrama, it stirred the audience once more to a wild ovation.

After that night Yeigh would begin promoting the story that Pauline had been an "instant recitalist," suddenly transformed from "the bashful and frightened Indian princess-maiden" to an assured platform performer. Others would add to the legend, pointing out that she had been too shy to read her work in front of an audience on two earlier occasions, the reinterment of Red Jacket and the unveiling of the Brant monument. But as Foster described it, her failure to read her tribute to Red Jacket had nothing to do with "diffidence." She had been neither asked to prepare a poem nor scheduled to read it during the ceremony, and considering the rather strained relations that existed between the Mohawks and the Senecas, it would have been presumptuous of her to have insisted upon reading it. In fact, it was a gracious gesture on the part of the Senecas to include the tribute in their memorial booklet.

It was not shyness that overtook her on the occasion of the Brant unveiling either. Although Pauline's voice was clear and musical, it would not have been heard at that large outdoor gathering. William Faster Cockshutt was an old friend and he had been a chum of Beverly Johnson. At the time of the unveiling, he was running for Parliament as a Conservative and needed all the public exposure he could get. (He was defeated in the election, but kept trying until he became an M.P. in 1904.) He was quite used to making himself heard on the hustings and could be guaranteed to make a good showing on this occasion, both because he cared about Pauline as a friend and because he cared about his own future as a politician. His style of delivery gave the poem something of an election speech aura, but no one missed a word of it. Pauline got all the exposure she needed when she presented her scroll to the wife of the lieutenant governor.

Yeigh's instant recitalist story must have amused the people of Brantford and Hamilton who had seen Pauline perform from time to time over the preceding seven years. They knew she needed more experience to rank with the professionals but that she was certainly not the novice he described. She was, in fact, the only one of his recitalists with any acting experience at all.

Her success that night was a godsend for Yeigh, for he had been turned down by more than half of the established writers he had invited. Probably most of those who declined did so for a reason that had nothing to do with temperament; they turned him down because they were uncomfortable reading their own works before an audience. It may be painful for a writer to watch his work being performed by someone else, but at least he can hide during the performance if things are going badly; if he performs his own work he must accept criticism for both the work and the performance. Pauline, who probably did not know that so many had turned down the invitation, plunged into this experience with enthusiasm. She had learned to accept rejection slips with stoicism and had even survived the scorn of W. D. Howells; she did not realize that the form of criticism offered to an entertainer would be different. And it would be months before she learned this lesson.

By 1904 she was able to say:

> . . . but the adverse criticism does not hurt me now as it used to. I often think that a poet is like a mother with a family of small children. This is the baby, this is the pretty one and this is the cripple. Poems are our brain children—we love them too much to have them treated badly. Then, too, what will please one critic will not, with his line of thought, please another. [12]

In the meantime, she was showered with the loving appreciation of her audience. At the close of the evening, a soldier who had fought in the North-West Rebellion came to her. Deeply moved by "A Cry from an Indian Wife," he said, "When I heard you recite that poem, I never felt so ashamed in my life of the part I took in it!" [13]

On Monday morning, the *Globe* said ecstatically: "Miss E. Pauline Johnson's may be said to have been the pleasantest contribution of the evening. . . . It was like the voice of the nations that once possessed this country, who have wasted away before our civilization, speaking through this cultured, gifted, soft-voiced descendant. . . ."

As he read the newspaper reviews, Frank Yeigh was clever enough to realize that though Pauline would be enormously pleased with Toronto's reaction, she would not know how to capitalize on it. But for Yeigh, the opportunity was too much to resist. He knew Pauline had been denied her ambition of a career on the stage, and she had confided her present ambition to support herself as a writer; he now realized that he could help her to reach both goals in a rather circumspect way, by using her present popularity as a springboard.

Less that a week later Yeigh, acting as Pauline's manager, hired

Association Hall in Toronto for the evening of Friday, 19 February. And on 27 January the Toronto newspapers carried advertisements for a recital by Pauline Johnson, the Indian poetess, with musical selections by Mrs. Maggie Bar Fenwick and Mr. Fred Warrington. The Johnson family had agreed that this concert was to be the beginning of a short recital career for Pauline and that it would continue only long enough to finance the publication of a book of her poetry.

Everything in her upbringing and every event in her experience had trained her for this career as a recitalist, yet she had never considered becoming one. Her mother had taught her how to deal with strangers graciously and to control her emotions at all times; wide reading had taught her a good deal about public taste; her amateur theatricals had developed her sense of timing and stage presence, and public acceptance of her poems had given her confidence. Yet the only career other than marriage that she had ever seriously believed possible was writing.

She had never considered becoming a recitalist or platform entertainer though she had attended many recitals and concerts, especially in the winter season. Many of them had been given by people she knew: ladies and gentlemen of her own social class who gave talks on travel in the South Seas, the wonders of Venice, missions in China, new inventions, or great literature, some of them accompanying their talks with lantern slides. Most of these speakers appeared under the auspices of a church or charity organization and so lost none of their respectability.

Professional recitalists or platform entertainers were usually not quite as acceptable in good society because they received money for performing and were itinerant. A conscientious, sober outlook on life and a well-established home were extremely important to all classes of society in the 1890s; anyone without roots in the community was considered somewhat morally lax. Of course, no one considered recitalists to be in the same class as actors, for everyone knew that actors were depraved.

Some of the professional recitalists did rise above the general ranks; these were the people who were acknowledged leaders in some other field or whose subject matter was intended to educate or uplift. Oscar Wilde was lionized when he toured Ontario speaking on "Decorative Art," even though society matrons were somewhat puzzled by his capricious behaviour and daunted by his caustic tongue. Preachers like DeWitt Talmage made regular rounds and were welcomed in the best houses. Educators, especially those who had taught at well-known universities, were treated with great deference.

In accepting Yeigh's career plans, Pauline was aware that maintaining her position as an "aristocrat" would be infinitely more difficult than it had been in the past. For the sake of her family, and especially her mother, she must always be welcome in the front parlours of Ontario.

Unfortunately, it was at this point in her life that the first rift occurred between her and her family, though none of them acknowledged that anything was wrong. Not one of them attended her career debut at Association Hall. They were all interested in her performance, but they kept their distance, as if unsure whether she would disgrace them. As a result Pauline turned more and more to Yeigh as her mentor and confidant; she began calling him "Yeigh-man" and called herself his "Star."

In return he worked hard on her behalf, feeding the newspapers snippets of information to provoke interest in her. On 13 February, the *Globe* told its readers: "Charles G. D. Roberts, the Canadian poet, says of Miss Johnson: 'She is the aboriginal voice of Canada by blood as well as by taste and special trend of her gifts.'"

A few days later Yeigh told the newspapers that Pauline had completed a new poem especially for this recital. It was the poem that made her name familiar to four generations of Canadian school children: "The Song My Paddle Sings." Convinced that the poem would be popular, Yeigh took it to the offices of *Toronto Saturday Night* who published it a week after the recital. (Many years later, Yeigh told how Pauline had sat on a little island in the Grand River writing the poem especially for that recital. He seemed to have forgotten that the recital took place in February.)

On Friday, 19 February, just one month after her appearance at the Academy of Music, Pauline faced a full house in Association Hall. These people had come fully prepared to be thrilled and enthusiastic. It was the knowledge of so many high expectations that caused a near catastrophe for Pauline.

Yeigh, as master of ceremonies, had just finished his introduction in which he outlined Pauline's lineage and the part played by her

grandfather in the War of 1812. He went on to praise her earlier
poetic works and predicted an impressive future for her. There was
prolonged applause.

Then Pauline swept onstage, dressed this time in a pale cream
gown with a small train. At centre stage, beside a table crowned with
a bowl of roses, she waited until her audience was silent. She began:

> West wind, blow from your prairie nest
> Blow from the mountains, blow from the west.
> The sail is idle, the sailor too;
> O! wind of the west, we wait for you.
> Blow! blow!
> I have wooed you so,
> But never a favour you bestow.
> You rock your cradle the hills between,
> But scorn to notice my white lateen.

She stopped. The audience, already caught up in the rhythm, leaned
closer. The pause stretched out second by second.

She reached out and took a rose from the bowl and tore a petal
from it . . . then another petal. There was nothing in her face to
indicate the panic she was feeling. (Later she said the only thing that
went through her head at that moment was "Oh, what's Yeigh-man
going to say to me?")

Then very deliberately she returned the rose to the bowl, and
asked: "Will the audience permit me to recite a different selection?"

There was silence, then applause. When it died, she began to
recite "In the Shadows." In the second half of the program she
returned to "The Song My Paddle Sings" and this time completed it
without difficulty.

A lawyer friend from the Hamilton Dramatic Society who was in
the audience that night said he had felt the blood rush to his face when
she forgot her lines and he held his breath while she tore at the rose.
He felt that she would somehow find a way out of her predicament,
but for the life of him he could not think how. "But I knew that girl
would recover herself!"

She was so successful in captivating her audience that few
remembered her lapse, and only *Toronto Saturday Night* remarked on
it. The *Globe,* having previously taken her to its journalistic bosom,

told its readers that "Miss E. Pauline Johnson scored another triumph at Association Hall on Friday evening!"

Within a month after this recital, she was embarked on the series of performances that was intended to finance a trip to London to find a publisher. For the next two years she would mount stages all over Ontario, the Maritimes and the New England states.

In the early months of her new career, many people in her audiences paid to see her mainly because they wanted to see an Indian. She was perfectly aware of this and though at times she felt like some kind of freak side-show attraction, she willingly capitalized on her Indian identity to keep bringing in the customers. She allowed Yeigh to bill her as "The Mohawk Princess" and she used the title for the rest of her career. But the people who came expecting to find a savage creature found instead a genteel young woman, in a fashionable but inexpensive dinner gown, who presented a refined literary evening. Although the poems based on Indian legends were unconventional, the rest of her program was composed of verses with traditional subject matter dressed up in traditional forms.

The customers who had come to have a peek at the savage came back a second time to hear the poetess. Even in this early period of her career, with neither experience nor training, she was far more exciting on stage than any other elocutionist they had heard. Since she had not had lessons, she never used the standard facial expressions or hand gestures of the popular Delsarte Method but instead allowed her face to mirror the emotions she was feeling. She had not yet discovered what to do with her hands so whenever she was in doubt, she held them behind her back, but this stance was not awkward. Her posture onstage was always graceful, and she managed to give the appearance of perfect self-control and calmness.

Her voice was her greatest asset. Her enunciation was distinct, and she projected her voice easily and naturally, so that she could be heard easily in any auditorium or village hall. But what reviewers remarked on most often, even in the early stages of her career, was her ability to convey the emotional content of her poems through her voice. Without a single gesture, she could leave her audience shivering and gasping when she recited "The Avenger," the story of a Mohawk who avenges his brother's death at the hands of a Cherokee.

"Last night, thou lent'st the knife unto my brother,
Come I now, oh Cherokee, to give thy bloody weapon back to thee!"
An evil curse, a flash of steel, a leap,
A thrust above the heart, well-aimed and deep,
Plunged to the very hilt in blood
While Vengeance gloating yells, "The Debt is paid!"

Throughout the remainder of 1892 and half of the following year, Pauline toured Ontario. Later, when counting up her performances, she said she had given 125 recitals in fifty different villages and towns between October 1892 and May 1893. This averages out to one performance every second night, but in fact she performed five or six nights in a row in a different town each night for two or three weeks at a time in order to have an occasional week at home in Brantford. Yeigh had arranged this gruelling schedule to capitalize on the success of each performance, always booking a hall in the nearest town for the next night's concert. Although it was his first experience in the entertainment business, he knew enough to follow the standard procedure for booking variety that was used until the advent of radio and television advertising.

He sent out advertising circulars and posters to each town about a week before the performance; these were turned over to the local bill-poster who collected his fee when Pauline arrived. The owners of the concert halls also printed their own advertising, called "dodgers," which they distributed around the town. These contained candid commentaries on the show based on word-of-mouth news from the other towns where it had played. Pauline's write-ups ranged from excellent to good, not like the unhappy lecturer who was preceded by dodgers announcing, "There have been no complaints . . . *as yet!*" [14]

In the summer of 1892 Pauline took a holiday, staying first with her mother in Brantford, then returning once more to Muskoka to visit with the Fred Wilkes family. Since she was somewhat more prosperous than she had been on earlier visits, she was able to undertake a canoe expedition up the beautiful Shadow River: "A stream of tender gladness, / Of filmy sun, and opal tinted skies."

Clarence Shaw provided locally made Ditchburn Brothers canoes for the trip and acted as guide for the group that went with Pauline. During the trip she wrote the rough draft of the poem

"Shadow River" and completed it after she returned to touring.

That fall she wore an Indian costume on stage for the first time. The *Toronto Globe* reported in early November that she had divided her program into two parts and was now wearing a charming buckskin costume to deliver her poems about Indian life. With a few modifications, this was the costume she would wear for the Indian half of her show for the remainder of her stage career.

The costume consisted of a buckskin dress fringed at mid-calf length to show a red woollen lining. The neck was round and cut very low, its edge decorated with silver brooches hammered out of coins; in later years she used these brooches to secure a set of ermine tails presented to her by the Hudson's Bay Company. At her waist she attached wampum belts, the Huron scalp she had inherited from her great-grandfather, and her father's hunting knife. Buckskin leggings and moccasins modestly covered her legs, and from one shoulder fell a red woollen cloak.

The most unusual feature of the costume was its mismatched sleeves. The right one consisted of a strip of buckskin attached to the dress at the shoulder and to a band at the wrist. From either side of this strip, ten-inch-long fringes of buckskin hung down gracefully. In her memoirs, Eva Johnson explained why the left sleeve was entirely different in design. According to her, she had come into the room where Pauline was making the dress, and found Pauline modelling it in front of the mirror.

"What do you think, Eva?" she asked. "Somehow I think the sleeves are going to be too . . . elaborate."

Eva stared at the dress for a few moments and then nodded. "Why not make one sleeve like that and use skins for the other one?"

And so the left sleeve became a simple drape of rabbit pelts hanging to a point slightly below her elbow.[15]

It was the custom on the recital circuit to team an elocutionist with a singer or an instrumentalist in order to give some variety to the program and to reduce the strain on the recitalist's voice. Yeigh usually chose musicians to complete the Mohawk Princess bill, though at times Pauline found herself on the same bill with the choir from the local orphanage or the band of the fire brigade. But in the fall of 1892 Yeigh began to team her quite regularly with Owen Alexander Smily. Smily was English and at the time Pauline first met him he was about twenty-three or twenty-four. He was physically attractive with blond curly hair and a trim body. He had a fine sense of the comic and loved to tease; Pauline, who tended to capitalize on the ironic rather than the comic, found herself badly outdistanced when they first worked together. He was an accomplished pianist, and quite capable of making up lyrics as he went along. On one occasion, he entertained reporters who had come to call on the Johnson-Smily team after a show, and answered a query about their tour plans by sitting down at the piano and putting their schedule to music. Pauline looked on totally bemused, graciously allowing him to upstage her. He was an elocutionist, a ventriloquist and an impersonator. He could do justice to Scottish, Irish, Yorkshire, Cockney and Yankee accents. He especially delighted his audiences by imitating the drone of the Scottish bagpipes.

On 25 November 1892 Pauline returned to Toronto's Association Hall, the scene of her earlier triumph, this time partnered by Owen Smily. The advance notices almost guaranteed a sell-out. A week before her appearance, the *Toronto Globe* reported:

> During her late tour of Ontario, Miss E. Pauline Johnson recited in Ottawa before a crowded house. In addition to some of the leading literary and political lights of the capital, Lord and Lady Stanley and the entire government suite were in attendance. It is very rarely that the vice regal party sit out an entire program and that they did so on this occasion is a tribute to the artist which she deserved.

After the Toronto concert, the *Globe* said: "Miss Johnson has improved her elocution by her studies since her appearance in the same hall earlier this year, and judging by the best standard she may now claim rank as an elocutionist."

Pauline's improvement was partly the result of her recent stage experience, but much of the credit belonged to Smily. Although nearly eight years younger, he was a veteran of five years in British music halls. When they met he had been making part of his living as an elocution teacher in the small towns of Ontario. Pauline had never studied elocution; she had simply studied what others were doing. Whether she learned technique by observing Smily or whether he gave her actual instruction is unknown. But after she teamed up with him her performance definitely bore the stamp of his style of showmanship.

The two of them were virtually isolated from the rest of society by their profession and by their constant travel. As a result, during the years they were together, their relationship came to resemble a marriage in many respects. They came to rely on each other completely when they were onstage; they listened to one another's complaints and turned to one another for humour and encouragement. In most of the halls they played, they had to share the only dressing room; they ate all their meals together, sat opposite one another in day coaches yawning and snoring, saw one another at their worst after late nights and long train rides, and suffered through each other's colds, headaches and indigestion.

Pauline had never been involved with a man at such close quarters. She had never seen one even partially undressed because her father and brothers had always been fully clothed in the presence of the ladies of the family. She had never heard a man discuss his indigestion before; such topics were never raised in her social set. And she had never before allowed a man to "lay a finger on her hand." She was forced to adjust to her new circumstances quickly in order to keep Smily as a partner. Because of her upbringing she tended to read more meaning into his casual physical contacts than he ever intended, and she rebuffed him as she had been taught to do. The young man's ego must have suffered badly while she was adjusting. Smily, of course, already knew what Pauline had to learn by herself: in the entertainment business, constant companionship and cramped quarters do not necessarily have to produce an intimate relationship.

There was undoubtedly warmth and affection between them, but there is nothing to indicate that they ever became lovers. For one thing, Pauline's upbringing was a strong moral deterrent. She was still hoping to marry within her own social class, and Owen Smily was definitely not of that class. Nor did he have any of her father's attributes. In the second place, Smily was probably not even remotely interested in Pauline or any other woman; events in his later career suggest that he was a homosexual. Pauline, of course, because of her lack of sex education, would have been the last person to understand what this meant or how it determined their relationship.

Quarrels between them were inevitable, especially when business was slow. In 1895 Pauline wrote:

This place [Montreal] is deadly dull, we have played to poor business, as have also the Coghlans who have been here all this week. There is absolutely nothing going on and Mr. Smily and I are forced to drive about the mountain daily, at the imminent threat of everlasting poverty in consequence of each extravagance, but if we did not do something, we would grow heartily tired of one another and probably quarrel. . . .[16]

Show business partnerships such as the one Pauline and Smily had require an enormous amount of generosity and co-operation if they are to succeed, for the partners are bound together not by love of one another, as they would be in a marriage, but by their mutual drive to obtain the audience's love and adulation. Unfortunately, no audience has an unlimited amount of love, so the partners walk a fine line between co-operation and competition.

In the winter of 1892-93, though Smily still played some of his dates alone, it was becoming evident to him that he drew better audiences whenever he teamed with Pauline. Consequently, by the summer of 1893 when they played the Maritimes, their partnership was firmly established. Here, their concerts were only a qualified success because Yeigh, being unfamiliar with that part of the country, could not book ahead for them.

Their program alternated a group of selections by Smily with a group by Pauline and culminated in a joint presentation. Smily introduced both his own selections and Pauline's so that they could dispense with the long-winded local masters of ceremony provided by the hall owners. From watching Smily, Pauline developed her own techniques for getting the audience's attention, making little jokes or throwing in unexpected bits of doggerel about some local event or institution. These tricks became a habit as time went by and eventually led to a great deal of soul-searching as she realized she was straying from the path of pure poetry.

Smily's half of the program came straight from his music hall days, and though many of his routines were rather shopworn, his performance was never dull. One of his best numbers was a ventriloquist sketch called "The Slumb'rous Citizen and the Midsummer Fly," but he also shone with "Major McStynger's Mechanical Arm" and "How Billy Atkins Won the Battle of Waterloo."

Pauline's contributions to the program consisted of six of her longer poems and one short prose piece. In 1893 the audience favourites were "The Song My Paddle Sings," "Ojistoh," "A Cry from

an Indian Wife," "The Sea Queen," "The Firs," and "As Red Men
Die." When she began touring, her only published prose selection
was "Indian Medicine Men and Their Magic," which was published
in the *Dominion Illustrated* in April 1892. But she followed this with
"A Red Girl's Reasoning" in the February 1893 issue of the same
publication and "Iroquois of Grand River" in *Harper's Weekly* in June
1893. "A Red Girl's Reasoning" had won first prize in the *Dominion*'s
short story contest in the fall of 1892 though it was not printed until
several months later; Pauline began using it in her program as early as
September of 1892. By the following spring she had rewritten it as a
playlet for herself and Smily, and thereafter they used it as the grand
finale to their show. The playlet, which was a great success, concerned the conflict between an Indian girl and a blond, blue-eyed
Englishman, a role exactly tailored to Smily's physical appearance.

In August 1893 Pauline once more broke the pattern of her tour
to attend the American Canoe Association Meet at Brophy's Point in
the Thousand Islands. With her mother as chaperone, she went at the
invitation of the Cataraqui Canoe Club; Pauline was to be the
highlight of their campfire entertainment. The club's campfire deco-
rations that year were unsurpassed in the history of the A.C.A. meets.
The glow from their campfire and their coloured lights lit up the
shoreline; Chinese lanterns in delicate tints hung from all the trees,
and the name "Cataraqui" in coloured lights left no one in doubt as to
who ruled the night. An orchestra of mandolins and guitars and
banjos serenaded the campers and provided background for the
Cataraqui Singers. But the main attraction of the evening came after
the Cataraqui "boys" announced in chorus: "Miss . . . Pauline . . .
Johnson . . . will . . . now . . . re-e-e-e-cite!"

And Pauline came gliding out of the shadows in full costume,
and in the glare of the fire recited "A Cry from an Indian Wife."

In a voice filled with bitterness and suffering, she clenched her
fists and began: "My forest brave, my Red-skin love, farewell; / We
may not meet to-morrow. . . ."

And sitting around the campfire, "the gentle American girls
shivered with something more than the chill of the night air."[17]
Pauline was called back for encores again and again, and then got a
special three cheers from her hosts who recognized what a prize they
had in her.

Bundled up in shawls, Emily Johnson delighted in her daughter's performance and enjoyed the attentions of the gentlemen canoeists who were most impressed by the old lady's exquisitely old-fashioned manners. One of the young men who danced attendance on Pauline and her mother that night was twenty-seven-year-old Arthur Henry (Harry) O'Brien. Pauline had met him the previous summer while canoeing, and both of them had looked forward to this opportunity to meet again. O'Brien was a barrister in a private firm in Toronto and edited the *Canadian Law Journal*. Intensely patriotic, he commanded a company of the 35th Battalion of Simcoe Foresters, later transferring to the Governor General's Foot Guards when he moved to Ottawa. For recreation he paddled a canoe, and when he met Pauline he was commodore of the Muskoka Lakes Canoe Association.

Pauline, when writing up canoe club meets for various publications after 1893, referred to Harry's "famous laughter and equally famous hat," his "square sportsmanship and his sunny personality." Though not handsome, he was a fine looking man and Pauline was very attracted to him. Their relationship was such that she felt free to borrow money from him in small amounts (which she always paid back), while he did free legal work for her, ran errands, and bought her railway tickets. They corresponded on a more or less regular basis and she valued his opinion of her and of her work, but nothing more than friendship ever developed between them.

Harry O'Brien was the first of her friends to criticize her recitals. It happened in early 1894. By this time she had become the darling of the entertainment pages in Ottawa and Toronto and, when she appeared in New Jersey, New York, Connecticut and Massachusetts for the Indian Historical Societies, the *New York Times* reported that she was "full of dramatic power and tragic motive," while the *New York Sun* said "she has taken Boston by storm. . . . She is perhaps the most unique figure in the literary world on this continent."

Harry O'Brien did not agree. He told Pauline that she was debasing herself in her recitals, not because she was on the stage, but because she was using tricks to keep the public happy and had strayed a long way from pure poetry. At first, Pauline denied his charges, then finally admitted that she "played to the public" and sought public favour "whether it reflected credit on [her] literary work or not." But she defended herself by saying that she had to do it in order to earn enough money to publish her book. Harry refused to accept this excuse and told her that the repetition of evil is what kills conscience, and the repetition of good is what makes moral heroes. Harry O'Brien pandered to no one.

Smarting from Harry's criticism, Pauline wrote to him a few days after their argument:

> More than all things I hate and despise brain debasement, literary "pot-boiling" and yet I have done, will do these things, though I sneer at my own littleness in so doing. Believe me, it is not degraded choice, nor do I wittingly and knowingly descend to smallness of expression in my work. —Now do not look that puzzled little way you have, I am not fencing with you. . . . You know well that I am honest in my desire to improve, and in my appreciation of my friend's keen sight and ear where perhaps my own are dulled with routine and the repetition that blunts one's finer senses of all things. . . .
>
> But where am I? Ah! I was writing of "Literary pot-boiling," and dramatic padding for which you feel a certain disappointment in me. You thought me more of a true poet, more the child of inspirations than I have proved to be. The reasons of my actions in this matter? Well, the reason is that the public will not listen to lyrics, will not appreciate real poetry, will in fact not have me as an entertainer if I give them nothing but rhythm, cadence, beauty, thought. You will not like your friend—(I am, am I not?) to bend to public favor, when she has the power and ability to rise above it, and yet you *know,* though thank your guiding star and saint you have never *experienced* my reason for this vulgar "catering" to an applauding crowd. Ye Gods, how I hate their laughter at times, when such laughter is called forth by some of my brainless lines and business. I *could* do so much better if they would only let me. I have had dreams of "educating" the vulgar taste to Poetry, not action. *I will* do it some time, when this hard, cold, soulless "reason" for bending to their approval ceases to exist.

Then, encouraging Harry to give her advice in her writing, she said:

> I do not accept all suggestions, nor would you or anyone else have me do so, but I hope I readily see the blur upon the sun, the little cloud that renders its rays less lustrous, and if it lies in my power, to sweep this cloud, this bitterness, the unworthiness away, and give expression to true poetry, clearer sentiment, in all my writings, I shall do so.

Pauline never openly accused her partner Smily of leading her astray, but she made it plain that he shared the blame for the way their recitals had developed and that together they would try to do better. She told O'Brien:

> You do not know, your life has never been touched by certain grimnesses that people such as Owen and I have been surrounded with. Grimness, did I say? So grim that the hollow comedy of it has often struck us so strangely that we have laughed together until we were exhausted. . . . Now? Well, now we are trying to look an audience more honestly in the face, with the confidence that success and demand always assures. . . .[18]

But none of this was really Smily's problem; he never claimed to be a poet. His job was to entertain with jokes, songs and monologues, and it was hardly his fault that she had borrowed his routines.

The "hard, cold, soulless reason" that Pauline blamed for forcing her to "cater to the applauding crowds" was the book of poetry she wanted to publish. O'Brien had apparently suggested that she could still earn the money to publish it without descending to the level of her audiences, but she argued that the public would refuse to come to her recitals if she gave them nothing but pure poetry, and the book would therefore be delayed. She insisted that the production of the book was urgent; she had the promptings of her public and her literary friends to prove it. Hector Charlesworth, writing in the *Canadian Magazine,* called her "the most popular figure in Canadian literature, and in some respects the most prominent one. There is something more or less remarkable in all this since her prominence and popularity were accomplished merely by a few occasional lyrics in fugitive publications."[19] A whole book of her poetry, he said, would be most welcome to Canadians. Charles G. D. Roberts, who had written her in December 1892 to ask if she had "enough good work done for a volume," wrote again in June 1893 to let her know how annoyed he was that two of her poems had been relegated to the appendix of *Later Canadian Poems.* Once more he urged her to bring out "a little volume of verse."[20]

However, though it was probably true that the book would appear faster if Pauline continued to play to the public, her real reason for doing so had more to do with her ego than with her literary ambitions. She had discovered that she needed the limelight. She loved the applause, the recognition in the streets, the bouquets of flowers from admirers, the special status of the star. In Ottawa, she was interviewed by the society reporter. In Newark, New Jersey, the gentlemen of the local canoe club marched in a body to her hotel to escort her to her recital and entertained her at a campfire reception the next evening. She knew she could not have become such an instant celebrity if she had simply recited lyrics in a ladylike fashion. But by putting the emphasis on her blood-and-guts poems—she even gave an offstage war whoop before her recitation of "The Avenger"—she had kept her audiences coming back for more, and had achieved celebrity status in less than two years.

Ironically, the faster Pauline accumulated the money needed to publish her book, the faster her career on the recital stage was destined to come to an end, because she had promised her family that she would return home when the book was in print. Consequently, as the time drew closer, she began to rework the agreement, explaining that she must keep herself before the public if she expected her book to sell. Her mother acquiesced, as Pauline knew she would, though this did not prevent Emily from writing wistfully from time to time of her happiness when Pauline would at last be able to attend church with her every Sunday.

In April 1894 Pauline had saved enough money to take her manuscript to London and find a publisher. After a final recital in Toronto, she left Smily to travel on alone and returned to Brantford to prepare for the trip and visit her family.

On Thursday, 26 April her Brantford admirers crowded into the main reception hall at Kirby House for a bon voyage party. For the occasion Pauline wore a mauve dress with a cream waist and a matching two-toned hat, and carried a bouquet of yellow roses. Her mother, her sister Eva, her brother Allen, and three of Brantford's leading hostesses who had organized the affair stood in the receiving line with Pauline.

The afternoon began with William Foster Cockshutt, the would-be politician, "reading an address" for a good half hour, the gist of it being that he and the rest of Brantford wished her Godspeed. According to the newspaper report of the affair, Pauline responded "prettily." Next Rural Dean McKenzie delivered a eulogy on Pauline's talent. He was followed by the Reverend Doctor Cochrane with another eulogy. Mayor Watts's turn was next. Wordily he wished her bon voyage, then presented her with a purse of English sovereigns which had been contributed by the citizens of Brantford. Finally he read out the names of the prominent persons who had written letters of introduction for her: Lord Aberdeen, Ontario Lieutenant Governor Kirkpatrick, W. F. Cockshutt, Reverend Professor Clark of the University of Toronto, Sir Charles Hibbert Tupper who was at that point minister of justice in the federal cabinet, Adam Brown, Mrs. Fairchild of Boston's artistic and literary community, and many more. The Bank of Montreal and the *Detroit Free Press* recommended her to "their opposites" in London. When all the refreshments had disappeared, Pauline's well-wishers sang the national anthem, then filed past her, each one wishing her a successful journey.

The following morning a group of her friends assembled at the Grand Trunk Railway depot to see her off. Eva and Allen boarded the train and went with her as far as Harrisburg, Pennsylvania. In New York she took passage on the Cunard steamship *Etruria* which would take her across "the awfulness of the intervening ocean"[21] to Liverpool. And in London, if everything went according to plan, she would find the publisher who would make her famous.

Chapter Four

London

PAULINE'S INTRODUCTION to England was disappointing. After enduring five days of seasickness on the *Etruria,* she arrived in Liverpool in a drizzling rain. There was no one at the dock to meet her. Like any other sightseer from the colonies, she had to travel up to London by train, and then found that there were no hansom cabs at Euston Station to take her to her lodgings; they were all out on strike. She had to carry her hand baggage aboard an omnibus.

But London, even seen through the grimy windows of the omnibus, was an exciting place. The stately brick and stone houses. The soot-layered monuments and statues. The throngs of horse-drawn carriages. The elegant shops and the noisy street markets. The parks and the broad avenues. The tenements and the twisting alley-ways. There was a special quality about London in that last decade of the century, "a suggestion of something a little daring, a hint of recklessness, of elegant abandon. . . . There was something in the air."[1]

Through one of her influential Canadian friends, Pauline had secured a small "studio" in an elegant house at 25 Portland Road, Holland Park West. These quarters must have cost at least fifty shillings a week, since hotels, even modest ones, charged twelve shillings a week and up per day (meals included). However, a good address was absolutely essential for what she had come to London to accomplish. She added her own personal touches to her rooms. "A bearded, goggle-eyed mask of a mystical medicine man" she placed on the mantel, over the screen she hung strings of wampum beads and her Indian costume, and on the wall she placed a picture in which a "Mohawk Indian brandishing a scalping knife in a most murderous attitude stood with his foot upon the throat of a writhing Cherokee."[2]

Once settled, Pauline tackled the problem of finding a publisher for her poems. Because she was totally unknown in London and few publishers would have even bothered to see her, she knew that she would first have to become known. She proposed to do this by giving recitals, which would not only establish her reputation as a poetess and an entertainer but would also provide her with money to live on.

However, giving recitals was complicated by the fact that, even if she had been able to afford to rent a hall, as an unknown she would not have drawn an audience. The solution was to find a patron. In the 1890s every artist, actor, writer and dancer in London had a patron to arrange gallery showings, pay for recital halls, subsidize publishing costs, finance study abroad, and pay the rent. A patron could be counted on to buy out the house on opening night, be conspicuously present himself, and bring all his friends. He could also arrange little suppers of several hundred influential people who all wanted to invest in art. A patron, therefore, was a necessity.

Somewhere among the minor nobility or the aristocracy Pauline hoped to find her own patron, and consequently she had come to London with her handbag crammed full of letters of introduction. She began delivering each of the letters by hand; in reply she received an invitation to attend an "at home," usually during the following week. Each of these forays into society was a trial for her, not because she was intimidated by aristocracy or even by royalty, but because, as she later confessed, the butlers and footmen in their livery and gold braid always made her feel so insignificant.

One of her first visits was to the Marquis of Dufferin and Ava. To him she carried a letter from the Earl of Aberdeen, the royal representative in Canada at that time. My lord of Dufferin with "his fine intellectual face and distinguished, dandified air"[3] peered at her intently, as was his habit, holding his pince-nez to his eyes, stooping a little as he leaned towards her condescendingly. Was this woman the same person who had curtsied prettily to him at Chiefswood twenty years earlier? Had time really passed so quickly? He shook his head in regret as she told him of her father's death and the family's departure from Chiefswood. Ah, but surely he could be of service to this loyal chief's daughter. . . . The marquis, unfortunately, was too old and too far removed from society to be a suitable patron.

She carried five letters of introduction to Sir Charles Tupper, Canadian high commissioner to London, who welcomed her to the small colony of Canadians in London society and invited her to the annual Dominion Day celebration at Westminster Palace Hotel. Tupper, by reason of his government status, was organizer and chairman of the event and, by reason of his egotism, was principal speaker there also. Always fond of the ladies, he was delighted to learn that he could be of service to Pauline by introducing her to society.

She called on the Marquis of Lorne (later the ninth Duke of Argyll) and his wife, Princess Louise, reminding them of their visit to Chiefswood in 1879. She called on Deputy Lord Chamberlain of London Edward Piggott, with a letter from the Reverend Professor Clark, and since Clark obviously regarded the Indian lady so highly, Piggott promised to assist her when required.

Lord Aberdeen had provided her with a letter to Lord Ripon, former viceroy of India (1880-84) and presently Britain's colonial secretary. When Pauline arrived in London, Ripon was recovering from a serious illness and was not receiving guests, but at the beginning of June Sir Charles Tupper made good his offer of help and introduced Pauline to the lord and his lady. Immediately after this introduction, Pauline was invited to have tea with her ladyship, and it was arranged that Pauline should recite at the Ripons' next major dinner party. She had at last found the patron she required. She wrote Harry:

> I was at a large dinner party at Lady Ripon's last week, and I wore a very fine gown and was taken to dinner by Mr. Somebody—I forget his name—but he is deputy speaker of the House of Commons, I sat next to Lord Ripon, and between them I had a very jolly time, I talked politics and Constitution and told them there was *no* government existing save the confederated government of the Iroquois, that Hiawatha was the only statesman who ever solved the problem of perfect government, and economy—They were delighted, they had got hold of something new to them. Oh! I disported myself with due credit to my country and I ate a disgracefully large dinner, and recited in the drawingroom later on, much to the detriment of my voice. The result is, however, that Lady Ripon wished me to find her an entire

evening of readings, so it seems that not withstanding my dissertation on statesmanship and my unusually large appetite, that I scored a success.[4]

Lady Ripon also introduced Pauline to Lady Helen Blake whose husband would become governor general of Jamaica a few years later. Pauline found Lady Blake delightful; she was "whole-souled and Irish," she wrote Harry, and she "spoils me dreadfully."[5] Lady Blake introduced her to Lady Helen Munro-Ferguson, the Duchess of Montrose, and the Countess of Derby. All of them invited the Indian maiden to recite in their salons.

She had arrived in London when the "social evening" had just begun to decline in popularity among hostesses of the upper classes. For more than twenty-five years, prominent ladies had vied with each other to provide their guests with evenings of stimulating entertainment. In the beginning this had simply meant presenting a bosomy soprano and her tailcoated accompanist or some visiting Austrian violinist. But in time, more was required. The entertainment sought out had to be both stimulating and unusual, and as a result, some of the evenings began to have a circus atmosphere. When the California poet Joaquim Miller had come to London in the seventies, he entered the salons dressed in the buckskins of a plains scout, threw a buffalo robe down on the floor, and stretched out on it to recite his poetry. He was a sensation in salon society.

The more refined and higher-class hostesses, however, were content to hire entertainers who were simply uniquely talented. These were the women who took Pauline under their wings, hiring her to entertain their guests.

On one occasion, Arthur, Duke of Connaught was in her audience, and at the end of her Indian performance he sent an aide to ask Pauline what had become of her father's ceremonial blanket. Pauline had been only seven years old when the duke was made a chief of the Council of the Six Nations, but she knew he was referring to the red blanket that had been placed on the ground for him to kneel on during the ceremony.

"Will you tell his Highness," said Pauline, "that the mantle that I wear was once honoured by his feet!"[6] She never told him that when her mantle had not been serving as a ceremonial blanket, it had been used as a piano dustcover at Chiefswood.

When Pauline had carried all her letters to the pillars of society, she began the rounds of the literary community. She took a letter of introduction to the dramatist Hamilton "Cynicus" Aide and recited in his Hanover Square drawing room before George Alexander, John Davidson, Percy White, "dear old Mr. Watts" (the artist George Frederic Watts), the artist Burne-Jones, Sir Frederic Leighton, Sir Henry and Lady Stanley, the artist Lawrence Alma-Tadema, and playwright Jerome K. Jerome.[7] She attended a soirée at the home of painter Sir Frederic Leighton and impulsively made him a present of one of her invaluable wampum belts. She met the actress Genevieve Ward and went to tea with the famous actor-manager of the Haymarket Theatre, Herbert Beerbohm Tree, and his wife, the actress Helen Maude Holt. George Alexander sent her complimentary tickets to his St. James Theatre and the Beerbohms sent tickets for the Haymarket.

She went to visit Alma-Tadema and his wife Laura Epps, also a painter, in their studio in St. John's Wood. Alma-Tadema's paintings of ancient Roman and Greek idylls were at that time the rage of London, and the success had grossly inflated his ego, but Pauline turned on her charm.

"Sir," she told him, "your art is very beautiful!"

"So is yours, madam," he gallantly replied and kissed her hand. "Write me a poem about them!"[8]

And she did, sending him a copy before she left England. It begins:

> There is no song his colours cannot sing,
> For all his art breathes melody, and tunes
> The fine, keen beauty that his brushes bring
> To murmuring marbles and to golden Junes.

The artist was duly impressed, though he never offered to paint her picture.

She went to Daly's Theatre to see Eleanora Duse starring in "La Signora dalle Camelie"; the English critics found the Italian production rather inferior to the French version of the play which they understood considerably better. Duse, however, was magnificent. Ellen Terry and Henry Irving were playing at the Lyceum in *Faust;* after the Prince and Princess of Wales went to see it on 10 May, absolutely everyone in London had to see it. Lillie Langtry opened a new play called *Society Butterfly* at the Opéra Comique. Said the *London Times* with delightful malice: "Mrs. Langtry's intermittent attention to the stage has not tended to improve her acting! Rose Leclerq gives the best acting in the piece." And then to cap the season, the divine Sarah Bernhardt arrived in London to follow Duse at Daly's Theatre with a whole season of plays: *Tosca, Phèdre, Les Rois, Fedora, La Femme de Claude, Izeyl,* and her challenge to Duse—*La Dame aux Camélias.*

For Pauline, the evenings of theatre were like hours spent in the classroom. She studied the technique of each actress, memorized the movements and the gestures. But she learned most from the costumes that the women wore, especially those of Lillie Langtry. Thus inspired, Pauline visited Westbourne Grove to order four ball gowns to wear on stage during the "lyric" portion of her program. They were in white and pastels, and in satins, brocades, taffetas and laces. They were far more elegant than anything she had ever owned, even though they could not compare with Mlle Rhea's Queen of Holland gown.

Pauline was the hit of the society season, appearing in some of the best homes in London as both guest and performer. She was as thrilled and excited as a child attending her first grown-up party, though were there some aspects of it that intimidated her. She was extremely conscious of her lack of education.

I have met all sorts of Lords and things—and found them for the most part interesting, but I much prefer *thinking* London to *aristocratic* London. Tho' I feel more at my ease in the latter, *thinking* London is so very clever, so far beyond me, so great, so penetrating that I seek refuge in my own blood and the land of my birth, and they are good enough to be blinded by my posings and mistake my fads, my love of race, my Indian politics for exceeding brightness, and the outcome of extreme originality and talent. Bah! and I without enough education to pad my intellect, let alone form the substance. After all they cannot be clever to be deceived so easily. But the great minds make me feel uncomfortable, illiterate, woefully lacking, terribly ignorant and insufficiently read—they do not mean to, but they do, not so with my Lord and my Lady. They invite me to their houses as "a great American Indian authoress, an astoundingly clever poet, a marvellous new interpreter of verse" etcetera, and I go and am looked up to, and dined, and wined, and I amount to a little tin god, for the titled people pretend not to literature. Therefore I am great. Ah! I feel quite a giant, a King in the Nobleman's drawingroom. I feel a worm, a veritable *nothing* in the critic's den or author's library. . . .[9]

But her main purpose in London was the publication of her book, and it was in the salons that she made contact with the professional people who could introduce her into publishing circles. At the end of June, she wrote: "Everyone is good to me, and I shall know at the end of the week if my first attempt with my book is satisfactory, if not I go to another publisher. Naturally I am a little anxious about it but very hopeful."[10]

Before she made the first attempt, she had arranged to have her longhand manuscript typed. Romantically, she decided that the typist would be

> some worthy girl who has a mother and a little brother to support. . . . I did not go near an agency bureau but spent five days hunting up my worthy girl. . . . She said her charge was a guinea–I had expected to pay two–I gave her one and a half. But when I looked at the work–Oh, it was awful! I do not know how long it took me to correct it. There were words spelled wrong, whole lines left out, dreadful punctuation and other things you can imagine. I determined not to have it done over, however, so I took it to Clement Scott, the great English critic. I had a note of introduction and recommendation from Professor Clark of Trinity University. . . .
>
> On inquiring for Scott I was told that he was busy.
>
> "I must see him," I said, and finally was shown into his den.
>
> He was a regular lion and glanced up through an awful scowl, growling out: "Well?" There is only one way to deal with a man–that is through his vanity–so I turned to the door again saying, "I'm afraid to come in!"
>
> "Come back here!" he growled louder. "What are you afraid of?"
>
> I went back. "I'm always afraid of a man who can make one or ruin one with a stroke of his pen," I answered.
>
> He looked over my work then scribbled a line of recommendation to John Lane, the best London publisher. I went to Lane and submitted my copy to him. As soon as he saw it he roared:
>
> "What do you mean by getting this copy typewritten?"
>
> "Why," I said, "I thought it was necessary."
>
> "No," he snapped, "it is not! I never take a book for publication without the expectation that my author will be great, and how would

this look in the British Museum labelled, 'Original Manuscript of Miss Johnson's first book?' "

I had expected to go to about twenty publishers before I could secure one, and had arranged to spend three months in England for the purpose; but Lane accepted it, with the result that I was made.

"I would not dare," he told me, "to refuse anything that Clement Scott recommended."[11]

For twenty-two years Clement Scott had been the *Daily Telegraph*'s drama critic, virtually controlling the theatrical opinions of the city of London. (For all those years he had praised and damned with impunity, until at last he had taken on a victim who thrived in spite of his opposition: Henryk Ibsen. To Scott's disgust, people liked Ibsen's plays and the style of acting they encouraged, and he had been forced to retreat.) When Pauline came calling on him and refused to be turned away, Scott was rushing to complete the manuscript for a new book of essays, *Pictures Round the World,* which was the result of his honeymoon cruise with the new Mrs. Scott. Under the circumstances, it is amazing that he took the time to give Pauline a recommendation.

John Lane, however, did not accept Pauline's poems as quickly as she has described. He actually sent her manuscript to two well-known critics, John Davidson and Percy White, for their opinion on its saleability; then he submitted it to his company's own editor-critic Richard le Gallienne. It was the verdict of these three men that Pauline was still awaiting when she wrote that she would know at the end of the week if her first attempt with the book had been satisfactory.

John Lane was the part owner and senior editor of the Bodley Head. The company had been founded by himself and Elkin Mathews who shared Lane's passion for collecting rare books. By the fall of 1891 the Bodley Head was acknowledged to be the premier publisher of all new English poetry. Being appreciative of the exceptional workmanship and quality of materials that had been used in the rare books with which they had begun their business, the partners set out to introduce new poets to the public while maintaining a "rare books" standard. In the beginning they did this by limiting their editions to a maximum of 550 copies and lavishing endless care on the printing, illustrating and binding. Frequently an edition would number as few as one hundred books, but since each copy was signed by the author they attracted both poetry lovers and collectors of first editions, even when the author was totally unknown. As a result the partners had no problem selling out each edition. Book buyers became aware that they could expect experimental and creative poetry, superb illustrations and designs, and finely crafted bindings in Bodley Head books.

Over the next two years, the company published the works of le Gallienne, Oscar Wilde, John Davidson, Kenneth Grahame, Michael Field, Herbert Beerbohm Tree, William Hazlitt and A. H. Hallam, as well as the famous *Yellow Books* and the books of the Rhymers' Club. They were illustrated by artists such as Aubrey Beardsley, Charles Ricketts and E. H. New.

Clearly, Pauline had been directed to the finest publishing house in London. But when she arrived there, the inner circle of the Bodley Head was in turmoil. Lane and Mathews had been an ill-sorted pair from the beginning of their association: Lane was aggressive, fond of a semi-Bohemian and somewhat risqué life style, whereas Mathews was rather conservative and sedate. In the spring of 1894 it became obvious to Mathews that Lane was trying to force him out of the business, or at least into the role of the silent partner. The first edition of *The Yellow Book,* the famous "half-book, half-magazine" that brought Aubrey Beardsley instant infamy, had just reached the booksellers. The critics had pounced on it in horror. "We frankly confess," said one, "that we have found among the contents of *The Yellow Book* much to weary and disgust and little to admire. All that this literary cackling has produced is a jaundiced-looking indigestible monster. . . ."[12] For Mathews, this reception simply verified his contention that some of the materials in the book were in bad taste, and gave him further ammunition in his battle with Lane.

More bitter disputes followed, and in the early summer of 1894 Lane and Mathews agreed to break up the partnership. The formal dissolution took place at the end of September, with Lane taking the company name, while Mathews kept the premises. Each partner took an "unequal half" of the authors presently under contract, dividing them according to which partner had recruited them.

Because of this, Pauline's book of poems stayed with Lane, though in the years that followed the breakup it was Mathews who continued to promote poetry. He published John Masefield, W. B.

Yeats, Ezra Pound and Bliss Carman, and introduced to the world the work of J. M. Synge, Lord Dunsany and James Joyce. Lane's interests continued to be on the side of the avant garde and experimental, so that if Pauline had come to London six months later, he would probably have rejected her poetry. As it turned out, his acceptance of her manuscript meant a year's delay in completion of the book, because once Lane was on his own the Bodley Head's priorities changed and poetry volumes waited while more innovative works were published.

The White Wampum, as Pauline's book was named, contained only eighty-eight pages. The cover was red-brown with the design of a ceremonial hatchet and a wampum belt engraved above her adopted Indian name, Tekahionwake. This and the title page depicting an Indian encampment and crossed tomahawks were the work of the black-and-white artist E. H. New, who became famous for the illustrations in the 1895 Bodley Head edition of Isaak Walton's *The Compleat Angler.* Pauline's book was published simultaneously by the Bodley Head, Copp, Clark Company of Toronto, and Lamson Wolffe and Company of Boston. This was a fairly common arrangement, with all three companies using the plates prepared by the Bodley Head.

Although no copy of Pauline's contract exists, similar contracts signed by the Bodley Head in that period illustrate the terms that the company usually demanded. More than most publishers of his day, John Lane was known as a shrewd man of business; in fact, where business was concerned he was keen almost to the point of meanness. His hard bargaining resulted in the Bodley Head offering three types of contracts, graded according to the renown of the writer. Popular authors were offered a half share in the profits after printing and binding expenses had been paid. Authors who were just becoming known shared expenses and were given a royalty on the number of volumes sold, usually ten per cent of the selling price. New writers were offered a flat fee of twenty pounds or so in exchange for surrendering their copyright; these writers derived most of their satisfaction from seeing their names in print.

Pauline's contract was probably of the second kind because she was not unknown in North America by this time and had come with excellent references. She must have been forced to pay all editing, proofing and illustration costs herself; printing and binding would be the publisher's share of the costs. And she could expect no financial return from the book for at least a year.

Pauline did not stay in London long enough to see her book completed, only long enough to finish her portion of the work. Lane assigned John Davidson to select the poems to be included and then to edit the final work. Davidson, already a recognized poet, was a "very brusque man with a broad Scotch accent and characteristic frankness in expressing his opinions. Some of her lines he would damn emphatically, but would raise his voice in acclaim at the originality of others."[13] Pauline grew to admire him and in the end was content with the selection of the poems he allowed to be published. She had little recourse in any case, for Davidson was not the kind of man to be conquered by an appeal to his vanity as Scott had been.

On several occasions she joined the tea parties held in John Lane's rooms which, though adjoining the Bodley Head on Vigo Street, were entered through a private door on Albany Street. Lane was still a bachelor at this time so the teas were unrestrained bohemian affairs which attracted quite a cross section of London society, though most of the guests had at least some artistic pretensions. It was not uncommon for writers who had been turned down by Lane at his Vigo Street premises to follow him to the Albany Street rooms, determined to get a hearing. Then they would corner him, teacup in hand, to read their entire masterpieces aloud. Poetesses like Pauline came by the dozen to slip scented manuscript sheets into his hand. And the critics came in order to be able to announce that they had met the newest literary sensations before the rest of the world was aware of them.

Sooner or later everyone in the literary world came to Lane's rooms. One afternoon Pauline met her illustrator, E. H. New, the critic Arthur Symonds who translated Gabriele D'Annunzio, Richard Watson Gilder who was the editor of New York's *Century Magazine,* and the poet William Watson. And they talked of the collapse of Richard le Gallienne's prized mulberry tree at his home in Brentford. For Pauline, an ocean away from Brantford, it seemed like the Mad Hatter's Tea Party.[14]

When July came there were no more social evenings scheduled.

Society had moved into its garden party phase, and Pauline was left in London to complete the proofing of *The White Wampum*. The season had been very wet, far wetter than anything she had known in Ontario, and she had suffered almost constantly with sore throats and bouts of laryngitis. In mid-July, her throat wrapped in flannel, she took the train to Liverpool and embarked for home. She had accomplished her objective: *The White Wampum* was ready for the printer, and she had been promised the first copies by October.

On the trip home, nursing her sore throat and feeling quite unwell, she found herself unable to avoid a large, talkative American woman. The lady was extremely upset about many of the customs she had found in England.

"Why," she said, "when I asked for ice water, they looked at me as if I were a North American savage!"

"Do you know," said Pauline quietly, "that's just the way they looked at me."

"Oh," said the woman, not at all abashed, "was your father a real wild red Indian?"

"Yes," Pauline answered.

"Why, excuse me," said the woman. "You don't look a bit like that!"

"Oh?" replied Pauline. "Was your father a real white man?"

"Why, sure," said the puzzled lady.

"Excuse me, but I'm equally surprised," said Pauline and sought refuge in her cabin. [15] This encounter had been all she had needed to remind her that she was heading home.

Chapter Five

There and Back Again

ON THURSDAY, 26 July 1894, in the middle of the afternoon, Pauline arrived once more on the doorstep of the little old-fashioned house on Napoleon Street in Brantford. No one had been at the station to meet her, but she had not expected anyone. Eva had forbidden her to send word of her arrival time. Pauline, she said, changed her plans too often without notifying her family; she did not want her mother disappointed again.

This was the longest that Pauline had been away from home, and Emily had been waiting anxiously for her return. Pauline, however, had already made plans for a new tour and had allowed herself only three days in Brantford. Little of this time was spent with her mother; there were courtesy calls to make on the local people who had arranged her bon voyage party and there were interviews to give to the press.

The *Brantford Expositor*'s reporter gushed: "She is the picture of good health and spirits and in that charming manner, peculiarly her own, chatted most pleasantly of her experiences in the great city of London."[1] Pauline explained that her tour would begin in Orillia and follow the CPR to the coast. "I don't know whether I'll go south to San Francisco or not, but I'll return to commence the Ontario season in October," she told the reporter.

Emily Johnson had slowly come to accept the fact that her daughter was going to continue her career on the recital stage. She had allowed herself to be convinced that *The White Wampum* would not sell on Pauline's past performances alone. But Emily's health was deteriorating rapidly and she resented Pauline's long absences. She looked forward to the time when Pauline would end her travels and settle down again in Brantford.

On Monday morning, 30 July, the steamer trunk and one small valise that were to be Pauline's standard travelling equipment for the remainder of her career preceded her onto the train for Toronto. There she booked into the Rossin Hotel to wait for Smily. Later she complained to Harry O'Brien:

> As I started on this tour I joined Mr. Smily at Toronto, I was only there one night, and spent the entire evening and dined alone—positively *alone*—not a sole [sic] to talk England to, or to help me not be lonely. The next morning I learned by telephone just before I left at one o'clock that you had returned from the meet and had been in town for some days. Need I say how utterly furious I was that I suffered myself to spend that evening alone, when I might have induced you to come and help me? It is this sort of thing that makes life unfit to live.[2]

She had always been the kind of person who needed, expected and received an enormous amount of pampering from her family and friends. On this night she wanted someone like good old Harry to listen to her and be impressed by her adventures. His esteem and approval of her activities was important to her.

Ernest Shipman was the new manager of the Johnson-Smily partnership, since Yeigh's career now demanded all his time. Shipman never travelled with them because he had a number of performers under contract, but he seems to have made satisfactory tour bookings for them nonetheless. However, he may not have been altogether honest. If he was still managing the partnership in the summer of 1896, he would have been the person Pauline complained of when she told Horatio Hale that she had been left in "pecuniary troubles" by her manager's "default."[3]

By Yeigh's standards, Shipman's tour was rather sedately paced, and it was confined almost exclusively to railroad towns, all of them with reasonably large populations and fair hotels. Nevertheless, it provided a good trial run of the west. Pauline and Smily boarded the train for Orillia at one o'clock 31 July en route to the opening performance of their tour the following night in Orillia. By 23 August they were already in Rat Portage (Kenora), and Pauline's letters were optimistic about the trip ahead. She wrote O'Brien:

> These August days are gorgeous. The atmosphere is rife with ame-
> thyst, amber and opal tints, parented by the far off bush fires, and the
> thin north air. The sun lays like a ball of blood, and oh! the stillness,
> the silence, the magnitude of this country impresses me as it never has
> before. I cannot tell you how I love my Canada, or how infinitely
> dearer my native soil is to me since I started on this long trip.[4]

They played one night in Morden, Manitoba, and then moved
on to Boissevain, Souris and Carman. On the first of September they
played Manitou, on the second West Selkirk, then settled into
Winnipeg for a four-night run. The stops after that read like the
railway's timetable: Brandon, Medicine Hat, Pincher Creek,
Lethbridge, Fort Macleod, Calgary, Banff, Golden, Vancouver, New
Westminster, then across the Straight to Nanaimo and Victoria. On
the first of October they were ready to begin the long trip home again,
this time without any stops en route.

They had played to full houses and satisfied their customers. On
4 September the *Winnipeg Morning Free Press* said: "It is safe to say that
no such a celebration in recital has visited the city in years, and large
audiences are predicted for the rest of the week." On 26 September
the *Vancouver Daily World* told its readers: "Miss Johnson fully
justified all that was said about her in the advance notices. She has
dramatic cleverness, versatility, elocutionary ability and a pleasing
appearance particularly in Indian costume." Three days later the
Victoria Colonist matched Vancouver's enthusiasm: "The program was
an excellent one . . . and the audience called Miss Johnson before the
curtain many times to show their appreciation."

One of the products of this western tour was an article published
in the *Globe* on Saturday, 15 December of that year. Smily, calling
himself Mr. Prose, had written a lighthearted and highly facetious
account of their travels and into this Pauline, as Miss Poetry, had
inserted poems which commemorated various places they had visited.
The article covered six full page columns of the special Saturday
magazine section of the paper, and it is interesting for the light it
sheds on the difficulties of travel. They called it "There and Back."

After admitting that the reading public had been deluged with articles describing trips across Canada, Smily announced that they did not intend to write about the same old stuff:

> This article will leave the important events out. It is merely intended to be an impressionist sketch of the experience of two Torontonians who travelled from ocean to ocean making numerous pauses during their three months of travel for the noble purpose of furnishing divers dramatic and literary critics with items for their columns. . . .

At Sault Ste. Marie,

> Mr. Prose occupied his spare time at the locks, watching the stream of iron-clads, timber-clads, and mud-clads which filter through day and night. Miss Poetry, on the other hand, having vainly coaxed Mr. Prose to accompany her, nosed out a dusky Chippewa pilot and went tearing down the rapids, acquiring such a reckless taste for this sort of water-tobogganing that she narrowly escaped missing the train, arriving at the station out of breath, but spray soaked from head to foot, just in time to swing gracefully (perhaps) on the last car as it moved out. Miss Poetry caught some music from the rapids as well as a fine large cold in the head.

Pauline's expedition by canoe was photographed, but she and her guides appear rather indistinct in the photo. From Sault Ste. Marie the travellers took the train to Sudbury, then proceeded west again to keep a date at Rat Portage. There, Pauline had problems understanding the hotel proprietor.

> There is a hotel proprietor at Rat Portage, a Frenchman, and all who have been guests at his house laugh at his one peculiarity. He does not understand the meaning of the word "again" and puts it into his sentences in a most promiscuous manner, the result often being ridiculous. For instance, when Miss Poetry went down to breakfast he remarked:
> "Ah, good morning again!"
> "Good morning! Er—but I have not said it before!"
> "No, of course, you have just come down again."
> Miss Poetry (looking a bit startled), "Yes, I have just come down."
> "And you go in to your breakfast now again, eh?"
> "But I have not had breakfast before!"
> "No, no, of course not. You have it again, though, now?"

Before Pauline began touring she had attended church faithfully every Sunday with her mother and Eva, but travelling had changed all that. There was less and less time for the ordered occasions of her former existence.

We arrived in Port Arthur on Sunday and forgetting what day it was (as people often do while travelling) we went for a walk up the hill that overlooks the town. . . . It was only after we commented on the hush that seemed over everything and in the search for some expression that would fittingly describe it, had hit upon the phrase "Sabbath calm" that we realized it was the seventh day.

BENEDICTUS

Something so tender fills the air to-day
What it may be or mean no voice can say,
But all the harsh hard things seem far away.

Something so restful lies on lake and shore,
The world seems anchored, and life's petty war
Of haste and labour gone forevermore.

Something so holy lies upon the land,
Like to a blessing to a saintly hand,
A peace we feel but cannot understand.

The article also revealed some of the vaudeville-style humour that went on between the partners behind the scenes.

At Boissevain . . . the water is opaque.

In this place there are two factions: strict teetotallers and the more intelligent. It is a funny place. You cannot walk ten yards along the sidewalk without falling over a snake. This of course is one argument for the first party. On the other hand, some villainous smelling compound was provided us in the dressing room which we at first sight took to be lemonade. Mr. Prose remarked to the official that brought it that it was very kind of them to provide fancy drinks but that simple water was all that was required.

"Wal, that's what ye've got," replied Aquarius.

Mr. Prose looking around the room as if in search of this hitherto undiscovered object asked, "But where is it?"

"Why here, right here in this yer glass pitcher."

"Oh, this is water and I thought it was lemonade. But why did you rinse the milk jug with it?"

Aquarius (growing ruffled), "I ain't washed no milk jug in it. That there is the best water in Boissevaine and comes from the best well in town."

Miss Poetry (dramatic aside): "That explains the snakes!"

Performers who found themselves booked to tour the prairies in winter at the turn of the century counted themselves unlucky, but the summer could be just as treacherous.

After having worn a spring coat at Rat Portage, Mr. Prose had foolishly imagined that the summer was over. Now summer may be and is a beautiful season in its own way, but it does not lie in the direction of footlights, crowded auditoriums, and stuffy dressing rooms with windows that will not open.

Consequently, we in the characters of benign bestowers of matter for the dramatic columns aforesaid do not look upon this season of the year with the same appreciative fondness that summer hotel proprietors, boat builders, and fickle summer girls do.

Well, as remarked before, we had consigned summer to its annual bed of dry leaves and were prepared for cool weather when we struck the south branch[5] and there we sweltered for one week in the steam-pipe breath of the Chinook wind. . . .

Pauline and Smily did not always travel first class and sometimes found themselves sharing accommodation with immigrants in the colonial or colonist cars. These had wooden seats above which were wooden shelves intended for beds.

It's not until you wake up in Winnipeg that you are in touch with the plains and after a few hundred miles of piled up rocks you appreciate them, but long before the Rockies are reached you grow desperately tired of them again and turn from the view outside to your fellow passengers for something to interest you. There is such a variety of nationalities to be found in the colonial cars, that this is easy to discover. 'Arry's from England, Murphy's from Ireland, Sandies [sic] from Scotland are all there, but Chinamen seem to be in the majority most of the time. . . .

At Fort Macleod, with time on their hands before the next performance, Pauline and Smily played games in the wind and witnessed Indian pony races.

The west wind comes in its full force through this town. The west wind we feel in the east is not the original article, but a mere fragment of it. It scatters after it leaves MacLeod, but there it always blows; sometimes it blows a hurricane, sometimes a gale, sometimes a cyclone, but it always blows. If you drop a dollar bill say good-bye to it unless you are on horseback. The prairie is so flat that anything as light as paper keeps on the move all the time. We had some most exciting races with two pages of newspaper which we tore into small pieces and let the wind carry along. Mr. Prose's fragments won most of the contests, however, as he had a copy of the *New York Herald* while Miss Poetry was handicapped with a scientific journal which was so slow in comparison to the *Yankee Times* that to even matters up, she tore out all the more ponderous words, but even then the *Herald* took the jump over the cliff into the Old Man River (the goal) first every time.

They had a sort of miniature Buffalo Bill's Wild West at MacLeod the day we were there with an Indian race on Indian ponies that alone was worth five dollars to see.

The race usually ends in a fight between the various competitors but it is exciting enough without the fracas. The riders dispense with saddle and ride barebacked (both horse and jockey). An article resembling an apron is the only habit of the latter. When the word is given to go, they go! They do not temporize, neither do they dally. They are not trained jockeys and so understand nothing about pulling or any of those eastern wiles, but they get there, yea, verily, they get there!

It is the very opposite of an eastern race. There the onlookers do all the yelling, but the uproar of the spectators at MacLeod was as the snap of a toy pistol to the bang of a rifle compared with the sustained war-whoop of that mob of naked Indians as they whirled past. What a bonanza a dozen of them would be scattered through the audience in some of those towns where it is considered vulgar to applaud! Thus thought Mr. P.

Unfortunately, by the time they reached Vancouver Pauline was writing verses to please local audiences again. "Little Vancouver" which was included in "There and Back" is perhaps the worst verse she ever wrote.

> Little Vancouver was born in the west,
> The healthiest baby on Canada's breast,
> What matter if once in its cradle it lay
> Its life all but doomed on its christening day

The poor little body fire-fevered lay tos't,[6]
And Canada mourned her sweet infant as lost.
But little Vancouver just shook its small head
And said, "I'm laid up but you bet I'm not dead."

And motherly Canada nursed the wee youth
And bought it a railroad to cut its first tooth,
And soon it grew out of its swaddling bands
To slip from the lap and the old nurse's hands
To toddle away in its two little shoes,
While all its grown relatives soon heard the news
That the sturdy young westerner nothing depresses,
For little Vancouver is in its short dresses.

This doggerel goes on for two more stanzas. Smily concluded the article by explaining that his intention

> was to speak only of impressions and we have endeavoured to keep to this rule. Otherwise we might have told you of two nights during which Mr. Prose sat up waiting for a train that was ten hours late, or of the day we spent in the caboose of a freight train (from 9 A.M. to 8 P.M., travelling 83 miles) because the time-table had changed, or of the narrow escape at Nanaimo, where Mr. P. insisted on going to the best hotel in the place and the other one [the Royal Hotel] caught fire in the night and burnt to the ground, along with the entire surrounding block, cremating two human beings and causing another to break her back jumping from the window, or of the Grizzly Bear we saw at Medicine Hat. I say we might have discoursed at great length regarding these events, but we have not, and as our panorama is over, we will ring down the Curtain.

The success of the tour made it plain to Pauline and Smily that it would be profitable to go west again with a much-expanded itinerary. But as Pauline boarded the eastbound CPR in Vancouver in early October, her mind was on her mother in Brantford, not on business. While en route west, she had received a telegram announcing the death of her brother Henry Beverly. Only forty years of age, he had died of a heart attack on the street in Columbia, Pennsylvania. His body was taken to the local hospital and he would have received a pauper's funeral except for the intervention of a local man who realized who he was. This man arranged to send the body home for burial in the old Mohawk Cemetery. Pauline had just arrived in

Medicine Hat when she received the news, and was unable to return for the funeral. She wrote Harry:

> I have just lost my dear eldest brother. . . . No one knew he was ill, it was so sudden, and the shock to me is awful—I was too far west to get home in time, and so I go on night after night before the public—for when one is under signed contract they may not have a heart. It was worst while he lay dead, and I in gay gowns, and with laughter on my face and tears in my heart, went on and on—the mere doll of the people and a slave to money. . . .[7]

It is true that when the Johnsons were all young, Beverly had been very dear to her. In those days their unique family life bound all the Johnson children closely together, and their parents encouraged them to lean on one another. They canoed and camped and snowshoed together, and spent long evenings reading to each other or singing around the family piano. They formed an exclusive club.

Beverly had led the family sports and in later years became known in Hamilton as a lacrosse star. He was also musically talented and had become quite an accomplished flautist by the time he was in his teens. He was a good-looking young man. A contemporary of Pauline's who arrived in Brantford after Beverly had left home says that he

> was reported to be even more handsome and attractive [than his brother] and perhaps one can imagine something of his character by knowing that his second initial was said by his many friends to stand for a name he could hardly have been christened—Beverly Hell Johnson.[8]

But Beverly was the first to break away from the family. After graduating from Hellmuth College, he never returned to Chiefswood or to Brantford but took a position in Hamilton with the Life Association Company of Canada. His advance within the company was steady because he had an exceptional aptitude for finance. In 1883, when the New York Life Assurance Company opened its Canadian division, Beverly went with them first to Montreal, then Toronto, then the Maritimes, and finally New York City. There he changed employers. He was on an organizing and inspection tour for the Anglo-American Loan Investment Company when he died.

Long before his death, he had ceased to regard Brantford as

home, and after 1888 he had even stopped joining the family there for Christmas. His values had changed dramatically in the twenty years he had been away; he no longer understood or sympathized with the aspirations of his younger brother and sisters. He felt alienated from his mother and blamed her for the fact that he felt unable to marry. He told Pauline that their mother should have talked of the nobility and beauty of love and the honour of marriage instead of choking their human tendencies. "We'll all be waifs and strays one day," he said. "Not one of us will marry."9 In trying to be the aristocrat his mother demanded, Beverly had become an isolate, unable to find anyone to love him.

In his own world, though Beverly never denied his Indian heritage, he never drew it to anyone's attention. It had ceased to be a factor in his life because he had no inheritance among his father's people. He had difficulty, therefore, in acknowledging a sister engaged in a stage career based on her Indian heritage and featuring a flamboyant Indian act. Few letters passed between them. And though he was living in New York when Pauline set sail on the *Etruria,* apparently he did not see her off.

Allen was the "big brother" to whom Pauline had always turned. Although only three years her senior, he was the one whose advice she sought all her life and who spoiled her most. On her trips to Hamilton in the years before her career began, he had escorted her to the theatre, treated her to sittings with a portrait photographer, and tried to match her up with his gentlemen friends. Like Pauline, he had inherited his father's love of costume and pageantry, and took great pride in wearing Indian attire. He had the honour of dancing in full regalia in the ceremony that preceded the unveiling of the Brant Memorial. But when he attempted to maintain that side of his cultural background after he went to Hamilton to work, he ran into trouble. He made the mistake of inviting one of his employers' daughters to a party given in a room he had decorated with his Indian relics and he hosted the affair in his Mohawk costume. The next day he was fired. The experience was a sobering one; he became much more conservative and learned to keep his Indian heritage private and his interest in Mohawk affairs on an academic level. In later years he became an enthusiastic member of the United Empire Loyalists Association of Canada and served for seven years as its vice-president;

this involvement, he discovered, was a socially acceptable way to express his heritage. Allen was, therefore, somewhat uncomfortable with Pauline's determinedly Indian pose, while at the same time he experienced vicarious pleasure every time a white audience applauded her Indian costume.

Pauline's alienation from her brothers was insignificant, however, beside the yawning gulf that separated her from her sister Eva. Instead, all the bitterness, jealousy and distrust they felt was hidden under layers of polite intercourse. But though both women knew this alienation existed, in their younger years neither would express it for fear of hurting their mother.

The rivalry began with Eva's fear that her parents did not love her. A wiry, articulate, determined little girl, she was fairly contented until Pauline was born. After that her parents lavished most of their time and attention on the new baby because she was sickly. Eva did everything to regain her parents' attention when it seemed to her that they preferred the new child. Her resentment grew with the years, but she bottled it up; no one in the Johnson household expressed unpleasant emotions openly.[10]

By the time Pauline was in her teens, she had become strikingly beautiful and was already recognized for her theatrical talents. Eva was good at mathematics at school and was a model student at Hellmuth, but no one had made a fuss over her. And no one ever said she was beautiful. In time, she became so convinced of her own ugliness that she took scissors to all the family photographs she could lay hands on, carefully cutting out her own face.

Eva never married. One account states that at the age of twenty-three she was engaged to marry an Indian doctor, but after his sudden death she refused all offers of marriage. But T. S. H. Shearman, in a *Vancouver Province* article in 1939, had an alternate explanation. He claimed to have been a good friend to the whole Johnson family at the time of Eva's engagement, and wrote: "Passing his [the young Indian doctor's] residence one day she [Eva] found a drinking party in progress and instantly cancelled the engagement."[11] Shearman's story has two things in its favour. First, he prided himself on being Eva's close friend and does not seem to have intended to malign her. Second, the Brantford newspapers, which normally celebrated the fall of the smallest sparrow with columns of grief-stricken prose, never mentioned the death of the unfortunate young doctor.

After his "death" Eva suffered once more in silence because her mother did not allow discussion of love and marriage. The years passed and the opportunity to marry never came to Eva again. She embarked on a career as compensation. The Indian Affairs office allowed scope for her mathematical ability and her managerial skills; she developed a high regard for money and began practising stringent economies in her personal life in order to put money aside.

She was convinced that Pauline was profligate both with money and family heirlooms. Pauline denied it and told a friend, "Do you know what I would do if I had only two dollars in the world and I knew it would be my last? I'd spend half on my body and half on my soul. With one dollar I would buy a whacking good meal, and with the other a dozen cut carnations. Then I could die happy looking at my lovely flowers."[12] Pauline simply believed that worldly wealth was meant to be shared. She loved to give presents: a wampum belt to Sir Frederick Leighton, a statuette to her friend Jean Morton, poems to artist Alma-Tadema and poet Charles Roberts, a wolf-clan talisman to writer Ernest Thompson Seton, her moccasins to editor Lionel Makovski, her time to worthy causes, nicknames to beloved friends, advice to fledgling writers. Once she paid out several hundred dollars which she could not afford to save a young bank clerk friend from jail when he had been caught embezzling. He never repaid her.

This gift-giving horrified and angered Eva, but there was little she could do about it except remonstrate with Pauline since she did not wish to antagonize her mother. Eva was also appalled by Pauline's treatment of presents that she had been given: she revelled in them and kept them around her to remind herself that people loved her. By the same token Pauline could not understand Eva's lack of pleasure in gifts. She wrote:

> I always use the things that are given to me; my sister has a habit of placing gifts away carefully in a box or drawers. She keeps them unsoiled and unused . . . consequently she has quantities of excellent articles tucked away in a state of good preservation. . . . I have the constant and daily aura of my friends about me . . . and I think I have the gold of treasure, and get the most out of life.[13]

The one thing that the two of them did agree on was their Indian heritage, but even this caused friction between them. Eva's forte was recording Mohawk history, especially that of her direct forebears. She was one of the leading members of the Brant Historical Society and wrote articles concerning the Mohawks for the Ontario Historical Society's journal. But in her efforts to show her ancestors to the best advantage, she romanticized some of their stories beyond credibility. Pauline, by dramatizing the same stories in poetry, did not purport to be writing historical fact even if people chose to look upon it that way.

After Pauline began touring in 1892, the household on Napoleon Street consisted of Eva and Emily, but though Eva looked after her mother with absolute devotion, it was Pauline the old lady pined for. Eva, realizing this but still determined to be appreciated, attempted to mimic her mother's concern for Pauline's welfare; however, because of the difference in motivation, most of what she offered Pauline was nagging and bossing. Friends who saw Pauline's annoyance over Eva's apparently well-intentioned thoughtfulness began to comment on how fame had made Pauline less appreciative of her old friends and family. And they noticed that her visits home were becoming shorter and shorter.

At the beginning of October 1894 Pauline returned from her western trip and went directly home to Brantford as she had promised her mother. At last, Emily could share her grief over Beverly's death, and the two women went to the cemetery to visit the new grave beside that of Chief Johnson. But if Emily had hoped that Pauline might be induced to stay home to console her, she was mistaken; Pauline was gone before a week was out, embarking on a tour of Ontario towns that would last until Christmas.

On 18 January 1895 *The Week* reprinted a brief item that had originated with the *St. Thomas Evening Journal* under the byline of a critic named "Malcolm." Offended by the tone of "There and Back," Malcolm had accused Pauline of "masquerading as a poetess." He had taken the entire article seriously and recommended that in future Pauline stick to elocution.

Pauline and Smily had already embarked on their second western tour by the time *The Week* reprinted Malcolm's criticism, so Yeigh took it upon himself to respond. In the next edition of the paper, he scolded Malcolm in a letter to the editor: "One whose verses have been published (and paid for) by such high literary journals as the New York *Independent, Harper's Weekly,* London (Eng.) *Public Opinion,*

Outing, and others can hardly be said to be 'masquerading as a poetess.' " [14]

The affair might have ended there, but two weeks later another contributor to *The Week* criticized Pauline's use of slang in several of her poems, most notably "Little Vancouver." The writer protested: "I have heard that poets cannot always sustain themselves on the level of their highest flight; but I cannot recall one worthy of the name who has descended to the region of *slang!*" [15]

Yeigh rode to the rescue again, but in the 1 March issue where his next letter appeared, two other contributors also had their say. The first commended the Johnson-Smily article and suggested that there would have been no criticism if her fame and name had already been established. The second was from Thomas O'Hagan, the editor of the *Detroit Daily Tribune* and one of Pauline's earliest fans. He closed the issue as far as *The Week* was concerned by saying: "You cannot get the whole world to agree on the absolute value of Milton nor even Shakespeare. How then can we hope to see all Canadians recognize Miss Johnson as a poet of real worth?"

It was not until July 1895 that *The White Wampum* was finally released. By this time, Pauline had almost despaired of seeing it, but, though she was seething with frustration, there was little that she could do from Canada to speed the publishing process. And every month had brought new promises and new disappointments from Lane.

However, when the book finally appeared, Pauline's career received the boost she had been waiting for, because the reviewers sat up and paid attention. Virtually the earliest and best review was written by the critic for *The Week*. "We have read them all," said the reviewer, "—some more than once — and we have not found a bad or indifferent poem in the collection!" He remarked on the

> power of lucid, picturesque, forcible expression possessed by Miss Johnson. No one can fail to be struck with the musical rhythm of her lines, and she has great power of rhyming—no slight accomplishment, and one which we venture to think constitutes a very considerable ornament to English poetry. A good example of charming word painting—word music rather—is "The Song my Paddle Sings."

The reviews from Britain were mixed. From the *St. James*

Budget, "Miss Johnson reaches a high level in both thought and expression in the later and more personal poems." *The Literary World* of London said:

> The authoress has no original way of wrapping her subjects up in words. She follows models that are not particularly deserving of the compliment that is implied by imitation. It is when she does not aim herself at the redskin, so to speak, that we like her most. When she is restful, she charms, and there are a few poems in this little book that deserve to be honoured by critics of all sorts and one of these is "Sunset." Another is "Overlooked."

The *Glasgow Herald* disagreed. "The best things in the book," they announced, "are some Indian tales which fairly breathe the spirit of the redman and his home in the great forests and the illimitable prairie." The *Guardian,* unaware of her lineage, declared, "The idea of posing as an Indian bard cannot be counted among her happiest inspirations," but a week later another reviewer in the same paper decided that he quite liked her work. The *Pall Mall Gazette* was commendatory; the *Sketch* was ambivalent, and the *Westminster Gazette* could find nothing in the volume that it "would be doing justice to the writer to quote."

Pauline presumably suffered the usual pangs that a creator feels when his work is maligned or commended, but she has left only one comment. On the back of a clipping of a review that referred to her as a "Bostonian," she wrote: "God forgive the slanderers. Why, oh why am I called a Bostonian?"[16]

The new western tour on which Pauline and Smily embarked in 1895 was considerably more venturesome than their first one had been, and it included many settlements that were far from the rail lines. This made financial sense, since the people of the more isolated towns and villages were starved for entertainment. The few entertainers who took shows into these places found that everyone was quite happy to pay whatever was asked and most of the audiences could be counted on to applaud every item on the program, good or bad.

The pace on this tour was just as wearying as that set by Yeigh two years earlier, but it was the usual pace of all the one-night-stand artists who headed west expecting to make a profit. They had to play settlements of every size, a different place every night, five nights a week, appearing in little halls (which were invariably called "Opera Houses"), theatres, hotel dining rooms and lounges, churches, Masonic chambers, warehouses and even sheds. Sometimes, when the only community building was a schoolhouse, they hired that for their show and faced an audience seated in the children's desks. On later tours they hired pool halls once or twice, and even played in a bar.

The usual hiring arrangement in these settlements was for the owner of the hall to take his share of the admissions first; anything left over went to the performers, so when it was a small "house," they could end up with empty pockets. Sometimes, however, entertainers were sponsored by a society or lodge, and then they worked for a percentage of the take. For example, in Winnipeg on their previous tour, Pauline and Smily played four nights, each one for a different organization: the Winnipeg Grace Church, the Rover Bicycle Club, the Winnipeg Church of Zion, and the North Presbyterian Congregation. After a performance, touring people were either "entertained," that is, accommodated for the night in the home of a member of the sponsoring group, or sent to the local hotel. In towns large enough to provide some choice of accommodation, they stayed at hotels that had been recommended by the experienced travelling theatre companies or by salesmen (known as "commercials") who knew where the cockroaches were hiding.

These small-town tours could be a terrible ordeal for show people. Many of the prairie farmers had never seen an entertainment before and talked throughout the show, commenting on its merits to the entire throng. And as everybody in the community wanted to see the show, mothers were forced to bring along their babes-in-arms who could be counted on to provide competition. During one concert in Nakusp, British Columbia, Pauline found herself deadlocked for the audience's attention all evening with an infant who had considerably more lung power than she had.

But babies were no problem at all compared to boys. The leader of the Webling Sisters act wrote:

> Boys were the disturbing element, or tried to be, at every entertainment. In some places the grown-ups had weakly given way to them for so long that luckless troupes were wholly at their mercy.
>
> They would gather round the hall long before the doors opened. They sat in the back rows, where they imitated cocks, dogs and cats in

a spirited and lifelike manner; they cracked nuts and aimed the shells at the shades of the footlights or the pianist; they threw hard peppermint sweets on the stage (known as conversation lozenges with compliments stamped on them); they greeted our appearance in costume with frantic howls of amazement; they climbed and scrambled onto the backs of seats, up to window ledges and over doors; they yelled "Angcore! Angcore!" till they were hoarse.[17]

Even Pauline suffered from the "boy-problem." She told an interviewer of one occasion when she was interrupted by constant heckling from the gallery of a small-town opera house. In a lull, she said to the audience: "When I see a crowd of boys having a good time in the gallery, I am always sorry—"

The boys, expecting the usual reprimand, refused to let her finish. She stood smiling at them until their noise died down again, then said: "I always wish I were among them!"

This apparently ended the interruptions for that evening.[18]

Women recitalists faced one problem in the small towns they played that they seldom faced in the cities. It was not uncommon for them to be ostracized by the wives of the farmers and miners who lumped all women performers into the "stage actress" category. For these unsophisticated, morally upright women of the pioneer areas, an actress was a dangerous woman who could have an evil influence on the whole community. Besides, the glamour of some creature in a lacy gown and feather boa was galling for women who owned one "best dress" and whose hands were as raw and work-stained as a man's. They welcomed the entertainment, but they did not want the entertainer hanging around any longer than necessary. The men of these communities generally regarded actresses somewhat differently than the women did; they propositioned them.

Peggy Webling told the story of the caretaker's wife at one small-town "opera house." The woman stood watching the three teen-aged Webling Sisters from behind the scenes while they rehearsed their performance, then said, "I don't know as it's right for me to be here, as I've just come from the Revivalist meeting in town!" Then she smiled at the youngest Webling who was just fourteen. "Ain't she real sweet? Do you think it will do me any harm to watch *her?*"

Some of the women of the stage really were "dangerous" women, hardened and cheapened by the difficult life style. Theirs was a precarious existence: monotonous train rides followed by stony-eyed audiences and a pitifully small "take" at the door, the profits from each night's show wiped out by the hotel bill the following day. For these women, holidays were synonymous with unemployment, and exhaustion was the normal way of life. And they all knew that losing their looks was tantamount to suicide. To stay employed, most stage women had to rely on keeping in favour with the men who controlled the touring companies, the talent agencies and the theatres. The simplest expedient was to marry the tour manager, though leading ladies of this type had a high mortality and divorce rate. Other women found security in family companies where fathers and brothers assured them of stage roles. This was true of companies like the Coghlans from New York, in which three generations of a single family controlled the company. In this case, Rose Coghlan, one of the second generation, was the company's star. And then there were the handful of tough-minded, aggressive leading ladies with superior acting ability who controlled their own companies and chose their leading men mostly for their talents after the lights had been turned off. Pauline's friend Mlle Rhea was one of these.

Many female performers never set foot on the stage of a big-city theatre in all their years in the business; for them life was just a succession of one-night stands in mining towns and prairie settlements, ending in a hopeless marriage to some stagestruck farmer, or perhaps in the comparative financial stability of some mining town cathouse.

Smily was Pauline's first line of defence on their small-town tours. Although he could not have given much resistance to a determined physical attacker, his presence discouraged the men who thought that Pauline might be a lady of easy virtue. Her deportment was her second protection. The aloofness and hauteur that had made other children call her "proudy" now was useful in convincing both farmers and their wives that she was not to be regarded as a "stage actress." In addition, she had picked up a few tips from the English upper class on how to keep people at a distance. As a result women always considered her a lady and became her staunch supporters.

Pauline's tours of the west were an enormous change of pace after London. A month after she returned, she had mourned: "Well, I have left England behind me, left it and its warm hearts, its applause, its possible laurel wreaths, and out here I am forgetting it. The little island has dropped many thousand miles behind me, many, many days away from me." But Pauline never forgot London. Her experiences there influenced her conduct for the rest of her life, because London had spontaneously granted her the status that she had been trying so hard to establish in Canada. They had taken her "Mohawk Princess" billing seriously, had decided that she was exotic foreign royalty, and had thereafter accepted her as both the cultivated lady and the princess from the primeval forests.

It was a difficult image to maintain once she was back in Canada. The educated audiences of Toronto and Ottawa were willing to accept her dual role without too much persuasion, but in the rest of the country she could not assemble this kind of audience. The people beyond these two centres of culture saw her either as a cultivated lady or as an Indian. They could not see her as both at the same time, and Pauline would surrender neither role. In the end, because she could not expect to make a living by reciting only in Toronto and Ottawa, she compromised by giving her small-town audiences two separate people. Tekahionwake, the Indian maiden, dressed herself in buckskin, wore scalps at her belt, and gave them war whoops and stories of warring braves and heroic Indian women. Pauline, the aristocrat, wore satin and lace and recited lyrics. To make them both more palatable, she made wisecracks, invented funny stage business, and composed bits of doggerel to celebrate local events and characters. From this kind of performance she hoped to build a following that would gradually accept the Indian as aristocrat and vice versa, as her London audiences had spontaneously done. In time, she believed, she would even be able to give up the "brainless lines and business" which Harry O'Brien despised.

In the cities of the east, the Canadian aristocracy welcomed Pauline as one of their own after her trip to London, and she revelled in being lionized by the wealthy. In Montreal, she lunched with Sir William and Lady Van Horne: " 'They put up something very good' as the out-west senator said. His pictures are glorious. Rousseau, Corot, Doré, Reynolds, Daubigny—all the great names—Ah! it was a feast worth having—that hour with his beautiful pictures!"[19]

When she was touring, Pauline gave herself the royal treatment.

In the big cities, she made a point of staying in the best hotels, the Russell in Ottawa, and the Windsor in Montreal. She did, however, complain of the latter: "Horrors! What a life. The hotel is as usual, big, dull, ponderous. The waiters profound in their majesty, and refusing to run even for a 'quarter.' "[20]

In Winnipeg, Pauline established her home from 1896 to 1899 in the Manitoba Hotel which at that time was considered to be on a par with the Chateau Laurier. In Vancouver, she checked into the Hotel Vancouver, considered the only decent stopping place for the gentry. And she did all this whether business at the box office was good, bad or indifferent. Her disparaging remarks about the Windsor were made, in fact, when she and Smily were in the middle of a week of almost empty houses.

In the small towns, of course, she was reduced to sleeping in whatever hotel was available, but as she became more experienced she learned to find herself a better bed for the night by ferreting out the local aristocracy. In every town and hamlet across the country, there were a few souls who had known better days before they came to Canada and a few more who had left eastern Canada to invest where they could see new potential. These were the people who welcomed the opportunity to provide a roof for her.

On the prairies she found little pockets of marooned upper-class men and women, the last of the remittance men and their families. On one occasion, she was invited to play to a whole audience of English gentry in the town hall of Cannington Manor. This unique settlement, forty miles south of Moosomin, Saskatchewan, was the brainchild of Capt. Edward Pierce, an English gentleman who had lost most of his money through a bank failure. He took up a homestead with his wife and eight children, and then induced the sons of upper class Englishmen to emigrate to attend his "Agricultural College." Pierce also lured a large number of retired professionals and gentry who were intrigued by the wide open spaces and new opportunities.

The settlers arrived with maids, valets and butlers; they brought great quantities of expensive furniture including grand pianos which had to be trundled over the precipitous Moose Mountain trail from the railway. Then, once settled, the inhabitants of Cannington Manor set about creating a replica of the life they had known in

England, complete with a rigid class system that did not allow them to mingle with the ordinary Canadian settlers in adjacent townsites.

They imported foxhounds from the Isle of Wight and organized a hunt club. Hunts were conducted in proper hunting kit, and the ladies rode sidesaddle in skirted riding habits. They established an annual Hunt Dinner and Dance in Cannington Town Hall; they had Race Week, Tennis Week and Cricket Week on carefully prepared grounds. Evenings were spent in literary and artistic pursuits and in amateur theatricals.

When Pierce died in 1888, the leadership of the colony passed to the Beckton brothers—Ernest, Billy and Bertie—who had built Didsbury, a twenty-two-room mansion, and maintained a prosperous racing stable with imported thoroughbreds. The Becktons, however, were not great businessmen, and it was only nine years before they found themselves ruined. By 1900, after the CPR's new branch line bypassed the community, Didsbury was already abandoned, and most of the settlers had scattered, the young men going off to the Klondike or the Boer War.

Although the exact date of Pauline's concert at Cannington Manor is unknown, it is recorded that the Beckton brothers sent their coach to Moosomin to fetch her and her partner. This places the event sometime between the spring of 1895 when she first toured the smaller prairie settlements and 1897 when the Beckton brothers went bankrupt. For Pauline, every aspect of the affair from the formally attired audience to the uniformed coachman was a re-enactment of her experiences in England, so that she found it difficult to leave Cannington Manor and return to the "opera houses" and pool halls of the other prairie settlements.

In Fredericton, New Brunswick, her hosts on several occasions were the members of the prestigious Roberts clan. The family head, the Reverend George Goodridge Roberts, was rector of St. Anne's Church and canon of Christ Church Cathedral in Fredericton, as well as a distinguished scholar and degree examiner in Latin, Greek and French at the University of New Brunswick. By the time Pauline began her tours, his son Charles G. D. Roberts and his nephew Bliss Carman had become recognized as two of Canada'a foremost poets.

Although Pauline had been corresponding with Charles G. D. Roberts since her first success in *The Week,* she did not meet him until she toured New Brunswick in the summer of 1895. After she had given her recital in Fredericton, she accepted an invitation from Canon and Mrs. Roberts to stay at the rectory. Their son, though now living in Windsor, Nova Scotia, where he was professor of English at King's College, brought his family to stay at the rectory for the occasion of Pauline's visit. The next morning he and Pauline went for a drive along the Saint John River, crossing over into the parish of Douglas to end up at Crock's Point, a high bluff ten miles beyond Fredericton. From here, Roberts was able to point out the house where he was born.

That afternoon, before Pauline caught her train, Roberts presented her with the manuscript copy of his book *Songs of the Common Day* which had been published in 1893, and the pen with which it had been written. Later, she returned the compliment by sending him the poem she had written to mark the occasion of their drive together; she called it "The Douglas Shore" in honour of his birthplace.

But during most of Pauline's travels across the country, the only oases of culture she was likely to find were the North West Mounted Police outposts where many of the officers were younger sons of British gentry. She claimed a special affinity with these "riders of the plains" because, as guardians of the British Empire, they were allied to her Mohawk forebears who had also fought for the Crown.

She guaranteed herself a respectful welcome in the social circles of the Mounted Police posts by introducing herself as the granddaughter of John Smoke Johnson, the brave warrior who had fought beside Joseph Brant. But she converted the police into devoted fans by eulogizing them in poems such as "The Riders of the Plains" and in short stories such as "Mother o' the Men" which was inspired by an incident in the lives of Major and Mrs. Constantine in the Yukon.

In the spring of 1895 she used her friendship with a police inspector to parlay her Indian heritage into a donation from an Indian chief. It happened in Fort Macleod where Pauline and Smily had returned to give their second concert; the morning after the event, she stood with the post's inspector and his wife watching an Indian chief riding in from the southeast:

> He was followed by at least fifty of his tribe—the Bloods of southern Alberta. They all wore fringed buckskin leggings, and were stripped to the waist, the bodies stained and painted in soft pastel tints and

overlined with streaks of scarlet and dark brilliant blue. At his belt the Chief wore, by actual count, seventeen scalps, all taken in wars across the border when the Bloods invaded the territory of the Sioux and trouble continued for years, that had first been stirred up by wars in Sitting Bull's time. This particular chief was a great "Britisher" and an American Indian scalp was, to him, a veritable Victoria Cross.

The desire of my life had been to possess an Indian scalp, a Sioux scalp particularly, so I interviewed the inspector and asked what chance there was of securing the treasure.

He shook his head gravely. "None, I am afraid," he replied.

Then I offered a sum of money far in advance of what I was able to spare, but the Inspector said that money would not count with the great Blood Chief; that he was already worth about fifty thousand dollars that he had made in cattle.

"However," said the policeman with the gallantry and effort to please that so strikes the Easterners when they first meet any of the force, "I shall try my best to secure one for you, perhaps we can appeal to him through your ancestors. The Mohawks always fought for the British, did they not?"

"Always," I affirmed. "My great grandfather fought against Washington for King George, my grandfather fought as a boy of sixteen under Sir Isaac Brock at Queenston Heights. My father carried dispatches from Niagara Falls to Hamilton during the Fenian Raids."

"Then we've got our good friend the chief, and I think you have got your Sioux scalp," laughed the inspector.

Afterwards I heard how it happened. The inspector approached the Chief and diplomatically opened negotiations. The Chief sat and smoked for a full hour in silence, then he asked thoughtfully:

"You say the lady's father and his fathers before him were great warriors?"

"Yes, great warriors," replied the inspector.

"Who did they fight for—Yankee or Queen?"

"Oh! the Queen always, and the British Crown before the Queen was born," the inspector assured him.

The chief removed a single scalp from his belt and rising to his feet said:

"Send this to the lady who comes from the Land of Morning and tell her I take no money from the daughter of fighting men."

"But you never would have got it," the inspector told me, "no matter how well your ancestors may have fought had they not fought for the British."

It is a beautiful braid of long brown-black hair, the flesh cured and encased in tightly stitched buckskin, and coiled about it close rows of turquoise Hudson's Bay beads.[21]

In 1931 Foster, Pauline's first biographer, described the acquisition of the scalplock as "her joy in the possession of this relic of by-gone valour."[22] To the modern reader, the story smacks of the tourist's pride in having returned from the land of the aboriginals with a genuine artifact. She had simply used her Mohawk ancestry as a bargaining lever to get a trinket which she wanted to add to her costume. There is no evidence that she identified with the Blood chief in any way or regarded the scalp as he did.

The same kind of condescension is apparent in a story by Hector Charlesworth in his *Candid Chronicles*.

> A most interesting experience was to drive through the Six Nations Reserve in Brant and Haldiman counties with Pauline Johnson and her brother. All the Indian farmers, of course, knew them. One summer day we were driving along . . . when Pauline said to me: "Did you know there are still pagans in this part of Canada?" On my expressing surprise she said, "Most of them here about are pagans; we will go into one of their houses, and over the fireplace you will see a turtle rattle; that is the instrument they use in their worship; but be sure not to comment on it." I forget whether the people were Onondagas or Tuscaroras. We alighted and Allen Johnson spoke in Indian to the housewife, who knew no English, asking permission to enter. It was accorded. . . . By a sign Allen showed me a turtle rattle on the wall,—the shell of a great "snapper" with the neck pulled out to serve as a handle had been scooped and filled with dried peas.[23]

Beginning in the year 1892, Pauline began turning out articles which explained the Iroquois people to the reading public. Of all of them, the most interesting is "The Iroquois of the Grand River" which appeared in *Harper's Weekly* accompanied by seventeen woodcuts prepared by the artist H. H. Heming. (One of these depicts Allen Johnson in full Indian costume, complete with a ring in his nose.) Pauline's language in this essay is simple and direct, almost completely devoid of the poeticisms found in her poems and later legends. She makes a plain statement of the Iroquois condition, explaining their life style in a strangely unemotional appeal for greater understanding. In this one article she seems to stand with the Iroquois instead of outside their community.

But in "A Glimpse at the Grand River Indians"[24] her tone is condescending. She makes the pagans seem quaint, their ceremony of the Burning of the White Dog rather crude. Nearly half the article is taken up with moralizing and admonitions to cultivate the pagan red man. She concludes: "One has but to look into the beauties of the pagan faith, pagan honour, and pagan poetry to realize the boundless possibilities to which the Redman may gravitate if he is once placed upon the right road that leads to high civilization."

She told an interviewer from the London *Sketch* in June 1894 that given a chance any Indian could do what she was doing.

> Go to my home on the Grand River Reserve in Ontario and you will find my countrymen under a free constitution framed more than four centuries ago by that greatest of Indian statesmen Hiawatha, no god as dear and dead Longfellow pictured him. Here our chiefs are elected, our councils are conducted and our civil policy is decided as nearly as possible by the laws of the ancient league. The tokens of the bear, the wolf, and the turtle form part of a coat of arms older than many European devices and represent a free commonwealth older than any in Europe, except England and Switzerland and perhaps two of the little republics hidden away among the Pyrenees and Apennines. These are my people, the six nations that form the Iroquois. All Indians are not, of course, so progressive. Some are as far behind the Iroquois as the Turks are behind you English people, but the quality is there if only a chance for advancement be given, and the taint of the whisky-bringing white outlaw be kept away. Put a pure-blooded Indian in the drawing room and he will shine with the rest of you. [24]

But as the years passed, she lost some of this faith in the Indian's adaptability. Her tone became paternal. In 1907 in a letter to Sir Wilfrid Laurier, she begged him to consider with care the successor to the Six Nations Indian superintendent who had just died.

> My people are a peculiar nation and one odd thing is their indifference to persons they know too well. An absolute outsider, an utter stranger, gains their allegiance and their confidence and loyalty to a far greater degree than those they know about the Reservation or its Environments. They are an exacting difficult tribe to govern, often malcontent, often I fear apparently ungrateful but never *really* so. [26]

In 1911 she asked and was granted permission to send young

Chief Mathias Capilano to be presented to Sir Wilfrid. Her letter reads in part:

> Once more the young chief assured me that what he desired most was to "shake hands with the government"—his own expression—and to assure you personally of his allegiance to his majesty, King George.
>
> If you could have witnessed this wonderful transformation from anxiety to delight that his face underwent when he heard of your gracious consent, I think you would have felt rewarded for your kindness.[27]

Yet in spite of the fact that her patronizing disparaged the Indian people, it was absolutely essential to Pauline that the world should accept her as an Indian. And it annoyed her that, because of her mother's white blood, she was sometimes considered white. She expressed her unhappiness to O'Brien in a letter written in 1894: "We are getting into the Indian country now. Every town is full of splendid complexioned Ojibwas, whose copper coloring makes me ashamed of my washed out Mohawk skin, thinned with European blood. I look yellow and 'Chinesey' beside these Indians."[28]

For Pauline, there was an ideal against which she measured all Indians; they must look, think and act like that ideal. History told her that men like Hiawatha and Tecumseh had achieved this ideal in the past, but she had personal knowledge of only two Indians who typified the ideal as she conceived it: her father and her grandfather. But her grandfather was already an extremely old man when she was born; she learned of his exploits only through the stories he told her of his romantic past. He was therefore not much more than a repository of legends. And though her father had mostly Indian blood in his veins, he was actually a hybrid. She underlined this herself when she wrote of his first meeting her mother:

> As the horses drew up before the porch the great front door was noiselessly opened and a lad of seventeen, lithe, clean-limbed, erect, copper-coloured, ran swiftly down the steps, lifted his hat, smiled, and assisted the ladies to alight. The boy was Indian to his fingertips, with that peculiar native polish and courtesy, that absolute ease of manner and direction of glance, possessed only by the old-fashioned type of red man of this continent.

But in this excerpt, the same individual prepares to go to church for his wedding:

> An hour or so later he stood at the hotel door a moment awaiting the cab that was to take him to the church. He was dressed in the height of fashion of the early fifties—very dark wine broadcloth, the coat shaped tightly to the waist and adorned with a silk velvet collar, a pale lavender flowered satin waistcoat, a dull white silk stock collar, a bell-shaped black silk hat. He carried his gloves, for throughout his life he declared that he breathed through his hands, and the wearing of gloves was abhorrent to him.

After the wedding ceremony is over, two witnesses, "the major" and his wife, compliment the white bride on her choice of a husband:

> "My dear," whispered the major's wife, "he's a perfect prince —he's just as royal as he can be! I never saw such manners, such ease. Why girlie, he's a courtier!"
> "Confound the young rogue!" growled the major in her ear. "I haven't had an officer on my staff that can equal him. You're a lucky girl. Yes, confound him, I say!"[29]

Although Pauline wrote this as if it were fiction, she added a note in which she said that it was the story of her mother's life, "every incident of which she related to me herself. . . . I have supplied nothing through imagination, nor have I heightened the coloring of her unusual experiences." The man she described was her father as she (and her mother) saw him. Although all the evidence suggested that he was not a typical man of his people, Pauline preferred to believe that he was, and she used him as the standard against which she measured all Indians, and the model for all that appeared in her poems and stories. Without exception, her fictional protagonists were noble, fearless, proud, motivated by the highest ideals, loving and hating with equal passion, at home in the depths of the forest and in society's drawing rooms.

For example, "As Red Men Die," based on the story of one of her forebears, tells of a warrior who was captured by the hated Hurons. When he is given the choice of walking over a bed of coals singing the

Mohawk war song until death claims him, or living as a slave among the women:

> His eyes flash like an eagle's, and his hands
> Clench at the insult. Like a god he stands.
> "Prepare the fire!" he scornfully demands.

The poem ends:

> Then loyal to his race,
> He bends to death—but *never* to disgrace.

A modern reader can be forgiven for seeing the warrior as a classic example of someone cutting off his nose to spite his face, but for Victorian readers (and later audiences) he was only a slightly different model of the heroes they found in the works of other authors. They knew that whereas ordinary mortals had to live by the rules of expediency and practicality, the heroes of literature, especially soldiers and warriors, were expected to place honour above all else. And in addition, there were enough real life heroes of this kind, such as the men of the famous Charge of the Light Brigade in mid-century and the more recently butchered General Gordon at Khartoum, for the reader to confuse real life and fiction.

Pauline's Indian women were fitting consorts for her heroic men. They are unbelievably selfless and morally pure. In a series of articles she wrote for *Mother's Magazine* in 1908, she described them in all their "beautiful old-fashioned womanliness"[30] making cornbread, weaving rugs from rabbit pelts and begetting "tiny copper-coloured children." They are women to whom "the grace of motherhood is a primitive glory" and they are a moral influence and inspiration to their menfolk. In addition, when they take it upon themselves to live as white people do, these women can compete with any white woman in cooking and sewing skills. At no point does Pauline concede imperfection in their characters—they never gossip, strike their children, hate their husbands, or commit adultery—and though Pauline never lived as an Indian woman or among Indian women, she convinced herself that this was a true picture of their lives. If she knew of any blemishes, she never betrayed them to white readers.

She was angrily critical of the attempts of non-Indian authors to portray Indian women in fiction. In an article published in the 22 May 1892 *Toronto Sunday Globe* and preserved by the Mills Memorial Library at McMaster University, she left few authors of her day unscratched. The article was called "A Strong Race Opinion on the Indian Girl in Modern Fiction."

Every race in the world enjoys its own peculiar characteristics, but it scarcely follows that every individual of a nation must possess these prescribed singularities, or otherwise forfeit in the eyes of the world their nationality. Individual personality is one of the most charming things to be met with, either in a flesh and blood existence, or upon the pages of fiction, and it matters little to what race an author's heroine belongs, if he makes her character distinct, unique and natural.

The American book heroine of to-day is vari-coloured as to personality and action. The author does not consider it necessary to the development of her character and the plot of the story to insist upon her having American-coloured eyes, an American carriage, an American voice, American motives, and an American mode of dying; he allows her to evolve an individuality ungoverned by nationalism—but the outcome of impulse and nature and a general womanishness.

Not so the Indian girl in modern fiction, the author permits her character no such spontaneity, she must not be one of womankind at large, neither must she have an originality, a singularity that is not definitely "Indian." I quote "Indian" as there seems to be an impression amongst authors that such a thing as tribal distinction does not exist amongst the North American aborigines.

The term "Indian" signifies about as much as the term "European" but I cannot recall ever having read a story where the heroine was described as "a European." The Indian girl we meet in cold type, however, is rarely distressed by having to belong to any tribe, or to reflect any tribal characteristics. She is merely a wholesale sort of admixture of any band existing between the MicMacs of Gaspé and the Kwaw-Kewliths of British Columbia, yet strange to say, that notwithstanding the numerous tribes with their aggregate numbers reaching more than 122,000 souls in Canada alone, our Canadian authors can cull from this huge revenue of character, but one Indian girl, and stranger still that this lonely little heroine never had a prototype in breathing flesh and blood existence!

It is a deplorable fact but there is only one of her. The story writer who can create a new kind of Indian girl or better still portray a "real live" Indian girl will do something in Canadian literature that has never been done but once. The general author gives the reader the impression that he has concocted the plot, created his characters, arranged his action, and at the last moment has been seized with the idea that the regulation Indian maiden will make a very harmonious background whereon to paint his picture, that he, never having met this interesting individual, stretches forth his hand to the library shelves, grasps the first Canadian novelist he sees, reads up his subject and duplicates it in his own work.

After a half dozen writers have done this, the reader might as well leave the tale unread as far as the interest touches upon the Indian character, for an unvarying experience tells him that his convenient personage will repeat herself with monotonous accuracy. He knows what she did and how she died in other romances by other romancers and she will do and die likewise in this (she always does die, and one feels relieved that this is so, for she is too unhealthy and too unnatural to live).

The rendition of herself and her doings gains no variety in the pens of manifold authors, and the last thing that they will ever think of will be to study "The Indian Girl" from life, for the being we read of is the offspring of the writer's imagination and never existed outside the book covers that her name decorates. Yes, there is only one of her and her name is "Winona." Once or twice she has borne another appellation, but it always has a "Winona" sound about it. Even Charles Mair, in the masterpiece of Canadian-Indian romances, "Tecumseh," could not resist "Winona." We meet her as a Shawnee, as a Sioux, as a Huron, and then, her tribe unnamed, in the vicinity of Brockville.

She is never dignified by being permitted to own a surname, although, extraordinary to note, her father is always a chief, and had he ever existed, would doubtless have been as conservative as his contemporaries about the usual significance that his people attach to family name and lineage.

In addition to this most glaring error this surnameless creation is possessed with a suicidal mania. Her unhappy, self-sacrificing life becomes such a burden both to herself and the author that this is the only means by which they can extricate themselves from a lamentable tangle, though, as a matter of fact, suicide is an evil positively unknown among Indians. To-day there may be a rare instance where a man crazed by liquor might destroy his own life, but in the periods from whence "Winona's" character is sketched self-destruction was unheard of. This seems to be a fallacy which the best American writers have fallen a prey to. Even Helen Hunt Jackson[31] in her powerful and beautiful romance of "Ramona" has weakened her work deplorably by having no less than three Indians suicide while maddened by their national wrongs and personal grief.

But the hardest fortune that the Indian girl of fiction meets with is the inevitable doom that shadows her love affairs. She is always desperately in love with the young white hero, who in turn is grateful to her for services rendered the garrison in general and himself in particular during red days of war. In short, she is so much wrapped up in him that she is treacherous to her own people, tells falsehoods to her father and the other chiefs of her tribe, and otherwise makes herself detestable and dishonourable. Of course, this white hero never marries her! Will some critic who understands human nature and particularly the nature of authors, please tell the reading public why marriage with the Indian girl is so despised in books and so general in real life? Will this good far-seeing critic also tell us why the book-made Indian makes all the love advances to the white gentleman, though the real wild Indian girl (by the way, we are never given any stories of educated girls, though there are many such throughout Canada) is the most retiring, reticent, non-committal being in existence!

Captain Richardson, in that inimitable novel, "Wacousta,"[32] had his Indian heroine fall madly in love with young de Haldimar, a passion which it goes without saying he does not reciprocate, but which he plays upon to the extent of making her a traitor to Pontiac inasmuch as she betrays the secret of one of the cleverest intrigues of war known in the history of America, namely the scheme to capture Fort Detroit through the means of an exhibition game of lacrosse. In addition to this de Haldimar makes a cat's paw of the girl using her as a means of communication between his fiance and himself to get herself despised by her own nation and disliked by the reader. Unnecessary to state, that as usual the gallant white marries his fair lady who the poor little red girl has assisted him to recover.

Then comes another era in Canadian-Indian fiction, wherein G. Mercer Adam and A. Ethelwyn Wetherald have given us the semi-historic novel, "An Algonquin Maiden." The former's masterly touch can be recognized on every page he has written; but the outcome of the combined pens is the same old story. We find "Wanda" violently in love with Edward McLeod; she makes all the overtures, conducts herself disgracefully, assists him to a reunion with his fair-skinned love, Helene; then betakes herself to a boat, rows out into the lake in a thunderstorm, chants her own death song, and is drowned.

But, notwithstanding all this, the authors have given us something exceedingly unique and novel as regards their red heroine. They have sketched us a wild Indian girl who kisses. They, however, forgot to tell us how she learned this pleasant fashion of emotional expression; though two such prominent authors who have given so much time to the study of Indian customs and character must have certainly noticed the entire ignorance of kissing that is universal among the aborigines.

A wild Indian never kisses; mothers never kiss their children, even, nor lovers their sweethearts, husbands their wives. It is something absolutely unknown, unpracticed.

But "Wanda" was one of the few book Indian girls who had an individuality and was not hampered with being obliged continually to be national first and natural afterwards. No, she was not national; she did things and said things about as un-Indian-like as Bret Harte's "M'liss"; in fact her action generally resembles "M'liss" more than anything else; for "Wanda's" character has the peculiarity of being created more by the dramatis personnae in the play than by the authors themselves. For example: Helene speaks of her as a "low, untutored savage," and Rose is guilty of remarking that she is "a coarse, ignorant woman, whom you cannot admire, whom it would be impossible for you to respect"; and these comments are both sadly truthful; one cannot love or admire a heroine that grubs in the mud like a turtle, climbs trees like a raccoon, and tears and soils her gowns like a mad woman.

Then the hero describes her upon two occasions as "a beautiful little brute." Poor little Wanda! not only is she non-descript and ill-starred, but as usual the authors take away her love, her life, and last and most terrible of all, reputation; for they permit a crowd of men-friends of the hero to call her a "squaw" and neither hero nor authors deny that she is a squaw. It is almost too sad when so much prejudice exists against the Indians, that any one should write up an Indian heroine with such glaring accusations against her virtue, and no contradictory statements either from writer, hero or circumstance. "Wanda" had without doubt the saddest, unsunniest, unequal life ever given to Canadian readers.

Jessie M. Freeland has written a pretty tale published in *The Week;* it is called "Winona's Tryst" but Oh! grim fatality here again our Indian girl duplicates her former self. "Winona" is the unhappy victim of violent love for Hugh Gordon which he does not appreciate or return. She assists him, serves him, saves him in the usual "dumb-animal" style of book Indians. She manages by self-abnegation, danger, and many heartaches to restore him to the arms of Rose McTavish who of course he has loved and longed for all through the story. Then "Winona" secures the time honored canoe, paddles out into the lake and drowns herself.

Charles Mair[33] has enriched Canadian Indian literature perhaps more than any of our authors, in his magnificent drama, "Tecumseh." The character of the grand old chief himself is most powerfully and accurately drawn. Mair has not fallen into that unattractive fashion of making his Indians "assent with a grunt," or look with "eyes of dog-like fidelity," or to appear "very grave, very dignified, and not very immaculately clean." Mair avoids the usual commonplaces used in describing Indians by those who have never met or mixed with them. His drama bears upon every page evidence of long study and life with the people whom he has written of so carefully, so truthfully.

As for his heroine, what portrayal of Indian character has ever been more faithful than that of "Iena." Oh! happy inspiration vouchsafed to the author of "Tecumseh," he has invented a novelty in fiction—a white man who deserves, wins and reciprocates the Indian maiden's love. . .

The reader has but one regret, that Mair did not let Iena live. She is the one "book" Indian girl that has Indian life, Indian character, Indian beauty, but the inevitable doom of death could not be stayed even by Mair's sensitive Indian-loving pen. . . .

One learns to love Lefroy, the poet-painter. . . . Oh! Lefroy, where is your fellowman in fiction? Iena, where your prototype? Alas, for all the other pale-faced lovers, they are indifferent, almost brutal creations, and as for the redskin girls that love them, they are all fawn eyed, unnatural, unmaidenly idiots and both are merely imaginary makeshifts to help out romances, that would be immeasurably improved by their absence. . . . Half of our authors who write up Indian stuff have never been on an Indian reserve have never met a "real live Redman," have never even read Parkman, Schoolcraft, or Catlin [sic][34]; what wonder that their conception of a people they are ignorant of, save by hearsay, is dwarfed, erroneous and delusive.

And here follows the thought—do authors who write Indian romances love the nation they endeavour successfully or unsuccessfully to describe? Do they like Tecumseh say, "And I, who love your nation, which is just, when deeds deserve it," or is the Indian introduced into literature but to lend a dash of vivid coloring to an otherwise tame and somber picture of colonial life; it looks suspiciously like the latter reason, or why should the Indian always get beaten in the battles of romance, or the Indian girl get inevitably the cold shoulder in the wars of love?

Surely the Redman has lost enough, has suffered enough without additional losses and sorrows being heaped upon him in romance. There are many combats he has won in history from the extinction of the Jesuit Fathers at Lake Simcoe to Cut Knife Creek. There are many girls who have placed dainty red feet figuratively upon the white man's neck from the days of Pocohontas to those of little "Bright Eyes" who captured all Washington a few seasons ago. Let us not only hear, but read something of the North American Indian "besting" some one at least once in a decade, and above all things let the Indian girl in fiction develop from the "dog-like," "fawn-like," "deer-footed," "fire-eyed," "crouching," "submissive" book heroine into something of the quiet, sweet womanly woman she is if wild, or the everyday, natural, laughing girl she is if cultivated and educated; let her be natural even if the author is not competent to give her tribal characteristics.

This was not quite Pauline's final word on the subject of the Indian girl in fiction, for just six months later she won the *Dominion Illustrated*'s prize for fiction with her short story, "A Red Girl's Reasoning."[35] In a space of five thousand words, she presents two Indian women, one wild and one cultivated, proves that neither were "squaws," permits one to live happily ever after with her white husband, and allows the other to place her "dainty red feet" upon her white husband's neck.

But for all her idealization and defence of the red man, she did not change the average white man's attitude. So she found herself introduced to the audience in one small Manitoba town as follows: "Now, friends, before Miss Johnson's exercises begin, I want you all to remember that Injuns, like us, is folks!"[36]

Chapter Six

Winnipeg

IN THE WINTER of 1896-97 Pauline Johnson and Owen Smily decided to try their luck south of the border. Crossing into Michigan at Sault Ste. Marie, they made the Morton House in Grand Rapids, Michigan, their headquarters for the first three weeks of November, hiring halls in the surrounding towns and picking up sponsors wherever possible. Moving gradually south, they played Indianapolis at the beginning of December and Terre Haute a few days later. In the first days of the New Year, they began a tour of Ohio, then in early February doubled back to play Iowa.

Although the tour was a financial sucess, it marked the beginning of Pauline's verbal war with the Yankees. Americans, she said, seemed to want their entertainers to make them laugh, nothing more. They saw Johnson and Smily as an Indian elocutionist and an English song-and-dance man, not as conveyers of culture, so they sat on their hands and waited for the laugh lines. Pauline, who had found the "sporting" Americans she had met at canoe races to be delightful people, reacted with hostility to the people she met on this tour. For the first time she began to disparage her audiences for their lack of culture, though they were probably not one bit less cultured than her audiences in rural Canada.

The Johnson-Smily partnership limped haltingly through 1897 as they toured western Canada again but broke up that December. It had lasted five years. In that time they had travelled Canada from coast to coast three times and established themselves as genuine box office hits. There had been a warm friendship between them at first, but it had worn thin in the last few months. There was little talk in the dressing room or over the breakfast table now.

The problem had existed from the first day of their partnership, but surprisingly it had taken five years before it grew out of control. That problem was professional rivalry. Smily had grown tired of taking second billing. Pauline, as the headline attraction, had always taken the lion's share of the applause and the reviews. A standing ovation for Pauline, a good round of applause for Smily. A paragraph in the morning newspaper for Pauline, a single sentence for Smily. A typical review ran like this one from the *Regina Leader* on 21 September 1897:

> An entertaining audience greeted Miss Pauline Johnson and Owen A. Smily at the concert they gave in the Regina Hall on Tuesday evening. The entertainment on the whole was much enjoyed, but sympathy was claimed for Miss Johnson who was suffering from a very heavy cold which prevented her filling some of her numbers. The selections she succeeded in rendering were "Ojistoh," "The Cattle Thief," and "His Sister's Son,"–all original compositions, given in the dress of her native people, the Mohawks, which added greatly to the dramatic effect. Mr. Smily in his humourous sketches and mimicry kept the audience in continuous merriment.[1]

She had given only half of her share of the program so that Smily had to do more than his share to keep the customers happy, but the critic had devoted almost all of his review to Pauline. Smily must have been desperately tired of this treatment, of getting the second best dressing room in every theatre, the second best room in the hotel. And he must have grown tired of Pauline getting star billing while he carried her bags, especially when he felt that she had learned most of her tricks from him.

On 31 October 1897 Johnson and Smily stopped briefly in Winnipeg on their way east. Although there was no press announcement, the partnership was finished. What took place in private between them is unknown, since Pauline never discussed Smily in any of her writing or even mentioned him in interviews after 1897. If there was any kind of row, it never came to the notice of the theatrical critics who would have had a heyday with it. It was not in Pauline's character to make displays of her emotions; she handled disagreements with ladylike discretion.

They said good-bye in Toronto. Pauline had a month of engagements to fulfil in Ontario before she went home to Brantford for Christmas. Smily spent the following month in Toronto assembling his own troupe of performers. For the next few years he travelled with Miss Ella Bridgeland, contralto, and Miss Mildred Walker, soprano (whose voices the *Winnipeg Tribune* described as "modest, unassuming, and well-trained"[2]). They were the perfect background for Smily's vaudeville-style act. From time to time, Stewart Huntingdon, the first tenor with the Laurier Male Quartet of Toronto, joined the company to beef up the masculine department. By 1900, Smily and his company had travelled Canada coast to coast two more times, and had established a following in the northeastern and north central states. When he finally retired from the road sometime during the First World War he settled in Ontario as an elocution teacher, but he never succeeded in developing "anyone half as clever as he was himself"[3] when he was in his prime.

Meanwhile, in the early winter of 1897, things had slowed down somewhat on the Winnipeg theatrical scene after Johnson and Smily left town, and the *Daily Tribune*'s drama critic began to run short of gossip. So it was that on 9 December he ran an item concerning the career of a young man who would become an important element in the life of Pauline Johnson. Wrote the critic:

> Port Arthur is not a good concert town at present. The Port Arthur *Herald* says: Mr. J. Walter McRaye, humorous and dramatic reader, assisted by Miss Florence McLean . . . gave an entertainment in the town hall on Friday evening last. The concert was in aid of the fire-sufferers of Russell and Ottawa counties, but the poor sufferers will not profit any because there was not enough money taken to pay expenses.

The following week Florence McLean gave up the stage and married a Presbyterian minister. But McRaye did not give up. He had been just seventeen when he was bitten by the acting bug. It had happened in the grimy old Ottawa Opera House (appropriately called "The Grand") where he had seen "The Great Romantic Actor" Edward Vroom playing in *Ruy Blas.* From that night on, McRaye's life was suffused with magic and glamour. He spent every cent he earned on dramatic literature, plays and stories of the stage. He memorized great blocks of Shakespeare, Sheridan, Bulwer-Lytton, Hugo,

Molière and Racine, and imagined himself the star of every show.

His real life, however, was considerably more prosaic. His father had apprenticed him to the telegraph company when he was sixteen, and he spent his days tapping out other people's messages. But McRaye was a romantic who wanted his own adventures. At nineteen he set off for New York to become a "Great Actor" like Vroom. The year was 1895; Pauline had already played New York and Boston and gone on to make her name in London. McRaye, eager to get his start in theatre, studied elocution until he ran out of money; then he went to work in a wallpaper store. On his lunch breaks he made the rounds of the theatrical agencies and stage managers begging for a chance to act. When his lunch breaks got longer than his working hours, the wallpaper company dispensed with his services. After that, he found a job with a wholesale millinery outfit and continued his noon-hour searches. The milliner fired him. His next job was in a molasses factory, and only the fact that the factory was five miles from Broadway saved this job. The one bright spot in his life in New York was the boarding house where he stayed. The other boarders were mostly young interns from a nearby hospital and they were willing to let McRaye practise his vaudeville acts on them; in return for this free entertainment they paid his way into the Broadway theatres where McRaye so badly wanted to act.

At the end of a year, a little discouraged with New York's indifference to his talent, he went home to Ontario. There he changed his name from Walter Jackson McCrea (which he had answered to since his christening in Merrickville, Ontario, in 1876) to the more theatrical sounding J. Walter McRaye, and set out to conquer the Canadian stage.

He was now twenty years old and shorter than average, but he managed to look even smaller when he was feeling important because he puffed out his chest like an enraged pigeon and began swaggering. He was not handsome; his nose was prominent, his chin was weak, his eyes were small, and his hairline was already beginning to recede. But his temper was serene, his confidence phenomenal, and his smile absolutely engaging. Most men found him detestable, largely because of his inflated self-confidence. Many women found him contemptible because of his opportunism. But luckily for him there were others who found him lovable because of his smile.

McRaye landed his first role with the sleazy theatrical company of the aging Harry Lindley, which worked its way back and forth across Canada acting out pirated plays, losing actors and picking up replacements at every settlement along the way. Even with this motley company, however, McRaye was not an overwhelming success. According to his memoirs, one of his reviews read, "The only stage McRaye is fitted for goes about five miles an hour,"[4] and though this remark was made of many turn-of-the-century entertainers, it probably described McRaye's lack of creativity quite accurately.

Finally, on St. Patrick's Day, 1897, McRaye launched his first "Trans-Canada Tour" as an "Entertainer and Monologuist." His stock in trade was the sentimental poetry of William Henry Drummond which had just arrived in the bookshops of Canada in a collection called *The Habitant*. McRaye had found his métier in the recitation of "The Wreck of the Julie Plante" and "Little Bateese," which were written in Drummond's version of Quebec patois, and he combined these with excerpts from Shakespeare and Victor Hugo to make a program. The tour began in Arnprior, Ontario; by the beginning of December he had landed in Winnipeg, not starving but certainly not wealthy. He then backtracked to Port Arthur to fulfil the less than successful engagement reported so gleefully by the columnist of the *Winnipeg Daily Tribune*. This experience left him penniless, but since he was not easily discouraged, he simply returned to Winnipeg to find a new partner and set out again on the road to fame.

Winnipeg had grown enormously in the three years since Pauline Johnson and Owen Smily had first seen it. Thirty-five thousand people had now settled at the junction of the Red and the Assiniboine and more of them were climbing out of the CPR's colonial cars every day. The town was having a construction boom; new hotels and banks and office buildings were climbing into the sky to rival those in Toronto. Not that Winnipeg had lost its frontier style completely; there were still just as many cowboys as city slickers on the streets, and there were still Indians sitting in doorways hawking buffalo horns and beadwork, and there was still that unmistakably western air of genuine friendliness about the town.

But the entertainment scene had changed. There were more theatres and more acts to fill them. The Winnipeg Grand Opera House had opened its doors earlier that year with the John Griffiths Company from New York performing *Faust* and *Richard the Third*.

In October they were back with a replay of *Faust* and a "new" production of *In Old Kentucky* "as played in Chicago and Boston." The Giffen-Neill Company came to play the Winnipeg Theatre while round the corner the Josie Mills Company brought *An Unequal Match* to the Dominion. In November Katie Putnam's Company staged *Tom Tinker's Kid* and Francis Jones starred in *In Olde Madrid.* December saw The Merry Widow Company at the Grand, and Black Patti's Troubadours paid their second visit to the Dominion. All this activity came about when the American stage industry, looking for new markets, had finally noticed that Winnipeg was not very far by rail from Minneapolis and St. Paul, and that frontier Canadians were quite eager to put their money into the pockets of American actors.

But in the Christmas season of 1897 there was one Canadian more popular than all the American players put together. Pauline Johnson's 29 December recital at the Grand Opera House was sold out two days after the tickets were put on sale. Although she now had permanent rooms at the Manitoba Hotel and considered Winnipeg her home, it was nearly five months since she had played there. All her admirers were eager to see her again.

J. Walter McRaye was eager to see her, too. He had arrived in town on 14 December and sought out an acquaintance named Charlie ·Handscombe who sometimes made his living as a concert tenor and sometimes worked as the drama critic for the *Manitoba Free Press.* Presumably McRaye had hopes of teaming up with Handscombe, but the latter was unreceptive to the idea. Instead he introduced McRaye around the local entertainment colony hoping to match him up there; then, since Pauline had just dissolved her partnership with Smily, Handscombe hit upon the idea of introducing McRaye to her. With this as his object, Handscombe bought two tickets to Pauline's recital.

Pauline shared the program with Ernest du Domaine, a young violinist, and his accompanist Albert Betourmay. Unfortunately for them, they suffered the same fate as Smily, receiving a minimal share of the applause and a sentence or two in the reviews. The audience loved Pauline, calling again and again for encores, but in this they were disappointed. Contrary to her usual generosity, "she merely bowed her acknowledgements"[5] and left the stage. McRaye and Handscombe, eager to beat the crowd, scrambled out of their seats and headed backstage, but someone had beaten them to her dressing room door, and was standing guard in front of it with a proprietary air.

He was a man of well above average height, broad-shouldered and somewhat bullnecked. His thick brown hair was parted in the middle, and his heavy brows shaded piercing blue eyes. But it was the bottom half of his face that really defined his character. His lower jaw was slightly undershot, so that although his face was unmistakeably handsome his jaw gave it a bulldoggish, obstinate look. It was the face of a man who was on his way to becoming a tough, aggressive businessman, a financier.

Charles Robert Lumley Drayton came from British stock. His father, Philip Henry Drayton, had been an officer in Her Majesty's 16th Rifles and had served first in Ontario and then in Barbados. When he resigned his commission in 1874, he brought his family to live in Ontario. His elder son, Henry Lumley, had been born there in 1869, and the younger one, Charles, had been born in Barbados in 1872. Both boys were sent to private school in England, but their father allowed them to complete their education at Upper Canada College in Toronto. Upon the resignation of his commission, Philip Drayton read law and became a lecturer and examiner at Osgoode Hall. He expected his sons to be equally successful and plotted their careers accordingly. Although his elder son had shown an early aptitude for finance, he took him into his office to read law. Henry was called to the bar in 1891 and two years later was appointed assistant solicitor for the city of Toronto, an influential post which he held for seven years. At that time he resigned to become involved in Ontario's railway problems and in politics. Having satisfied his father's career demands, he proceeded to marry a girl from a prominent Toronto family and settle into the upper echelons of Ontario society. (Henry was knighted in 1915 for his work on the Dominion Railway Commission. In 1919 Sir Henry was elected an M.P. and served two years as Canada's finance minister and another seven as a backbencher.)

Philip Drayton had less confidence in the capabilities of his younger son Charles, so in 1890 he arranged an apprenticeship for him as an office boy with the Western Canada Savings and Loan Company, which a few years later became the Canada Permanent

Loan Company. At the same time, he allowed him to move from the family home to a boarding house at the corner of Jarvis and Huntley streets. A year later Charles was transferred to the company's Winnipeg office; by this time he was a cashier. Obviously his employer had put its stamp of approval on the boy and Philip Drayton began to relax. Charles would add lustre to the family name, after all.

In the summer of 1897, shortly after he had been appointed assistant inspector, Charles moved from his humble boarding house on Hargrave Street to rooms in the elegant Clarendon Hotel. His work now carried him to all parts of western Canada, often to areas far from the railways, and many times to the wilderness where roads were nonexistent. In a few years he had driven across most of the prairies and British Columbia by horse and buggy, and had established himself as one of the foremost authorities on property values in the west.

It must have been shortly after his promotion to assistant inspector that he met Pauline. How they met is not recorded, but since their hotels were adjacent to one another, it is quite possible that they met in the street. While such a casual meeting in Toronto would have been out of the question, in Winnipeg it was entirely permissible, even among the members of polite society.

Charles Drayton had just marked his twenty-fifth birthday. Pauline Johnson was thirty-six.

On the evening of 29 December 1897, when Drayton met McRaye and Handscombe outside Pauline's dressing room, it must have been fairly common knowledge in Winnipeg society that he was paying court to her. He was not, of course, the only man who sent her flowers or arranged dinner parties in her honour, but he was the only one she was openly encouraging. And Winnipeg smiled and nodded and waited for the big announcement. Drayton was not happy, therefore, to meet these interlopers outside her door on the first evening in months that he was to be alone with her.

Handscombe and McRaye managed to crash the late supper party which Drayton had arranged for Pauline that night at the Clarendon, and before the evening was over, Pauline had agreed to share billing with McRaye on a short tour that she had planned into Deloraine County. They would leave on 6 January and return to Winnipeg on the fifteenth. Her reasons for taking McRaye with her, even though she was aware of his minimal successes to date, were simple. With Smily gone, she had to provide an entire evening's entertainment herself or rely on local talent to spell her on stage. In Winnipeg, it had been safe to share the program with du Domaine and Betourmay because they were seasoned performers who would shortly go east to make their fortunes. But the situation was entirely different in the smaller settlements. The local acts were unreliable both in calibre of performance and availability. Recalled one ex-trouper:

> This local talent was a continual anxiety and exasperation. It was chiefly represented by young ladies, all self-confident in the morning and wretchedly nervous at night. They invariably rattled the minuet and played the Irish jig like a dirge. Local talent occasionally burst into tears before the audience and always forgot everything it had been told.[6]

McRaye may have been green, but Pauline could see that it was unlikely his confidence would ever desert him in front of an audience and that he wanted this chance badly enough to do exactly as she told him. And then, of course, there was his smile; Pauline could not help but warm to such a "jolly, happy-go-lucky" little man![7]

Together they played Boissevain, Deloraine, Hartney and Souris, but when they returned to Winnipeg, McRaye headed south alone. In his memoirs he explained that he went because he was already booked for engagements in North Dakota, but this was a story he concocted to protect his ego and cover embarrassing details of Pauline's actions.

In fact, Pauline had not extended an offer of partnership to McRaye. Instead, on 15 January the Winnipeg newspapers printed a press release in which she outlined her plans for the following year.

> Miss Johnson finishes her Manitoba tour this month, and then goes as far west as Prince Albert to fill a special three nights' engagement there. She intends giving recitals in the different towns between Regina and Winnipeg on her return from Prince Albert, after which she goes to Ottawa to fill a postponed engagement there . . . afterwards going on to New York to publish a book of short stories which she has written and is anxious to have on the market for this year's trade. She will tour the States until September when she may possibly visit Manitoba on her way to Australia. . . .[8]

Pauline would have needed two secretaries and her own private railway car if she had really intended to complete this itinerary. To begin with, she did not have enough stories ready to fill a book. By 1898 "A Red Girl's Reasoning" was her only published short story. It had appeared in *Dominion Illustrated* in 1892. Four essays—"A Strong Race Opinion on the Indian Girl in Modern Fiction," "Indian Medicine Men and Their Magic," "Iroquois of the Grand River," and "The Organization of the Iroquois"—had appeared in various journals, but even if she included them in her book she would not have sufficient material. It is, of course, possible that some of her early stories have been lost, though this seems unlikely.

The idea of a book of stories was dear to her heart, and she laid plans on at least two other occasions to publish one. In June 1899 an inquiry to Harper and Brothers of New York brought the assurance that her manuscript would be welcomed there as soon as it was ready, but there is no evidence that she ever submitted it. In 1905 she told a reporter of her plan to bring out a collection of her stories, but again it never materialized. It was not until the publication of *Legends of Vancouver* in 1911 and *The Moccasin Maker* and *The Shagganappi* in 1913 that her stories were finally put into book form, but it is significant that few of the stories included were written during the first half of her career.

The press release came out just before her second Winnipeg concert on 18 January when she was already booked to play the west, instead of before the December concert when she had time for a holdover. The first concert had been a sell-out so that she could have made a real profit on a second one within the week. But Pauline had stayed in Winnipeg until 5 January without another public appearance. She had not intended to stir up a public response with this release. Her objective had been a private one, and she accomplished just exactly what she had in mind. On 26 January the drama critic of the *Toronto Globe and Mail* announced:

> Winnipeg, January 25 (Special): Miss E. Pauline Johnson, the Indian poetess, owing to a severe sore throat, was unable to leave this city to give entertainments in the Province. The announcement of Miss Johnson's engagement to Mr. Charles R. L. Drayton is made, and each of the principals is receiving the congratulations of their numerous friends in the city and in the east. The marriage will not take place

until next September. Miss Johnson intends to reside in New York next summer to superintend the publication of her new book of stories.

Pauline's press release a week earlier had been her warning to Charles Drayton that it would be a whole year before he saw his beloved again, and as she had calculated, he panicked. Young and relatively inexperienced with women, Drayton was afraid to take the risk that some other man might carry her off if he failed to lay claim to her before she left on her travels. He must have had his proposal well rehearsed by the time she returned from her short tour across the Deloraine line with Walter McRaye, and if there was any hesitation in her acceptance, it was only because she was an excellent actress.

Brantford was shaken by the news. Even if Pauline had refused to resign herself to spinsterhood, Brantford had long since consigned her to that state. She had become a local institution. The *Courier* expressed the town's concern on 27 January:

> The announcement of the engagement of Miss E. Pauline Johnson to Mr. Charles E. Drayton of Winnipeg came as a surprise to those not intimately connected with the family. That her rare accomplishments and pleasing personality should win many bids in the matrimonial market was to be expected, but Miss Johnson was enthroned by her genius far above the commonplace of life and getting married is such an ordinary thing to do that it was the last thing expected of her. "She will never be the same," said one, "she will lose her individuality."
>
> "Not a bit of it," I said. "An individuality like hers is not easily lost. Mr. Drayton is the one to be pitied in this respect. He will go through life as the husband of Pauline Johnson, the Indian poetess, you know. If it be that true love is the only immortal spring of true poetry, we may expect even greater things from Miss Johnson's pen in the future. To the fervour of her patriotic poems will be added a divine flame, the dainty colouring of her word painting will be coloured with a new and rosy tinge. And through her interpretation of nature's language, the throbbing of the human heart will itself speak. . . ."

Pauline had waited a long time for this "ordinary thing" called marriage. For nearly twenty years she had been hearing wedding bells every time a new man entered her life, but though there had undoubtedly been proposals during those years, no suitable man had asked for her hand. Charles Drayton, however, fitted Pauline's dream of the perfect husband and she was determined to marry him.

But she was ignoring all their differences in values and interests. Although both of them travelled the frontier country in the course of their work, Pauline saw the "yellow prairies rolling into the rose-gold westland"[9] and rivers wending "a lawless course . . . and breaking into torrents"[10]; he saw only the industrial development possibilities and the dollars per acre. He was a man looking for good solid value for his money, exactly the trait that had alienated Pauline from her brothers and sister; she never saved a penny in her life. For Pauline, life was poetry and the recital stage; all Drayton knew of literature and drama was embodied in Pauline herself.

Their age difference was an even greater stumbling block. At thirty-six Pauline was incredibly youthful in appearance with a smooth complexion, abundant hair, almost classic features, and the figure of a teen-ager. Foster says of her: "Contrary to the usual with Indian women, she had outrun the fading time of beauty by ten years at least, an English heritage truly, and was at her best in charm and looks at thirty-five."[11]

Portraits taken of Pauline at the time of the engagement confirm what Foster has said, but regardless of appearance, Pauline was still eleven years older than the man she intended to marry. In the end, it would matter little that she looked no older that he did on their wedding day, nor would it be important whether she had told him her correct age before he proposed, but it would be catastrophic to Pauline if Drayton, once married, found his aging wife unappealing and turned to younger, prettier women. For Pauline, the wedding was far less important than the marriage, because if that marriage produced anything less than the perfect relationship her parents had enjoyed, it would be intolerable to her.

Pauline also had to deal with the Victorian expectation that a woman would provide her husband with an heir, even though financial pressures often determined that middle-class couples did not marry until the wife was past her best child-bearing years. The mortality rate for both mother and child was therefore extremely high, and old cemeteries attest to the fact that a large percentage of nineteenth-century males went through more than one wife in the process of begetting a family. Pauline, at thirty-six-plus, with a history of illnesses and delicate health, was not a prime candidate to survive motherhood.

May-December marriages were generally accepted by the practical Victorians and the Edwardians who came after them. A young man on the way up could marry an older widow whose husband had left her a small fortune or a good business, or a wealthy old man could marry a beautiful young thing in order to "protect" her. But there was considerably less acceptance when the marriage was between a young man of means or social position and an older penniless woman, as in the case of Pauline and Drayton, because there was no practical reason for the match.

The public made a special allowance, however, for one category of female: the celebrity who married a younger man. Such an alliance caused a good deal of caustic comment in society circles, but newspaper polls showed that women in general gave their overwhelming support to stars like Lillie Langtry, Jenny Churchill, the much married opera star Madame Adelina Patti, and the Baroness Burdett-Coutts who at sixty-one married a man less than half her age. There is something about such behaviour that gives every mature woman the hope that someone will also find her glamorous and desirable. Pauline probably calculated quite correctly that her fans would consider her marriage to Drayton just one more proof of her continuing aura of glamour.

Although Pauline must have weighed all the problems and risks before she induced Drayton to propose, in the end the deciding factor was her need to be loved and her desire to act out her favourite romantic idyll: the Indian maiden marrying a fine young Englishman. She had acted it out a hundred times on stage with Smily playing Charlie MacDonald in "A Red Girl's Reasoning"; now she would have the real experience.

However, for Charles Drayton and, more importantly, for his family the paramount question was the social acceptability of the bride. Philip Drayton and his elder son were already listed in *Who's Who in Canada*, Drayton Senior was a K.C. (Henry became a K.C. in 1907), and the family had become politically and socially prominent. It mattered little to them that Pauline was the daughter and granddaughter of Mohawk chiefs, that she was the darling of artistic circles from coast to coast, or that she had been wined and dined by the Ripons and the Van Hornes. What mattered to them was the fact that she made her living on the stage.

The Draytons were essentially of the merchant class, hard-headed and sensible, who took their doses of culture like medicine. They went to the theatre or the opera because others did, not because they appreciated it. The elder Draytons had never seen Pauline perform and did not wish to; they already knew about her kind of woman. As far as they were concerned, women who made their living on the stage were lewd and immoral.

If Pauline had really chosen to be an immoral woman, she would have had endless opportunities on the road. There were always "commercials," lonely miners, stock actors, and stage-struck bank clerks who would have been more than willing to be her bed-partner, but not many of them would have had the temerity to approach her; she still had that hauteur which had frightened the boys of Brantford. And she was too much aware of her public image to have begun consorting with men in that manner. If news of her improper behaviour had got around she would have been shunned by her women supporters, and it was the women's groups, most of them associated with churches, that were her most frequent sponsors. And it was the women of her audiences, enthralled by her aura of purity, who mothered her and protected her from coast to coast.

(Foster, who prepared Pauline's first biography in 1931, adopted a very partisan approach to her subject but nevertheless did not quite trust the tales of Pauline's purity and unsullied maidenhood. She set out, therefore, to interview women who had known her, among them a number of Mounted Police wives who had met her at police outposts. None had ever heard a whisper of scandal about her. She concluded "I think we might as well give her a white robe."[12])

But more than any other argument in favour of Pauline's chastity in the year 1898 was the fact that she desperately wanted to be married, not just to any man who asked her, but to a solid middle-class man who would give her a solid middle-class home. And she knew perfectly well such men did not offer marriage to women whom they could bed without wedding.

The Draytons, however, could not differentiate between recitalists and actresses, nor between Pauline and other recitalists. They saw her as a half-breed actress who could not be presented to their friends.

The 26 January edition of the *Globe and Mail* precipitated an avalanche of letters between Toronto and Winnipeg, with young Charles attempting to defend his right to marry the woman of his choice and his father adamantly insisting he choose again. Pauline, however, was unaware of the problem. She had left Winnipeg on the twenty-eighth for the beginning of her prairie tour and had met with heartbreak quite separate from what the Draytons were concocting. When she arrived in Regina on 20 February, a telegram was waiting for her from her brother Allen. Her mother was dying.

She cancelled the rest of her tour and the following morning in the middle of a blizzard she was helped aboard the eastbound transcontinental. Again and again, as enormous drifts swept over the tracks, the train was forced to stop; it was more than forty-eight hours late arriving in Winnipeg. Here there was a six-hour delay, time enough for Pauline to have met with Charles and learn his bad news, but there is no way of knowing whether he did break it to her then, or if he was even in the city at that time.

Blizzard conditions continued as the train moved east again; five more days passed before it reached Brantford. Pauline, desperately trying not to disappoint her mother on this one final occasion, was unable to do anything but sit and wait. She "barely accomplished her desire. Three quarters of an hour after she arrived at the house, her mother passed away."[13] Pauline, in the last lines of *The Moccasin Maker*, gives a romanticized version of this death and its affect on her:

> She felt she must live until this youngest daughter grew to be a woman. Perhaps this desire, this mother love, kept her longer beside her children than she would have stayed without it, for the years rolled on, and her hair whitened, her once springing step halted a little, the glorious blue of her English eyes grew very dreamy, and tender, and wistful. Was she seeing the great Hereafter unfold itself before her as her steps drew nearer and nearer?
>
> And one night the Great Messenger knocked softly at her door, and with a sweet, gentle sigh, she turned and followed where he led— joining gladly the father of her children in the land that holds both whites and Indians as one.
>
> And the daughter who writes the verses her mother always felt, but found no words to express, never puts a last line to a story or a sweet cadence into a poem, but she says to herself as she holds her mother's memory within her heart:
> "She knows—she knows."[14]

In spite of the bitter weather, there was an enormous turnout for the funeral two days later. The Reverend G. C. McKenzie, rector of Grace Church, officiated at the funeral service at the family home, while the Reverend R. Ashton read the burial service in the old Mohawk Cemetery. Hundreds of bouquets and "floral emblems" covered the new grave; among them were cut flowers from Charles Drayton and violets from Mrs. Philip Drayton. Perhaps, Charles had one ally within his family.

A day or two later the *Toronto Globe and Mail* had the last word on Emily Susanna Howells Johnson when it printed her obituary:

> Elderly people, especially those who lived at that time in Kingston, will remember well the astonishment with which society received the news of the engagement and subsequent marriage of the popular and much admired Miss Emily Howells to a full-blooded Indian, Chief Johnson by name. That this unusual marriage should have turned out most happily is only another proof of the fact that what everybody says is not necessarily true. [15]

After the funeral Pauline stayed on in the little house at No. 7 Napoleon Street, mourning her mother. Allen returned to Toronto a few days later, but Eva stayed in Brantford with Pauline, partly because she had also loved her mother, and partly because she wanted to settle family matters with her sister. The barriers between the two women were higher than ever, especially since the world seemed to assume that Pauline was the only mourner. The morning after Emily's death the *Brantford Expositor*'s story was headlined, "Mother of Pauline Johnson Died Last Night After Lengthy Illness," and concluded, "The other members of the family are Miss Eva and Allen W. Johnson." The *Toronto Globe and Mail* said, "Very much sympathy is felt for Miss Pauline Johnson and the other members of her family. . . ." Although Eva was actually proud of Pauline in her fashion, she did not enjoy having her nose rubbed in Pauline's fame or having her own grief belittled.

Several weeks after her mother's death, Pauline became ill with a throat infection. Eva hovered over her, trying to settle the rest of the family affairs while Pauline was incapacitated, but they were still unsettled when Pauline went back to the stage at the end of March, travelling on a circuit from Toronto to Ottawa, northwest to Sudbury and back to Toronto. Work helped to dull the pain of loss. Because she did not believe in ostentatious displays of grief, she never wore mourning. Few, therefore, remembered that she had recently lost her mother, and she was spared daily doses of pity from the public.

In May she returned to the United States to give recitals for the Indian Association. Said the Johnstown *Daily Republican* on 27 May, "Miss E. Pauline Johnson is a wonderful woman of great ability as a reciter, also as a writer. Her compositions were all of a very high order and many of them display a talent and versatility that has never been equalled by any reciter appearing in our city." Two weeks later her throat condition recurred and she had to return to Brantford and submit to Eva's care.

On 7 July Charles Drayton's mother died in Toronto. She was only fifty-one years old. Pauline attended the funeral, meeting Charles for the first time since January. Although she stayed overnight at the Rossin, she returned alone to Brantford the next day.

During the next two weeks she packed her belongings, sending those things unsuitable for life on the road to be stored at her brother Allen's house or at the home of her cousin Kate, who was now married to lawyer Stephen Washington of Hamilton. On the last day of July Eva and Pauline left Brantford; No. 7 Napoleon Street had ceased to be the home of the Johnson family. On future visits she would stay with friends or at Kerby House. From now on Winnipeg would be her official home.

On the way to Winnipeg she stopped in Ottawa to fulfil a long-postponed engagement, then continued west. On 6 August the *Manitoba Morning Free Press* told its readers that Pauline would be embarking on "a trip through the NorthWest. After this, her marriage takes place in Winnipeg where she will permanently reside." The Draytons may have said no, but obviously Pauline was not conceding defeat. But before the western trip could begin, she became ill again and was forced to remain in Winnipeg for the rest of August and most of September.

There are hundred of kinds of streptococcus bacteria. Some of them, the most life-threatening ones, are hemolytic, that is, they break open the red blood cells. Of this kind the group known as A-Beta causes strep throat and diseases such as erysipelas. Now, since Pauline had had an attack of erysipelas in her childhood and her father had died of it, it is almost certain that the repeated sore throats and colds that constantly interfered with her recital schedule had been attacks of strep throat. But in the summer of 1898 her illness was something even more serious than that.

In certain people, when strep infections are left untreated, an allergic reaction occurs because the streptococcus capsule contains a highly irritating component. This allergic reaction does not occur at the time of the infection but comes on some two to six weeks afterwards, and like any fever that attacks the human body, it is most likely to appear in times of emotional crisis. It does not necessarily occur after the first strep infection or even the second but may suddenly occur after a fifth or sixth one. This reaction can be likened to the individual who does not have an allergic reaction to certain pollens until after he has been exposed to them many times. The allergic reaction in the case of strep infections may take the form of rheumatic fever, rheumatic heart disease, or the kidney disease which used to be called "Bright's Disease."

Pauline had been twice afflicted by sore throats earlier that year, both times seriously enough to force her to return to Brantford and Eva's bossing. She was under severe emotional strain because of the death of her mother and the Draytons' opposition to her marriage. And the period of time she lay ill in Winnipeg almost exactly corresponds with the time needed to recuperate from a serious case of rheumatic fever.

If any more evidence is needed to diagnose the illness Pauline had that summer, there is also the fact that as in the case of any other allergy, additional attacks of rheumatic fever may be triggered by a return of the irritant, that is, another case of strep throat. Since Pauline's medical history for the ten years prior to her first recital in 1892 is a blank, there is no way of knowing whether this was her first attack of rheumatic fever, but it was certainly not her last. Only two years later she was to have another one with much more serious consequences for her career.

In Winnipeg she was too ill to stay at the Manitoba Hotel, and friends took her to their home and nursed her back to health. Drayton's whereabouts are unknown during this period.

On 26 September she left Winnipeg on a tour of Manitoba under the management of Thomas E. Cornyn. He was her third manager, but unlike the first two, the management of actors and recitalists was his full-time occupation. Working out of Toronto and Winnipeg, this young ex-actor arranged tours for a string of clients and, in partnership with another young entrepreneur named Charles C. Lindsay, he operated a road company called the Bijou Comedy Company.

According to the publicity releases, Pauline's first tour under Cornyn's management was highly successful, but because she was still recuperating from rheumatic fever and still under enormous emotional strain, she must have relied almost entirely on her mastery of her material to be able to perform. She returned to Winnipeg on 5 November and stayed just long enough to do her laundry and pick up her mail before catching the Manitoba and Northwestern for Portage la Prairie, Minnedosa, Rapid City, Birtle, Binscarth, Russell, Yorkton, and every little settlement within fifty miles of the rail line. The *Manitoba Morning Free Press*, however, reassured its readers that "Miss Johnson intends to give a recital in Winnipeg in February just previous to her marriage, after which she will leave the stage and locate permanently in the city."[16] This may have consoled some of her fans, but any who read the drama column the next night would have been puzzled to learn that Thomas Cornyn had set off for the Dakotas where he "expected to book about fifty appearances for her" for the late spring. Pauline was leaving her options open.

In her entire career there was no lonelier time than this. Her new manager merely planned her itinerary, travelling the route as her advance agent, booking halls and setting up sponsors. Most of his communication with her was by mail or by notes left at hotels along the route. And although her tours with Smily had seemed exhausting, Cornyn's schedule required a superhuman effort on her part because now she seldom shared the program with local talent. Since audiences like a "full evening," this meant she had to perform for two or two and a half hours every evening beginning at seven o'clock with only one intermission to give her time to change her costume.

But the saddest aspect of Pauline's life in the years 1898 and 1899 was the knowledge that her future happiness was slipping away and she had no power to stop it. Perhaps if she had retained stronger family ties she would have had someone to turn to now while the Draytons tried to shed her, but Allen was in the throes of a long and patient courtship and had no time for her, and Eva had settled into the role of the disappointed and critical parent. T. S. H. Shearman even states that Eva was partly responsible for breaking up Pauline's engagement.

The winter of 1898 was a particularly harsh one on the prairies, and Pauline's tour came to a halt many times because of the weather. In early December she waited out one blizzard in a tiny hotel in Saltcoats, Saskatchewan. The temperature outside was forty below. The time was not entirely wasted, however, because the literary outcome of the delay was the short story "Where Horse Is King," which was eventually published in the *Vancouver Province*. It tells of a young Mountie, Trooper Hamilton, who rushes half frozen into the hotel to demand a fresh horse, then plunges back into the blizzard on his new mount to chase cattle rustlers. Since all of Pauline's stories were based on actual incidents, someone like Hamilton must have arrived during the storm. In early January she was delayed by another blizzard at Duck Lake. Here the hotel was unable to accommodate her so she was taken in by the wife of the officer in charge of the Mounted Police barracks. For Pauline, of course, it was no hardship to be quartered with the men in scarlet.

On 3 February, as the *Free Press* had promised, she was back in Winnipeg to perform at the Winnipeg Theatre on the same program with Charlie Handscombe and Miss Merrielle Patton, contralto. Charles Wheeler, writing in the *Tribune* the next morning, said: "In her own particular line, that of depicting Indian life and character, this lady stands to-day unrivalled. . . . but her 'Moccasin' stories are not original; there are many other versions." (He did not like the other performers either, and complained that Handscombe's ballads were "trashy, as empty as a dream" and that Patton "had one good song.") The *Free Press* critic was kinder. After outlining the program, he only commented: "Last night Miss Johnson was suffering from severe throat trouble," as if that excused all the shortcomings of the performance. It had been a bad concert, but the cause was more likely to be found in her emotional state than in her physical one. Charles Drayton was conspicuously absent from the city during her visit as if in irrevocable denial of all Pauline's wedding plans and announcements.

The following day she left town without announcing a new date for the wedding. She was off on a tour of the west arranged by Cornyn and she let it be known that she would not return to Winnipeg until she had completed a tour of Australia. On 8 February, shortly before midnight, the Manitoba Hotel, which Pauline had called home, caught fire and burned to the ground. This event marked the end of her love affair with Winnipeg.

Nevertheless, references to her wedding plans continued. In late March the *Macleod Gazette* reassured its readers that arrangements were being made to have a special recital by Miss Johnson in April or May "before her marriage and retirement from the stage."[17] In August her old friend Ernest Thompson Seton wrote her from Carberry, Manitoba, where he was researching wildlife:

> My well-beloved cousin,
>
> Here I am with my wife—gritting our teeth at having been so near and never knew it—What a shame—and all our plans are laid to return by Denver. I can only weep and look to the future—but in my tears I stop to smile and congratulate you heartily on your approaching entry into double bliss. I am writing this before I have had time to hunt up McKay—but others about the hotel describe Mr. Drayton as "a fine fellow."
>
> My wife unites in congratulations and hopes to have the pleasure of knowing you in the near future.
>
> We have followed and rejoiced in all your success. We shall be on this trip till December, then as before our address is 144 Fifth Avenue, New York.
>
> Ever your friend,
Ernest Seton-Thompson[18]

Even her friends were deceived by the journals of the day.

Chapter Seven

Halifax

In mid-March 1899 Pauline's travels took her into southern Alberta, then north to Edmonton for two recitals. From there her route led south to Calgary, then west through Banff and Kamloops to Vancouver, across to Vancouver Island and back, following the CPR with a side trip into the Kootenays, then over the Kicking Horse Pass to Calgary for a brief pause in late May. But the woman who appeared on stage along this route was not the fiery Pauline who had electrified audiences with her savage tales, nor the elegant London lady bringing culture to the hinterlands, nor even the wisecracking comic that Smily had educated in music hall techniques. This was a tired and disillusioned woman, struggling to maintain a following and make a living.

That spring her reviews ranged from tolerant to bitingly critical. Despondent over her mother's death and Drayton's rejection, and weakened by her attack of rheumatic fever, she went through the motions of performance. It was not until she reached Vancouver on 3 April that she made her first attempt to return to her old form; there she introduced a character sketch in which she played a newcomer to Ottawa society attending a reception. The sketch was a parody in verse on the guests at the reception, including a mining man, "an infant phenomenon who breathed hard and forgot her pieces in the middle," a shabby curate, and a pompous railway director who sang the praises of the CPR and of Vancouver. From the reviewer's description of the verses used for the last character, she appears to have salvaged them from that piece of doggerel, "Little Vancouver," which had been published in "There and Back" five years earlier.

In spite of this new material, the *Vancouver Province* complained: "The sketch, though in itself a clever bit of character work and in its parts altogether estimable, might be made somewhat more compact as its raison d'etre is in the types presented and not in any tale that is told."[1]

Pauline had borrowed the basic idea for the sketch from Smily, but she had not understood how to gauge the audience's interest span. The reviewer went on to compliment her on the new poems, "Canadian Born" and "Riders of the Plains," then resumed his complaining: "Miss Johnson showed a fault which she seems to have slipped into . . . that of relying on gesture and forceful delivery for effects of vehemence rather than by more intimate study, obtaining the result through intellectual means and aiding her own cause by the suggestion of reserve."

Now that she was performing alone, she had no one to give her constructive criticism and no one to measure her own performance against, and since she had never learned standard elocution she could not fall back on technique when her emotions ran dry. She had discovered that it was far easier to make a lot of noise than to give a controlled emotional performance. In the prairie settlements and in the mining camps, where audiences were glad of any entertainment, her show had been warmly welcomed, but when she reached the larger towns, she was competing against all the other acts and stage companies that had passed through, and she was subject to the criticisms of newspapermen who had learned their trade in Ontario or California or England. And like the reviewer for the *Province,* they wasted no time in telling her that she was not giving what they had come to expect.

Vancouver appears to have been the lowest point on her tour, after which the mechanical performances slowly gave way to shows that, though not up to her old standards, were at least more spontaneous and geared to the interests of the audience. For example, in Cranbrook three weeks later her show pleased the local citizenry well enough to be held over for an extra performance in the Presbyterian Church, but for these concerts she abandoned her Ottawa Tea Party sketch in favour of more serious works. The *Weekly Herald* was enthusiastic.

> To those who have never heard her, she is a most interesting revelation. Graceful in her movements, pleasing in her tone, and charming

in appearance, she holds her audience with perfect ease, while reciting her wonderful tales of nature. Her compositions are in nature's own language and she displays the true poetic instinct in the grouping of ideas and her rhythmical combination of words.[2]

In early June Pauline crossed into the Dakotas and spent the summer playing there and in Minnesota. By fall she was back in Saskatchewan (still part of the Northwest Territories at that time). Her recital style had become much more competent as the year progressed and she had learned to escape some of the pressure by diversifying her program and by including anecdotes of her adventures on the road. She had also picked up the knack of writing wherever the opportunity arose, and in the eighteen months since her return to the stage in late September 1898, she had written "Riders of the Plains," "Canadian Born," "A Prodigal," and possibly "Golden of the Selkirks."

"A Prodigal" was probably written during her convalescence in the summer of 1898. She had been wandering in the cemetery of the old St. Boniface Cathedral in Winnipeg when she saw a nun putting flowers on an unmarked but well-tended grave. When the nun finished her prayer, she exchanged a smile with Pauline.

> "No stone, no marking," breathed Pauline.
> "No name," returned the Sister, sighing softly. "She was just a girl. We never knew her name," she continued, fingering a crucifix at her side. "We respected her pride. We nursed her, and when she died we laid her here with her just born daughter at her side. But they seemed so lonely, those two in their sadness, that I come always to care for the spot and leave a token of flowers with a prayer to the Virgin, Mother of God."[3]

The text of the poem not only suggests the poignancy of the lonely deaths but also Pauline's own feeling of rejection that year:

> My heart forgot its God for love of you,
>   And you forgot me, other loves to learn;
> Now through a wilderness of thorn and rue
>   Back to my God I turn.
>
> And just because my God forgets the past,
>   And in forgetting does not ask to know
> Why I once left His arms for yours, at last
>   Back to my God I go.[4]

By the sixteenth of November she was in Qu'Appelle to play in a hall that "was crowded with an enthusiastic audience." Admissions that night amounted to fifty-five dollars, which means that the crowd numbered more than two hundred adults, an excellent house for a small rural settlement.

After nearly a year's absence, she returned to Winnipeg at Christmas, once more confident of her abilities. Travelling alone all those months, she had finally taught herself how to keep her audience entertained for her entire show; what she gave them now was a one-woman variety program. In the process of developing it she had to become a full-fledged comedienne, but she no longer seemed to despise herself for having stooped to her audience's level in this way. It was as if she had become reconciled to the essential commercialism of her work at last. She settled into her Winnipeg hotel room, bubbling with optimism. When she was interviewed by the reporter from the *Tribune,* she was in a playful mood as she told him of her plans for the future. He wrote:

> Miss Pauline Johnson will be the chief attraction at the Massey Music Hall in Toronto on Christmas night at a patriotic concert. Miss Johnson will be crowned poet laureate by the Brantford "Old Boys" on December 28th, and previous to filling an engagement in one of the large vaudeville theatres of New York will appear at the chief centres in Ontario. Her Australian tour will begin in April.[5]

It was true that during Christmas week that year, Brantford was celebrating its "Old Boys Reunion" when all the men and some of the women who had been educated in the town returned to demonstrate their success to one another, but the town was not offering to crown Pauline, and she had made no plans to be there to accept the honour if they had offered. Instead, she remained in Winnipeg until 8 January. She visited old friends and met Charles Drayton one last time and learned that he wished her to release him so that he could marry someone else. Having waited almost two years for this particular axe to fall, Pauline is unlikely to have succumbed to hysterics. Her pride had been abused once by the Draytons; she did not care to be humiliated again. She refused to lower herself to denounce him, nor did she even consider a breach of promise suit, the popular revenge of abandoned Victorian damsels. She parted from Charles with dignity, and then, in characteristic fashion, dedicated herself to work even harder; fortunately for her, January 1900 was the month that Canada became involved in the Boer War.

In October 1899 fighting had broken out in South Africa between the British and the Boers. From the outset the British, who were outnumbered almost two to one, had suffered defeat after defeat, crowning their disasters with "Black Week" in the middle of December when British troops were defeated in three separate battles.

The opening month of the new century saw Kimberley, Mafeking and Ladysmith besieged by the Boers, and British troops under General Buller defeated at Spion Kop. In Britain, shock and anger at these disasters caused a new wave of enlistment and the appointment of Field Marshal Lord Roberts to the position of supreme commander. Patriotic fervour also swept English-speaking Canada, encouraging thousands of young Canadians to enlist to fight beside the British. However, the Canadian government, trying to mollify French Canada, where feeling was running high against joining in Britain's battles, arranged for the Canadian troops to be paid by Britain. But their personal comforts, medical services, family and widows' benefits were the responsibility of "the folks back home."

To raise money for these benefits, patriotic concerts and "tableaux vivants" were organized by each regiment's auxiliary and by the Red Cross, and every entertainer in the country rushed to donate his services to prove his loyalty to the Crown. Ernest du Domaine, now a violin teacher at the Toronto Conservatory, played at a Red Cross concert in Ottawa under the patronage of the governor general and the Countess of Minto. Owen Smily arrived in Toronto from a tour to the Pacific Coast just in time to appear in a patriotic concert on 16 January. Walter McRaye, returned from his American journeys, organized the town of Cobourg's patriotic concert in Victoria Opera House. Frank Yeigh pounded lecterns all over southern Ontario espousing the cause. Regimental bands got little rest as they marched out to blow martial airs night after night in opera houses and church halls. Prominent ladies and gentlemen posed in tableaux vivants while public-spirited sopranos and elocutionists challenged the Canadian public to GIVE! And at every concert, there was someone to recite or sing Rudyard Kipling's new poem, "The Absent-Minded Beggar," which set the tone for the most important part of the evening: passing the hat around.

> Duke's son—cook's son—son of a hundred kings—
> (Fifty thousand horse and foot going to Table Bay!)
> Each of 'em doing his country's work
>   (and who's to look after their things?)
> Pass the hat for your credit's sake,
> and pay—pay—pay!

Pauline arrived in Toronto on 11 January with just enough time to check into the Rossin before she was due to perform at her fund-raising concert at Massey Hall. The first part of the evening's entertainment featured tableaux "with well known ladies and gentlemen taking the part of personnages [sic] represented by the various pictures"[6] while a military band played suitable music. The second part of the program starred Pauline reciting "Canadian Born" and "Riders of the Plains." A week later the concert was repeated.

In spite of the fact that Pauline received excellent publicity from these appearances, her primary reason for donating her services was her very real concern for the British cause. This was not surprising considering her family's history of allegiance to the British flag, but it was not until her trip to London in 1894 that Pauline herself had become a truly aggressive anglophile. After that time she became increasingly sensitive to criticism of Britain and her people, and totally intolerant of anything or anyone that was non-British. As Britain's champion, she stepped up her private war on the Americans, and vigorously thumped the Yankees in the articles she produced over the next few years.

In describing a journey from Saskatoon to Battleford in 1902 she wrote:

> We halted for dinner at the "Badger," a neat little sod-covered shack kept by two American women of rather wide experience. We dined off exquisite Japanese china, for the West is a place of surprises and incongruities. Of the sixty thousand Americans that have settled in our NorthWest this year there are two classes: those anxious to swear allegiance to the King and become good British subjects, and those—more numerous, alas! who flaunt their hatred of us and yet come to us to earn a dollar they cannot get in their own country. Our

hostesses evidently belonged to the latter class for during the meal hour one said to me:

"When next you come here you will see the Stars and Stripes flying over this shack."

In jest I replied, "If I do I will empty a shot gun into it."

She lifted her head proudly and said: "We can stand it. It won't be the first time the American flag has been shot at."

"No," I said, "nor the first time it has been shot at by an Indian. Did you ever hear of an Indian shooting at the Union Jack?"

She turned the conversation.[7]

Pauline's dislike of Americans never prevented her from appreciating certain individual Americans, or submitting her articles and poems to American publications, or accepting engagements in the United States. However, she made it plain that most of her American dates were something to be endured, rather like bad-tasting medicine. "We will however leave this state [Michigan] at the earliest possible moment, we dislike it so. The people are *very* uncultured, very ignorant, very illiterate. Daily I grow to be more and more of a 'Cannuck.' "[8]

Her attitude towards the French on the other hand was dictated by her father's great admiration for Napoleon, by her own respect for a few Frenchmen, and because she admired French elegance. But the French showed no inclination to reciprocate. Her Quebec concerts were, in fact, singularly unsuccessful.

One of the Frenchmen on whom Pauline based her judgement was Monsieur Paul Bluet, who was known in the entertainment world as Max O'Rell, wit and raconteur. In January 1900, during his "first" farewell tour of North America, he lectured in Toronto on "The Little Foibles of John Bull, Sandy and Pat: how other nations look at Great Britain." The concert was a sell-out among Toronto anglophiles because O'Rell could never find fault with the British. After the show, Pauline was one of the audience who went backstage to greet him, and while they chatted, she asked his advice for her forthcoming tour of Australia where he had recently toured.

The following day, Pauline took the train to Stewarton near Ottawa where she was booked for a one-night engagement, and then she settled into the Russell House in the capital city with the intention of staying "about a week." At the Russell, the gossipy "Marchioness" of the *Ottawa Daily Free Press* called on her for an interview, and Pauline confided to her that her departure date for Australia was now definitely set for June. The following day Pauline began the rounds of Ottawa society "at homes," and then on 30 January she slipped into the office of Clifford Sifton at the Ministry of the Interior for a brief interview.

For the next fourteen months Pauline's pattern of behaviour becomes a mystery, beginning with the Sifton interview. She continued to perform, touring in eastern Canada, but it is almost as if her life had become a jigsaw puzzle with some of the most significant pieces missing. There are enough pieces still in existence, however, to explain why Eva Johnson felt it was necessary to destroy all Pauline's personal letters and the documents relevant to this period of her life, and why Eva induced Walter McRaye to pretend that he began a partnership with Pauline in 1899. Fortunately, a number of Pauline's papers were beyond the reach of Eva and Walter and they tell a little of the story.

The Honourable Clifford Sifton came from a prominent Manitoba family of lawyers and politicians who had acquired money and influence by dabbling in railway building and then in provincial politics. Clifford was one of the second generation Siftons and he came to Ottawa in 1896 as the minister of the interior, a position which made him responsible for Indian Affairs and therefore indirectly responsible for collecting the rent from the Chiefswood tenants and then disbursing it to the heirs.

From the wording of Pauline's note asking for an appointment with Sifton, there is nothing to suggest that the two were friends; she merely asks if "he will find it convenient to name an hour, if possible today, wherein she may have a business interview of fifteen minutes with him."[9] But since he was still living in Winnipeg when she made her home there, and since he was a friend of Frank Yeigh, it seems likely that they were at least acquainted. This would have made it simpler for her to get what she wanted from him.

The following day Pauline called on Sir Wilfrid and Lady Laurier to solicit introductions to prominent people in Australia. It was her second contact with the Lauriers; she had given an afternoon recital for them in 1893. This time, Lady Laurier invited her to return the next day to recite at her afternoon reception. Pauline obliged in return for the letters she had requested.

On 9 February, returning to Brantford for the first time since her mother's death, Pauline wrote to Clifford Sifton:

My dear Mr. Sifton,

Will you grant me one more favour, one that is urgent, and will most greatly assist me—at this time when I am financially embarrassed—and seeking backing for my proposed Australian tour.

I called upon Supt. Cameron here to-day to learn if I could raise $500.00 *at once* on the rent of my share of our Indian Reserve property. He informed me there would be no difficulty in getting an advance on rent under official loan, *if the Department would approve of it* as the security under this lease is number one. Will you do me the inestimable favor of having the Department approve without delay if possible. I need this money very urgently. Mr. Cameron said he would write the Department at once about it.

If you will see that the Department sanctions this for me, I shall be most greatly in your debt, and you will be doing me a kindness inexpressible.

I have the honour to be yours most faithfully,

E. Pauline Johnson.

Six days later she wrote him again from her brother's address in Hamilton, to acknowledge receipt of the money "which came when [she] most required official favours."[10] This five hundred dollars represented her share of the rental monies for the next three and a half years. Since she was visiting in their homes, it is possible that she told her cousin Kathleen and her brother Allen that she had borrowed the money, but she certainly never told Eva, and this was to prove another bone of contention between them when Eva learned of it a few years later.

Although five hundred dollars would be inadequate today to finance a tour of Australia, it was a considerable sum of money in 1900. With that amount she could have travelled by rail from Montreal to Vancouver and back *three* times with a drawing room to herself and all meals supplied and had money left over for stopovers at the best hotels in the country. Or she could have renewed her entire wardrobe five times over; the finest silk blouse cost only $6.50, quality kid gloves were selling for $1.25, and there was not a bonnet to be found in the shops of Toronto for over $5. Even a made-to-order brocade ball gown could be bought for $30. With five hundred dollars she could have rented a home like Chiefswood and lived for more than a year in perfect luxury without giving a single recital.

But she did not travel back and forth across the country by rail, nor did she suddenly expand her wardrobe. And she did not spend the year in idleness.

For the next month and a half, Pauline made appearances in Ontario, usually backed by local talent; then in April she disappeared from the entertainment scene entirely. Now, according to the interview that she gave to the reporter from the *Winnipeg Tribune,* she should have been in New York in early April fulfilling her vaudeville engagement. But she was not. At that time of year, New York's theatrical season was beginning to overlap with its summer season, so Pauline would have had a choice of playing one of the vaudeville houses or one of the "summer gardens" where the vaudeville acts went in the hot summer weather. In either case, New York critics would have made note of her appearance since they were in the habit of documenting even the most insignificant acrobat or juggler. There is no mention of Pauline in any of their columns, and she did not advertise in the New York papers nor list her recital in the trade papers. She did not, in fact, perform in New York at any time during the year 1900.

The next time her name turns up in the columns of a newspaper is 2 June 1900. Under a Sydney dateline, the *Halifax Herald* announced that arrangements were being made for Pauline Johnson to visit North Sydney, Sydney Mines and Glace Bay to give recitals. And on the same date the *Herald* reported on an interview with a gentleman named Charles Wurz from New York who claimed to be "directing the Canadian tour of Miss E. Pauline Johnson." He had arrived in the city the previous day from Quebec and had just finished making arrangements for Pauline to appear in some two dozen Nova Scotia towns. After leaving that province, Wurz said, she would appear in a few cities in the United States, and in the fall she would leave for Australia and Great Britain.

On 4 June the *Herald* printed a large advertisement for her coming performances. Above her picture was a tomahawk crossed with a peace pipe. On the ninth an even larger ad appeared. It measured eight by fourteen inches and included a photograph of Pauline in Indian costume, the text of "Canadian Born," and the caption, "Canada's foremost Comedienne and Poetess!" The next day a four- by seven-inch ad appeared in both morning and evening papers to announce a concert in Dartmouth on 14 June and one in Orpheus Hall in Halifax on Friday, the fifteenth. The same day a publicity release listed her distinguished patrons for the Halifax event including His Excellency Vice Admiral Sir Frederick Bedford and Lady Bedford, His Honour Governor Sir Malachi Daly and Mrs. Daly, the Most Reverend Dr. O'Brien (archibishop of Halifax), the Honourable George H. Murray (premier of Nova Scotia), His Worship the Mayor of Halifax, Colonel Biscoe (chief staff officer of Her Majesty's Troops); the list went on and on. On the eleventh the June ninth ad was repeated. On the twelfth Haligonians were briefed on Pauline's schedule for the following month; the itinerary ended with a New York booking for 17 July.

While all of the publicity was totally uncharacteristic of Pauline, the most surprising part of it was the size of the photograph published on the ninth. In the past she had been content with a few lines in the "Music and Drama" columns of the local papers and a column-inch advertisement a week before her recital. For concerts in big cities such as Winnipeg or Toronto she also paid to have her program of events printed in the paper and placed a couple of ads which told where tickets could be bought. Whenever her picture did appear in the paper it was the publisher's response to her paid advertising, but in all her years of touring no newspaper had printed a picture of her as large as this one.

Haligonians must have been wide-eyed at the campaign. No recitalist had ever advertised on this scale in their newspapers. In fact, even in Toronto, photographs like the one in Pauline's 9 June advertisement could not be found touting the biggest theatrical companies. Occasionally celebrated stars or road shows would buy a three-by-four-inch ad that included a picture, but this was always done on the strict understanding that the newspaper would run pictures in the Music and Drama column free of charge. Although photography was becoming very popular and therefore fairly reasonable, the cost of transferring photographs to a print medium was still comparatively high.

Two things had been responsible for this abrupt change in Pauline's career style: five hundred dollars and Charles Wurz. Wurz was a small-time New York promoter whom she had probably met in the spring of 1898 when she toured for the Indian Associations. Still mourning her mother and anxious about the status of her engagement to Drayton, Pauline desperately needed love, and she would have warmed to anyone who seemed sympathetic and even more to someone who gave her admiration and encouragement. Sometime before Christmas of 1899 she crossed paths again with Wurz, and this meeting is what prompted her to tell the *Tribune's* reporter of a New York booking. It is possible that their second meeting coincided with a period of disappointment in Cornyn's management, and Pauline may have suggested that Wurz manage her career instead. The carrot was the Australian tour which she had been putting off since she first announced it at Christmas, 1897. When Wurz jumped at the chance to go to Australia with her, she had to arrange financing in a hurry and this is where Clifford Sifton came in. Sifton made it possible for her to get five hundred dollars, part of which was now financing her new and expensive publicity and her new and expensive manager.

Why Wurz embarked on this campaign is a mystery. If he knew anything about theatre, he would have known that the return on the investment would not justify the cost. And if he knew anything about Pauline, he would have known that she did not need this kind of build-up, especially in Nova Scotia where she had always attracted large audiences. It could have been stupidity on his part or a desire to do things in a big "show-biz" way, but it is also possible that he simply miscalculated if it was the first time he had actually played the role of theatrical manager. In any case, he seems to have been convinced that he could make money for the Australian tour by spending Pauline's five-hundred-dollar stake on her planned Nova Scotia tour.

Pauline allowed him to do it because she was totally inept with money. Time and again, she had been forced to borrow from friends and relatives and finally from the family estate. She had immense admiration for people who were money-wise—her brothers, her sister, Drayton, O'Brien—for it was an art that she considered beyond her grasp. Therefore, all Wurz had to do to convince her of his ability to manage her money and her campaign was to talk as if he knew what he was doing. Obviously, he talked well.

Events, however, took a turn that neither of them expected.

Pauline became ill. On the evening of 14 June she delighted a capacity audience at Dartmouth, but after the show she had to drive to Halifax to meet Wurz. She set out by buggy in a torrential rainstorm and by the time she arrived at the Halifax Hotel she was soaked to the skin. Within hours, the hotel had to summon a doctor, and the Halifax recital was cancelled.

In the press release that was printed the following morning, the doctor (whose name was Farrell) referred to her ailment as "acute rheumatism," but a doctor today would recognize it as rheumatic fever. This was the predictable second attack brought on, not by getting wet in the storm, as Pauline's doctor believed, but by some unrecorded streptococcus infection of a few weeks earlier. Dr. Farrell remained in constant attendance for several days and then a trained nurse was able to take over. Pauline lay in bed for twelve days. Wurz, who had arrived at the Halifax Hotel in time to meet her there, left after four days. Where he went is unknown.

When she was able to leave the hotel, she played some of the dates that had been scheduled and picked up a few more to keep herself going, but she was obviously not well enough to carry a full schedule. Meanwhile, all the money spent on the elaborate advertising campaign had been wasted.

On 27 July she wrote to Sir Wilfrid Laurier:

My dear Sir Wilfrid,
    Some months ago, when I called upon you, I was graciously promised letters of presentation to the various governors of Australia. I have not yet arranged the date of my trip there but I am intending to visit Newfoundland within the next two weeks.

(She then requests introductions from him to government officials in Newfoundland.)

I wish to make use of it in the matter of begging patronage of their Excellencies at one of my public recitals.
    I am my dear Sir Wilfrid,

Yours most faithfully,
E. Pauline Johnson
    Will you kindly address it to me at St. John's, Newfoundland where I shall arrive next week. [11]

By mid-August she was in Charlottetown; by late September

she fulfilled the promised dates in St. John's. She did enlist the patronage of Lady McCallum and a "party" from government house, no doubt with the aid of Laurier's letters.

The next recorded date in this censored year of her life is 19 November, when she gave a recital at the Church of England Hall in Fredericton, New Brunswick. The following day she travelled to Woodstock, taking the train from there to St. Stephen for a recital; then she began the long trip back to Fredericton for a second recital in the Church of England Hall on 24 November. This, however, was one concert that she missed. When she arrived at McAdam Junction she found the trains had been delayed because of the heavy snowfall which had begun earlier in the day. At noontime she was still sitting in the train station; another woman who was on her way to Halifax shared the lunch she had packed. Pauline was crocheting Christmas gifts and while she worked the two women talked, or rather Pauline talked and the woman asked questions, fascinated by the life of a celebrity and appalled at the hardships and difficulties of her career. Pauline told her that she had hoped to give a recital at Woodstock, but the local committee had not been able to promote it, and now with the trains delayed indefinitely, the recital in Fredericton would be cancelled and she would probably have to pay the hall rental anyway. It was dark when the train finally arrived.

Her next recorded appearance is in Saint John on 6 December at the Mechanics' Institute in aid of the New Baptist Tabernacle which was being erected on Haymarket Square. The next night she moved on to Elgin in Albert County to perform. One of the interesting things about these New Brunswick appearances is the enthusiasm of the newspaper reviews, especially that of the *Saint John Daily Sun* which said after an opening burst of raptures:

> The audience expected to find Miss Johnson an impressive reader of her own poetry. But her remarkably varied dramatic gifts, her power to personate all the characters in humourous stories came as a surprise. Her best known poems have something tragic in them, and there is a great power in her rendering of the Mohawk's wife who stabbed her Huron abductor while she whispered words of love in his ear. But for much of the evening Miss Johnson kept her audience laughing by her accounts of her own experiences, her description of life and people in various parts of the world, and her representations of some phases of society life. [12]

The effects of her illness had vanished and she was revitalized so that she was once again at ease with her audience and confident of her ability to make them laugh and cry at will. And although it seems that her material was basically unchanged—"The Mohawk's wife" is just "Ojistoh," a poem she had been reciting for a full seven years—she managed to mesmerize her audience. She even kept them happy with "her representations of some phases of society life," an improved version of the sketch for which she had been crucified in Vancouver nineteen months earlier.

Three and a half months go by before her whereabouts can be pinpointed again. Then, on 1 April 1901, on the stationery of The Graham House, Havelock, Ontario, she wrote the following to Frank Yeigh:

> My dear fond friend—
>
> Now—when I wrote you—or rather wired you not to bother about that loan I was begging of you I felt like an escaped convict—independent, free—everything that is glorious, albeit I am in a network of tragedy—too sad for human tongue to tell—Now—could you, *without* great inconvenience lend me the half of that amount I was so frantic about last week. That is—fifteen dollars to be repaid in a month's time—you could never quite imagine just "where I am at," or you would forgive me writing and asking this.
>
> Here I am, in Holy Week in Havelock,—an economical town to pray in—also to eat in, and I *shall* be here all week.
>
> This is all a horrid shame—and I would not have Mr. O'Brien or Miss Maracle know for *worlds* what I am asking of you. Someday, when I see you again, I shall tell you all of it, and grasp your good warm hands and congratulate you from my true Indian heart, that your own has anchored in the harbour of a fond woman's love.
>
> Will you write me here—*do*—if you can spare that little fifteen dollars, you will do more than churches, nor yet priests can do for me and yourself in the great Hereafter.
>
> Thine,
> E. Pauline Johnson[13]

What had happened in that three-and-a-half-month period? It seems impossible that Pauline could have been desperate for money so soon when she had received a lump sum of five hundred dollars only a year earlier. The clues are in the melodramatic expressions "an escaped convict" and "network of tragedy," the fact that she does not want certain friends to know what has happened, and her reference to Yeigh's safe and secure marriage. The "something" that caused Pauline to write to Yeigh again was a string of poor houses in the Peterborough area. Without someone to organize her tour, she had not given enough advance notice of her recitals and had played to almost empty halls. She had even inadvertently booked herself into one settlement where she had to compete with the local high school's spring concert.

It is more difficult to explain the rest of the puzzle, but it seems that the thirty dollars had been intended to facilitate her escape and by chance she had freed herself without requiring it. Was the person who held her in bondage the mysterious Charles Wurz? He did disappear from her life just prior to the date she wrote to Yeigh and he never re-entered it. From existing letterheads it can be proven that he managed her career, but if Wurz is the man she is alluding to in her letter to Yeigh, there was more to their relationship than manager and client. There can be no other reason for her to fear the disclosure of her financial problem to Miss Maracle (Allen's lady friend) or to Harry O'Brien. She had borrowed from O'Brien many times in the past without embarrassment. She also congratulated Yeigh that his heart was anchored in the harbour of a fond woman's love, which suggests that her own heart was anchored in a stormy sea. Did Wurz cause the storm?

The extent of her emotional involvement is indicated in three poems which she wrote during the period when she was associated with Wurz. The first, "Morrow Land" was written at Easter, 1900. The other two are not dated, but she apparently wrote them that summer.

MORROW LAND

In morrow land there lies a day,
With shadows clad and garments grey,
When sunless days will come my dear,
And skies will lose their lustre clear,
Because you will be miles away.

Has fate no other kindlier way,
No gentler hand on me to lay,
Than I to go, than you stay
In Morrow Land?

But oh, these days will be so dear
Through all the bleak and coming year,
This passion week of gold and grey,
Will haunt my life and bless my way
In Morrow Land.

HEIDLEBURGH

In Heidleburgh, where you were born,
The day dawn must wear strange disguise;
Since it has left its wealth of grey and melting shadows
In your eyes.
Did Fate decree your art and mine
Should weave into a future skein,
When you were born in Heidleburgh
And I was born in vain?

In Heidleburgh, where you were born,
The sunshine must be fine and rare
To leave its wealth of golden sunshine
In your hair.
Did Fate decree your promise hour
Greet mine of storm and stress and rain,
When you were born in Heidleburgh
And I was born in vain?

SONG

The night-long shadows faded into grey,
    Then silvered into glad and golden sunlight,
Because you came to me, like a new day
    Born of the beauty of an autumn night.

The silence that enfolded me so long
    Stirred to the sweetest music life had known
Because you came, and coming woke the song
    That slumbered through the years I was alone.

So have you brought the silver from the shade,
    The music and the laughter and the day,
So have you come to me, and coming made
    This life of mine a blossom-bordered way.

Pauline considered these poems so personal that she never
included them in any of her collections. It is probable they were

intended only for the eyes of the man who inspired them. They are very simple and uncomplicated, but there is no mistaking the passion in them. Or the resignation.

Even after allowing for the romanticism and exaggerations of poetic licence, certain things about the subject of the poems are matters of fact. First, Wurz came from Heidelburg, Germany. (The name is either Swiss or German.) Second, his hair was blond and his eyes were grey: the physical traits of the man in Pauline's classic fantasy of white-man-marries-Indian-maiden. Third, he arrived in Pauline's life when she felt most alone. Fourth, Pauline not only expected but was reconciled to the fact that this man would leave her. Finally, she felt that her relationship with this man from Heidelburg had completely changed her life, and even after he was gone, he would haunt her. With these facts in mind, it seems reasonable to assume that Wurz was the man in the poems and that he was probably a married man, or at least Pauline believed him to be committed to someone else.

They had little time together in private. Wurz never travelled with her and it appears they did not rendezvous regularly when she was touring. But more to the point, there is no record of Pauline offending the good ladies of some small town with her indiscretions and being ostracized as a result. She was still patronized by the governor of Newfoundland and his wife in September 1900, and by Ottawa's elite the following autumn. The best homes in the land still opened their doors to her.

At the same time, there is no question that the three poems which were inspired by her relationship with Wurz describe something more passionate than the feelings Pauline shared with Drayton. These poems tell of consummated love. Therefore, any explanation for her puzzling behaviour in the fourteen months that Wurz was her manager hinges on Pauline's departure from her rigid moral principles to become sexually and romantically involved with an unscrupulous small-time promoter. There is the possibility that her mother's death somehow released her from the strict Johnson code of morals, but if so it was a temporary release, for she never again let down the barriers of propriety. On the other hand, it is possible that she was simply overreacting to Drayton's rejection, rebounding into the arms of Wurz. The only clue to the answer perhaps lies in an expression found in her letter to Yeigh: an escaped convict—independent, free. These are not the words of a woman who has been in physical captivity, but rather they suggest psychological and emotional bondage, almost as if Wurz had completely dominated her life in the manner of a Svengali.

In all her previous experience, no man had manipulated Pauline as Wurz had done. She had always been the charmer, the one who had manipulated the men in her life. Hector Charlesworth, for example, had been just nineteen when he met her; she was thirty-one. As a new assistant editor on *Saturday Night* he dealt with her when her poem "The Song My Paddle Sings" was accepted by the magazine. In his memoirs he recalled that he had "never met any native-born Canadian who gave a more complete sense of aristocracy than Pauline Johnson. . . ."[14] Young Charlesworth's adoration helps to account for the extravagant praise he gave to *The White Wampum* when it appeared. She responded by parading him around to the homes of the literary set, and even took him backstage to meet Mlle Rhea. (That lady, realizing he was quite shy in these surroundings, announced, "You are a ni-ice boy; I am going to keess you!" And she did.) He accompanied Pauline to lunch with the beautiful Belle Archer as well, but he remained Pauline's adoring slave.

Men her own age were not as easily spellbound. Frank Yeigh actually made use of her to further his own career, though it must be said to his credit that he remained her champion all her life, responding financially on at least two occasions. The bachelor Harry O'Brien, whom she met through their mutual love of canoeing, was her staunch friend but never apparently succumbed to her charms. It took more than a decade of letter-writing, in fact, before they addressed one another by their first names.

She was much more practical in her approach to the influential men of the literary and artistic world. After her return from London in 1894 she had said, "There is only one way to deal with a man—that is through his vanity. . . ."[15] This was the policy she had followed with the critic Clement Scott in order to get his blessing on the poems for *The White Wampum*. She followed it again with the artist Alma-Tadema to gain a foothold in London's colony of painters and sculptors. After Theodore Watts-Dunton praised her early work, she confirmed him as her lifelong advocate by praising him in return. Of

John Greenleaf Whittier she said: "I owe to Whittier all I have ever accomplished for he first gave me faith in myself."[16]

She labelled William Douw Lighthall her "literary father" because he was responsible for *Songs of the Great Dominion* in which her poems and those of many of the other young poets were first given wide distribution. Sir Gilbert Parker whom she met in London introduced her to the literary world there. In return she dedicated *The Moccasin Maker* to him "whose work in literature has brought honour to Canada"; she never saw his response because it was printed after her death, but it certainly helped book sales.

> I am glad to have known this rare creature who had the courage to be glad of her origin, without defiance, but with an unchanging, if unspoken, insistence. Her native land and the Empire should be glad of her for what she was and for what she stood; her native land and the Empire should be glad of her for the work, interesting, vivid and human, which she has done. . . .[17]

Ernest Thompson Seton, though he was her own age, responded easily to her flattery, but he regarded her primarily as a subject for his canvas.

> How well I remember my first meeting with Tekahionwake, the Indian girl! I see her yet as she stood in all ways the ideal type of her race, lithe and active, with clean-cut aquiline features, olive red complexion and long dark hair. . . . We met at a private view of one of my own pictures. It was a wolf scene and Tekahionwake quickly sensing the painter's sympathy with the wolf claimed him as a Medicine Brother, for she was of the Wolf Clan of the Mohawks. The little silver token she gave me then is not to be gauged or appraised by any craftsman method known to the trade.[18]

She had bought Thompson Seton's loyalty with a silver charm.

Older men were more easily enslaved. The poet Charles Mair was almost sixty and a grandfather when they met, but he saw in her a "pagan yearning"[19] that stirred him to an overly sentimental appreciation of everything she wrote. In return, she praised his "magnificent" poetic drama, *Tecumseh,* calling it the result "of long study and life with the people whom he has written of so carefully, so truthfully."[20] In this way she primed him to respond quickly to her request for bears' claws and teeth for a necklace for her stage costume. From his home in northern British Columbia he obliged with alacrity, but in the meantime Ernest Thompson Seton had already sent her a necklace of teeth and claws, so Mair's collection never hung around her lovely neck.

But the group of men who received her most concentrated wooing—and most persistent demands—were the politicians. Her technique was simple: first she flattered them, assuring them she was helpless without their special patronage, then she pounced on them for favours. One of her earliest "flattery letters" was written to the Honourable A. S. Hardy in 1891:

> My dear Mr. Hardy;
>
> Your letter has been one of the sincerest pleasures, one of the most acceptable compliments I have ever received. I think I value the moments you have given me as much as I do your words of commendation, for I know what demands an exacting public make upon your time.
>
> Your kind notice of my little poem I will always regard as an imperishable laurel leaf in my tiny wreath, as well as a stimulant, a tonic and an encouragement to better things.
>
> I can scarcely tell you how often an author requires approbation or how dear is the handclasp of encouragement when it does come. Your praise and approval of my work will lighten many a hard road that I must needs tramp over before I reach the heights of Literature I mean to attain. Your letter may have seemed a little thing for you to do—to me it means more than I can thank you for. I will only try to merit your kindness to me.[21]

Three years later, when she prepared to embark for England, Hardy was first in line to give her letters of introduction to influential friends. By the time she began sending letters off to Sir Wilfrid Laurier in January 1900, her technique had become more direct:

> My dear Sir Wilfrid,
>
> I am taking this liberty of recalling myself to your memory. You will perhaps remember that about three or four years ago I gave some recitations in the drawing room here at one of Lady Laurier's receptions. I am the Indian girl who writes you sometimes. May I beg that you will name an hour to-morrow that will be convenient for me to present my compliments and beg my favours.
>
> I am most faithfully yours,
> E. Pauline Johnson[22]

And a number of years later, she pounced again:

> As I am a ward of the Canadian government and a member of the Six Nations Indians, I would attain much, could I meet Mr. Chamberlain. Perhaps you and Lord Strathcona would arrange it. This is asking much of a busy prime minister but you have always encouraged my advancement, and I dare to hope you would do what you could to help both a Canadian and an Indian while in England. . . .[23]

Laurier could hardly refuse her request since she made it sound as if it was his responsibility that she had gone to England in the first place! But she was always careful to be properly grateful after she got what she wanted. "Gratitude," Watts-Dunton said of her, "was with her not sentiment merely, as with most of us, but a veritable passion."[24] In 1906 she thanked Sir Wilfrid for recent favours with these words:

> I feel that you will be interested and gratified to know that your gracious and flattering letter introducing me to Lord Strathcona has been the means of practically giving me a place in London that I could never have attained without your introduction and his responsive and kindly aid.
>
> I have always so much to thank you for, but this has been the most helpful thing that you have ever done for me, and has given me a confidence and strength to battle away here and achieve success. . . .[25]

From a present-day point of view it is easy to condemn Pauline for this outrageous scheming and manipulation, but she lived in a completely male-dominated world where women's rights were derived from their male protectors. A middle-class wife cajoled and manoeuvred to get an increase in the housekeeping money from her husband, she wheedled permission to attend concerts and meetings, she used subtle persuasion to influence his decision-making. From their mothers, daughters learned these techniques to practise on their own husbands, so that in return for outwardly docile behaviour they were given security.

Single women had to find alternatives to the security guaranteed by marriage. One way was to submit to the dominance of a father, and when he died, to a brother. Another was to join the small band of emancipated women who, though subject to discrimination, battled for their rights in the world of men. Pauline could not turn to a male relative for protection; Allen, the only surviving one, had never learned the art of asserting himself and Pauline was actually a much more aggressive person than he was. On the other hand, the image she maintained for her stage career would never have allowed her to become a suffragette. She chose instead the elegant courtliness of the upper-class woman who distributed compliments in flowery phrases, expecting them to be taken sincerely but not literally. The recipients, while appreciating the beauty of the compliments, recognized the convention contained in them. So when Pauline showered men with compliments and dealt with them through their vanity, she was only fulfilling her half of the convention. They in turn, by acknowledging her helplessness and vulnerability, accepted their roles as protectors and bestowed on her the "favours" she demanded. In this way she derived rights through a great number of surrogate fathers, brothers, and husbands.

But in spite of her success in manipulating men, Pauline allowed herself to be manipulated by a man who spent all her money and gave her only a brief love affair in return. When it was over, she returned to her career with the bitter knowledge that life would probably never again offer her love. She was forty years old and destined never to marry.

She returned to the fold of Thomas Cornyn, apparently without any recriminations from him, but this time, either to provide her with a chaperone or to take some of the performance pressure off her, he teamed her with his wife. Clara (McDonald) Cornyn was a classical pianist who had married her manager while on tour in Minnesota, but since her keyboard talents were not suited to the Bijou Comedy Company's format, she spent much of her time travelling alone to give recitals. Sharing a program with Pauline seemed like the ideal solution to both their problems, but it was not. In the first place, her musical taste centred on classical music so that Pauline was required to provide all the lighter moments on the program. For Pauline, this meant that since she had only half her former time on stage, she had to drop some of the dramatic pieces she most enjoyed reciting. In the second place, two female performers were less of a drawing card than a male-female combination.

On 27 August the two women arrived in St. John's, Newfoundland, where Pauline had played the year before. The timing of their arrival seemed most fortunate; a British warship had just entered the harbour and a levee was to be held the following afternoon at Government House. Although the two women were not included in the event, the governor general and his wife, Lady McCallum, and the admiral from the British warship acted as patrons at the Johnson-Cornyn recital that evening in St. Patrick's Hall, thereby encouraging a large audience to attend. The next afternoon, "a dance was given on board the flagship which was the event of the season. So great was the enthusiasm of the sailors over Pauline's dramatic numbers that one of them, Percy Billington by name, took off his tie of black silk and presented it to her, a souvenir which she always prized."[26]

Flushed with success, Johnson and Cornyn gave their second concert on the thirtieth; the hall was almost empty. The next morning, attempting to recoup their losses, they had dodgers delivered all over town announcing a Saturday matinee performance. This too was a financial disaster. On Monday the two set out for Bell Island to begin three weeks of one-night stands.

They left Newfoundland almost penniless in mid-September to begin touring New Brunswick. They played to half-full halls. Their program was simply too heavy to draw the general public in the manner that Pauline had drawn them when she toured alone or with Smily. At last, broke once again, Pauline wired Clifford Sifton on 9 October from Campbellton, New Brunswick:

CAN YOU ARRANGE FOR THREE TICKETS FROM HERE TO MONTREAL VIA INTERCOLONIAL WANT TO LEAVE AT FOUR TO-MORROW MORNING WILL BE IN OTTAWA SATURDAY AND REMIT PAYMENT WANT TICKETS IN ADVANCE PLEASE REPLY IMMEDIATELY HERE.[27]

He sent the tickets. On Saturday, 11 October, she wrote him from the Grand Central House, Vankleek Hill, Ontario.

My dear Mr. Sifton,

I hardly think you can ever know what a favour you did for me when I telegraphed you from Campbellton. I shall not attempt to thank you—But I am grateful.

Will you kindly have me informed where and to whom I am to remit, also the amount for those three tickets. I committed an error in telegraphing you I was to be in Ottawa today. I find it is *next* Saturday. My manager corrected me by wire later. I shall be in Rockland,

Ontario, Tuesday and Thursday nights, Buckingham, Ontario, Wednesday night, Ottawa (Russell House) Friday night. May I hope for information from your secretary regarding the above remittance. Again I shall not even try to thank you for a most inestimable favour, but Indian-like, I shall not forget.

I am, Honourable Sir,

Yours faithfully,
E. Pauline Johnson.[28]

Safely returned to Ottawa, the scene of her earliest triumphs, it must be assumed that she soon earned enough to repay Sifton. It was there, too, that she parted company with Clara Cornyn without regret, and notified Thomas Cornyn that she had no further need of his services. She was about to begin an eight-year partnership with J. Walter McRaye. Unable to find herself a husband, she had found herself a child.

Chapter Eight

Regina and Points West

THE JOHNSON-McRAYE partnership debuted at Ottawa's Orme Hall on 6 November 1901 with the prime minister and Lady Laurier and the Siftons seated in the midst of Ottawa's high society. Pauline was uncharacteristically nervous before she went on stage. She had played to far more aristocratic audiences than this one, of course, but on those occasions she had not been breaking in a partner who had never set foot on a big-city stage. She was worried about the reaction of the capital city's audiences and what the critics would say. But most of all she worried because McRaye was *not* worried. He appeared to be totally confident and absolutely convinced that the audience and the critics would adore him.

He was not entirely correct in this assumption, but he erred only in degree. The Orme Hall audience was certainly pleased to welcome a new talent; the critics had reservations, but they were willing to give him time to improve. They were offended by his elocutionary technique. Why was his voice so harsh? they asked. Was he trying to make himself sound older? Why did the pitch of his voice rise on the end of every line? Then they relented and complimented him on his "considerable talent and sympathy" and on his "insight,"[1] and generally forgave him his technical sins. He had passed the Ottawa test.

Pauline did not fare as well. The reviewers scored her on the lack of new material in her program, citing her one new piece as her best offering. This was a playlet called "At the Ball" which is set in an "insane asylum" where two visitors mistake each other for patients. It had been part of Owen Smily's repertoire, but Pauline had rewritten it for herself and McRaye. The *Ottawa Citizen*'s critic reported that her style of performance had become mechanical. It was "vigourous and energetic although rather exaggerated from an artistic standpoint"[2]; he missed the depth and passion of her earlier performances.

Pauline relaxed. After the unflattering reviews, it would be years before she could play Ottawa again, but she was unconcerned. More important to her was that McRaye had been accepted by the reviewers of the nation's capital. At the same time, she found it disconcerting that he paid so little attention to their criticisms, especially when she knew they were valid. But J. Walter McRaye, the ultimate opportunist, had not a worry in the world. He knew he had a safe berth at last in the theatrical world.

At this point in his career, McRaye was ready to acknowledge that he was not star material. It had not been a difficult assessment to make. He had simply read his own reviews and counted the heads in his audiences. Even in the limited field to which he usually confined himself—the habitant poems of Dr. Drummond—he had been considered unspectacular. As the *Vernon News* was to say candidly in 1902: "Mr. McRaye can hardly be placed in the same class as his clever companion [Pauline], and there are not a few here who say that Charles Christien of this city could do the Drummond poems better justice."[3]

McRaye had collected a few laudatory reviews in his time. A reviewer from the St. Louis (Missouri) *Globe Democrat* had called him "a second Mark Twain"[4] when he played in that city in 1899 while working his way back to Canada from California. And a few years later, the *Vancouver Province*'s reviewer decided he was "considerably better than the average comedian that is seen on the stage."[5]

By being careful never to play the same town twice, and by giving plenty of exposure to the St. Louis plum in his advance bills, McRaye had survived from the spring of 1897 when he had made his unspectacular entry into show business until the day he met Pauline again in the spring of 1901. For this entire four-year period he had been searching doggedly for success, though since he was a practical young man, it had not been his own success he searched for. He was on the lookout, instead, for someone successful enough to allow him to tag along for the ride. A pair of coattails, as it were. An established entertainer who needed a warm-up act or an intermission routine, a well-known figure who would guarantee the full dinner pail that Walter McRaye had been missing.

From time to time he had found himself on the same bill with a "name" entertainer and had been able to promote a few more concerts on the same bill, or he had filled in for a show with a sick "act," but none of these encounters had produced any lasting arrangements. There were simply too many second-rate elocutionists already stumping English-speaking North America.

By the winter of 1900-1901 Walter McRaye had taken refuge in Peterborough in the run-down Oriental Hotel, paying his rent by giving elocution lessons to the children of the socially ambitious middle class. He had almost begun to doubt that he would ever find the comfortable niche he was seeking in the theatrical world, when Pauline popped into his life a second time in March 1901. This was McRaye's moment. Although she had turned him down once before, he could see that her circumstances had changed. He set off confidently to visit her.

There is some question as to where the fateful meeting between them took place. Pauline did not record the event, and McRaye himself is contradictory. In his book *Town Hall To-Night,* in the chapter entitled "En Tour," he says: "Pauline Johnson was appearing in Peterboro when I met her for the second time. We gave several programs together, and in the autumn started an association that was to last for nearly ten years." Seven pages later in the chapter called "East and West with Pauline Johnson," he says that after their 1897 meeting, they "separated to meet again in Havelock, Ontario two years later when we opened a tour at Ottawa. . . ."

With McRaye's reminiscences, there is a constant problem of deciding whether he suffered from a tragically failing memory or whether he was simply an out-and-out prevaricator. *Town Hall To-Night* was composed of articles written fifteen and twenty years after the events described in them. Under these conditions it is quite understandable for McRaye to have confused dates and places, but these are the least of his inaccuracies. Although he never recounts the ignominious events in his own career, he tells wonderful stories of his days with Pauline, all of them adding glory to his own image. He knew he was safe in telling them because he did so long after Pauline's personal papers had been destroyed by her sister, and after the memories of other witnesses to the events had been dulled by time. It may be unkind, but entirely within reason, to assume that many of McRaye's memories were nothing more than lies. For example, he recalled reciting at Cannington Manor with Pauline and being entertained at Didsbury, but Didsbury was closed four years before he became Pauline's partner. It was Smily who accompanied her to Cannington Manor. McRaye recalled having Christmas dinner with Pauline in Winnipeg in 1897, but she only arrived in town on December 28. She had Christmas dinner with her ailing mother that year. And though he claimed to have done so, McRaye did not perform with Pauline in Peterborough or its environs in the spring of 1901; her dates that spring were played as a single.

McRaye is correct in one detail: in the autumn after their spring meeting in Peterborough (or nearby Havelock), he did team up with Pauline to begin a collaboration which was to last seven and a half years (not ten years, as he was fond of saying). What possessed Pauline to form a partnership with this strange little man with his slight talent? Eva Johnson's explanation is perhaps the best: "He was very bright and jolly and fair entertainment, and his jolly disposition attracted her. . . . She was looking . . . for an entertainer and took him up when he called a second time. He was quite young, boyish . . . amateurish but could recite well. . . ."[6]

Eva loathed McRaye, but she seems to have summed up the situation fairly dispassionately. Pauline was at a very low ebb in her career. Her health had suffered another serious setback as a result of her "acute rheumatism" in Halifax the previous June. She had been rejected by Drayton and cheated by Wurz so that her ego was badly battered. She had added very little material to her act. Although she had become a master of technique and could stage a slick show, her heart was not in it. It was a very tired "Mohawk Princess" who donned her buckskins every night.

What she needed at this point was a good manager and a good stage partner, people who would look after the business end of touring and relieve her of the burden of carrying a whole show by herself. In the spring of 1901 she thought she had found these things in the husband and wife team of Tom and Clara Cornyn. It took her until midsummer to admit that she was wrong. Tom Cornyn was still running his Bijou Comedy Company, touring with it through the central states and most of Canada. At the same time, he managed a half dozen other performers besides Pauline. In spite of this workload he was efficient and businesslike, but from half a continent away he could not be on top of schedule changes and missing posters and forgotten newspaper advertising. He could not select hotels in towns that sprang up overnight, or find alternate transportation when the local stagecoach driver left for the gold fields, and he was never around to carry the star's bags through the gumbo of some prairie main street.

Clara Cornyn was an even bigger disappointment to Pauline than Tom Cornyn was. She did not wish to play the role that Pauline's partners had played in the past, nor did she wish to act like one of Pauline's female fans, fawning over her and mothering her. Clara Cornyn wanted to be the star of the show and was prepared to battle Pauline for top billing. This rivalry affected the quality of their concerts.

Whether Pauline had promised to give McRaye a trial run as her partner when they talked together in the spring in Peterborough/ Havelock, or whether this was a decision she made as the summer progressed and she grew disenchanted with the Cornyns is unknown. But it turned out to be one of the most important decisions of her career, and *the* most important event in the life of J. Walter McRaye. He had at last found the coattails he needed, and he never let go of them until the day he died. In 1924 Eva Johnson would write scornfully, "Pauline carried Mr. McRaye everywhere on her name and individuality. . . . Since Pauline's passing, Mr. McRaye seems to find it impossible to do without the use of her name. Some years after she passed, he was advertising his entertainment as a collaboration with the late E. Pauline Johnson."[7]

Allen Johnson also detested the little man, but Allen's love for Pauline and his inarticulateness prevented him from telling her how he felt. As a result, he found himself sharing her with McRaye on a camping trip in the summer of 1903. After that summer, however, she saw less and less of her brother, and when she did go to visit him, she went unaccompanied by McRaye, presumably at Allen's request.

In a letter to Harry O'Brien describing the camping trip, she says: "Mr. McRaye sends his very kind regards. He so frequently expressed a wish this summer that you could have been out camping with us."[8] O'Brien must have winced. He too found McRaye detestable. When the beautiful Belgian Mlle Rhea did not welcome Pauline's new young man as she had welcomed young Charlesworth, the friendship between the two women cooled. Rhea found McRaye uncouth. Years later, when he took up writing nostalgia pieces for magazines, McRaye retaliated by writing of her in disparaging terms. Friends and family all looked upon him as a vulgar little sponger, and gradually their contempt and dislike became the wedge that drove Pauline finally and irrevocably away from them all and away from the east.

Pauline was not blind to McRaye's inadequacies and his faults. She knew that he was second-rate. She had looked him over in December of 1897 and had even taken him on a brief tour in January 1898. Having seen just about every kind and calibre of performer on the boards during the years since she stepped onto the recital stage, she could not misjudge McRaye's abilities. Therefore, if excellence on stage had been her criterion for selecting a partner, McRaye would never have made it. But she chose him for quite different qualities.

First of all, he was no novice in the business. He had played every dilapidated stage and crummy hall from California to Ontario, and he knew every rickety back-street hotel along the way. What better companion for the endless one-night stands than someone who had already been over the route and knew where the pitfalls lay? McRaye was perfectly aware that he was not going to set the world on fire, and Pauline could see he was looking for a safe berth. And when you are in the market for a back-up act, what better than someone who is content to be just that? McRaye had toured with Harry Lindley's seedy company, he had booked his own halls across two-thirds of the continent, and during the Boer War he had done his bit organizing patriotic concerts. With a man like this to book her tours, there would be no more unpaid hotel bills in Havelock, no more expensive half-page ads in the newspapers, and no more desperate cries for financial help to Yeigh and O'Brien and her brother.

Therefore, despite the views of her friends and family, McRaye was precisely what Pauline needed. And as if to prove it to them, two years after she accepted McRaye as a partner, she wrote to O'Brien: "Through all this time that we have been associated, he [McRaye] has been just the same unselfish, considerate boy you saw him to be in

Ottawa. His management has indeed proved a great thing for me, and my freedom from business cares and anxieties has rejuvenated me beyond words."[9]

At last, Pauline had found the right man to carry her bags.

She nicknamed him "Dink." Although it has since acquired other connotations, at the turn of the century this Scottish term simply meant small and neat. The nickname was soon picked up by others who knew him, and even his lady friends addressed letters to him as "Dearest Dink."

McRaye was good company on the endless train and coach rides. Secure in his new role, he was almost always good-humoured. He loved puns and jokes, and entered into games with the enthusiasm of a child. And just as lonely children sometimes do, he invented playmates for himself and Pauline. Foremost among them were "The Boys," four elflike creatures who went along on their tours, sleeping on bedrolls which they spread out on the overhead hat racks of the trains. From this vantage point, they made comments on the performances of their human companions and on the audiences, comments which neither Pauline nor McRaye would have themselves ventured to express.

After a recital in Berwick, Nova Scotia, where the hotel's cat had insisted on sleeping in Pauline's dressing case, an imaginary cat joined their entourage. They christened it Dave Dougherty for the hotel's proprietor. An insect named Felix the Bug was next added to the menagerie; he acquired the surname Joggins when they passed through the settlement of Joggins Mine, Nova Scotia. In time, Felix gained a wife named Jerusha. When the newspapers reported that mongooses were being experimentally imported into Jamaica to exterminate rats, McRaye introduced an imaginary mongoose to their company. They named him Baraboo Montelius, after two more towns with names that appealed to them. "The Boys" welcomed Baraboo and enjoyed lifting him up by his tail to their hat rack hideaway, while Felix and Jerusha scurried over the seats in wild excitement.

Now on the endless journeys to Newfoundland fishing settlements and farming centres in Saskatchewan, Pauline would invoke this whimsical invisible company to entertain herself and her partner. Or she would command, "Dink, do Munyon for The Boys!" Obediently McRaye would stand and solemnly hold up one admonitory forefinger just as the great Dr. Munyon of patent medicine fame did in his newspaper advertisements. Then he would begin a wild parody of Munyon, extolling the merits of his cures for arthritis, rheumatism, cancer, catarrh, erysipelas, consumption, and every other disease that afflicts man, exaggerating the benefits and the side effects of each medicine. Tears of laughter would run down Pauline's face, and up on the hat rack, The Boys and Baraboo would hold their sides in helpless silent delight.

The Johnson-McRaye partnership, however, came close to dissolution before it achieved this comfortable, mutually dependent state. During that first winter, Pauline fell ill again.

They had been playing the smaller towns of Ontario while Pauline eased McRaye into Smily's old shoes. Each day as they travelled she held line rehearsals, and in the evening whenever possible they squeezed in full rehearsals in the halls where they would entertain a few hours later. It was a tiring schedule for Pauline. She had been under continual emotional stress since the death of her mother and now she had taken on the additional burden of an inexperienced partner. She knew he was no match for Smily and there were times in those first weeks when she had to face the possibility that he would never be an asset.

In the third week of December, shortly after they arrived in Orillia, Pauline was stricken with erysipelas. She must have known instantly what it was. She had watched her father die of it and she had suffered with it herself as a child. The first morning she must have looked in a mirror to see a raised patch next to her nose, then watched throughout the day as it spread, its crimson rim creeping across her face, the small blisters which pocked its surface growing rapidly into large watery ones. She must have known as the chills and pain and fever set in that she would not be performing in Orillia or any other town for quite some time.

McRaye probably felt considerable frustration as he set off to cancel the hall; he was scarcely established as Pauline's partner when it appeared that she might die. And it was even more frustrating that the doctor he called to the hotel could do little except confirm Pauline's own diagnosis. He told her to stay in bed, gave her morphine for the pain, and promised to come back the following day. At her request, he agreed not to make any public statements about her illness.

McRaye now waited patiently while the disease ran its course. Unfortunately, as in her father's final attack of erysipelas, Pauline suffered a complicating illness—"brain fever." This could have been caused in one of two ways. Either there was such a devastating localized infection that it broke through into the bloodstream, causing systemic toxicity—the probable cause of her father's death. Or Pauline in her feverish state may have scratched or manipulated the blisters or boils around her nose and mouth, as children with chicken pox are prone to do, causing an irritation of the veins that go from the nose to the sinus and into the brain. The result would have been cerebral thrombo-phlebitis. Both of these complications cause delirium and extremely high fever. In many cases the patient loses all his hair; Pauline was one of those cases.

She spent Christmas Day, 1901 in her hotel room in Orillia, only vaguely aware of the world around her; then, to McRaye's immense relief, the fever began to subside a few days later. Just before New Year's Day, they left Orillia quietly, having kept the news of Pauline's illness out of the headlines to avoid another circus of bulletins as in Halifax. It is not recorded where they went next, but it seems most likely that they took refuge with Pauline's cousins in either Kingston or Hamilton. This stay would have given the cousins ample time to develop a dislike for McRaye.

The partnership was in serious financial difficulties by this time. Even though their six weeks of touring in Ontario had been reasonably successful, the funds they had earned were not sufficient to carry the two of them through a long layoff. And Pauline's plea to Frank Yeigh only nine months earlier establishes that she had no reserve funds. Her published work had provided no income for more than two years, and she was not entitled to a further share of the Chiefswood rent until the spring of 1903. Nor was there a possibility of borrowing against it again; Eva, as eldest member of the family, would have prevented that. It is therefore likely that the partners lived off the charity of Eva, Allen and the cousins during the period of Pauline's convalescence. This fact probably explains why Pauline was back on the stage by 7 February in London, Ontario, only six weeks after the onset of her illness.

The effect of erysipelas and brain fever were still very noticeable. Although erysipelas does not leave scars in the usual sense, the outlines of the inflamed areas leave ridges which shrink and fade much more slowly than the patches themselves. Five months after the attack, newspaper reporters were still remarking on her "noticeable" scars. In the past, Pauline's beautiful complexion had often prompted compliments. One American interviewer had noted that she used neither lip rouge nor powder, though he noticed that she curled her front hair and manicured her nails. "In fact," he wrote, "she does pretty much everything that a real Indian would not be expected to do and leaves undone everything that one would expect of a child of the Iroquois."[10] After this attack of erysipelas, Pauline began applying make-up to camouflage the ravages to her face, and continued to use it for the rest of her career even after the "scars" had disappeared.

Her lack of hair, however, was her most serious problem, and required much more elaborate camouflage. For this, Pauline ordered wigs. Unfortunately, the one designed for her to wear with her Indian costume, though cosmetically successful, irritated her scalp so badly that she could hardly wait to yank it off at intermission. She gave up looking for a comfortable wig for the other half of her program and elected instead to wear a "picture hat" with her evening gown, just as the Broadway chorus girls did. She told friends: "People say it is very becoming, and no one suspects the tragedy underneath."[11]

The only photographs of Pauline from this period were taken by Edwards Brothers in Vancouver in September 1902. Though she posed full face, her hair appears very short and quite sparse. It may have been bobbed in the fashion that became popular about ten years later. Pictures taken eight months after the Edwards photos show abundant hair, but it still had not grown to the length she customarily wore it. Her hair in both photos appears to be curlier than in earlier photographs, which could mean that she now curled more than her front hair, or that her new hair was curlier than the crop she had lost. All photographs taken after 1902 show her with darker hair.

By May of 1902 Johnson and McRaye had become a solid partnership. They were now in northern Ontario, back to the old routine of one-night stands with scarcely a break for relaxation. On 27 May they arrived in Copper Cliff, where they were to be the house guests of "Kit" Coleman who wrote for the women's page of the

Toronto *Mail and Empire*. A tiny intense Irish woman with a mass of copper-coloured hair, she had long been one of Pauline's most avid fans, and had boosted her career with her highly partisan interviews and reviews. Kit had married a doctor who was employed by the mining company at Copper Cliff, thereby condemning herself to live in this desolate place where the fumes from the smelter had killed off every blade of grass and the leaves on every tree. Determined, however, to put on a good show on the occasion of Pauline's visit with McRaye, she had ordered a bouquet of roses from Toronto to present to Pauline at the conclusion of her performance. To preserve the flowers, she put them in her icebox, only bringing them out for the short drive to the auditorium. But Copper Cliff's smelter fumes turned them limp and brown during the trip to the hall. Kit's beautiful gesture was ruined, and the two women cried together over the sad bouquet.

The concert was difficult, with more than the usual quota of crying babies, talkers and smart-aleck boys. Outraged, Kit recommended that some of the "native geniuses" should be locked up whenever "clean wholesome entertainment" came to town, especially after one of these "geniuses" convulsed the local audience by stage whispering "Marvellous!" at a poignant moment in one of Pauline's recitations. "Funny wight!" wrote Kit. "He must have heard it from some other village goon who doubtless heard that fat-faced English magician say it. . . . But the splendid Mohawk girl scored her own. What a genius she is!"[12] Disappointingly, Kit does not elaborate on how Pauline scored her own, but it is obvious that the performer had fully recovered her wits if not her hair by this time.

Walter McRaye also won Kit Coleman's heart and she wrote the best review he would ever receive:

> As for Miss Johnson's fellow artist Walter J. McRaye, he is a young man whose name and fame are yet to be made in Canada, but are already made in God's country, sweet California. He is richly armed for the fray. Humour, rare goddess, is his; his also is romance. He is par excellence the best reader of dainty and clear poems I have ever heard, and I pretty well know half the elocutionists the world over, and if he works he has a big future before him. He is a true artist and like all such needs words of encouragement and heart.[13]

Ten years later McRaye was still quoting from this review in his promotion material.

On 6 June Pauline and McRaye booked into the Leland Hotel in Winnipeg. They had not come to perform; they were only passing through. But Pauline took time to hold court for all her old friends and for the press, inviting them up to her suite where in her "bright and pleasing manner" she entertained them with stories of her travels and her famous friends. She told them of

> some English friends from whom she has just received letters. She told the story of their little daughter, a tot of four years. Like most English children the child had been most carefully reared, and had been taught that to have a second piece of cake or two helpings of jam was extravagance. A few months ago, twin babies arrived at the home. The little maid was taken to see her new twin sisters. After gazing mutely at the two midgets for a moment, she said, "Oh, mother, isn't this extravagant?"[14]

The story did not originate with Pauline; she was simply onstage as usual, making sure that everybody had a good laugh. She joked about her interchangeable hair and the hats which she used for her disguise, and made sure that McRaye appeared to advantage in front of the newspaper people. When they had all gone, she drooped with exhaustion.

But the effort had been worthwhile. It was her way of telling Winnipeg that she was doing all right, and that she had no regrets about the way things had turned out. Because she knew, though no one else did, that only thirteen days later the newspapers would carry the story of the wedding in Toronto of Charles Drayton to Lydia Howland in the Church of the Messiah, Avenue Road. The excellent match Charles had made pleased his father. The bride was the only daughter of the late Henry S. Howland, president of the Imperial Bank of Canada, the third largest financial institution in the young dominion. It was Howland's death that had delayed Drayton's wedding for six months, but now he would be bringing his bride back to Winnipeg where there were plenty of people to remember that he had jilted Pauline Johnson. But Pauline would be far away by the time he returned.

During her Winnipeg visit she had appeared nonchalant about

the ravages that her illness had perpetrated on her face and hair, but she was actually far from indifferent to her appearance, especially in situations where she was expected to make a celebrity appearance. After leaving Winnipeg she took McRaye into the Territories for a month, but she had planned to open the summer's tour officially in Regina, and had written to Madame Henrietta Forget, the wife of the lieutenant governor of the Northwest Territories, asking for the patronage of the Forgets at her Regina recital. Madame was more than willing. She wrote:

> You may advertise your entertainment under our patronage; moreover we shall be pleased to have you at Government House during your stay at Regina.
>
> But if it was at all possible, we would like you to come for Coronation day, for we propose giving a children's party and from all appearances over a thousand children are expected to attend. The public also being invited to witness the entertainment, there will undoubtedly be a large crowd. His Honour and Judge Prendergast will make short addresses and if you could be present, His Honour would ask you to say a few words also. Your own entertainment coming, let us say, the next day could not fail to bring in a full house. . . .[15]

Pauline was delighted with the response until she remembered her face. "Imagine," she wrote, "poor me 'dining' with my scarred face and cropped hair—Is it not awful?" The camouflage she had devised made the damage unnoticeable on stage by this time, but close encounters would continue to be an embarrassment for many more months.

The coronation to which Madame Forget referred was that of Edward VII, planned for 26 June 1902. All over the Empire, celebrations had been organized to coincide with the ceremony at Westminster Abbey, with special emphasis on festivities for children. But two days before the event, the king underwent surgery for appendicitis. Since this operation was relatively new, there was great concern for his safety and all over the Empire the celebrations were replaced by prayer services for his deliverance. Only the children's fetes went ahead as scheduled, at the king's express wish.

So Pauline's part in Regina's grand celebration was just a shadow of what it might have been. With McRaye, she spent 24 June at

Government House praying for His Majesty's life. It was altogether too soon for the Empire to lose another monarch, with Queen Victoria in her grave a scant eighteen months.

On 26 June the king was declared out of danger, but a new coronation date could not be set until it was known how soon he would be fully recovered. Since Pauline and McRaye could not afford to wait, they rescheduled their recital for the thirtieth. The lieutenant governor, true to his wife's word, "graciously accorded his patronage" and presented Pauline with an enormous bouquet which she carried onstage for her opening number. Fortunately the viceregal flowers did not wither and turn brown as Kit's had done. For the occasion, Pauline had written a "Coronation Ode" which she recited in spite of the postponed event, but the poem was never reproduced.

Two days later, in the midst of a torrential downpour, the partners boarded the CPR's westbound Number 1, headed for British Columbia. On the fourth of July, they pulled into Medicine Hat, long after dusk, to learn that there was a washout ahead. The train was to lie in a siding for the night.

> The Americans aboard fired their last bunch of firecrackers, and the porter, after the manner of his kind, bundled us all into our berths, and the following morning the C.P.R. did a great and memorable thing. It pulled us one hundred and twenty-five miles west and tied us up for forty-eight hours at Gleichen, in the heart of the Blackfoot Indian Reserve.
>
> No spot on the entire system of the great transcontinental highway could have been of so intense interest, and few more beautiful. We had come out of the East and its wheatlands of Manitoba, out of the drenching rain and unseasonable storms, into a perfect July day, with the prairie swelling away to the north; westward, a horizon fringed with a glory of glistening white peaks, where the royal old Rockies swept irregularly across the sky, southward the lonely habitations of an erstwhile powerful tribe of redmen. [17]

The Number 1 had been halted for only a few hours when it was joined by the Imperial Limited, and twelve hours later another Number 1 drew up behind it. The passengers were then told that two bridges on the Bow River, one east and one west of Calgary, were washed out. The Number 2 eastbound was stuck at Banff, and the eastbound Imperial Limited was waiting out the delay somewhere in

British Columbia. The CPR had come to a standstill, and for the first time the Imperial Limited would not make its run across the continent in its advertised ninety-seven hours.

There were more than six hundred passengers on the three trains at Gleichen, and they made the best of the situation, turning it into a holiday. On board Pauline's train were eight young NWMP recruits under the command of a Corporal Adams, all bound for service in the Yukon. Their presence was a considerable reassurance to some of the Americans who feared for their lives when they learned they were in the midst of an Indian encampment. The second-class carriages were crowded with settlers: Doukhobors, Galicians, Swedes, Italians, working-class Londoners and 150 "Chinamen." Lord Beven and his young wife aboard the Imperial became a point of interest on the immigrants' sightseeing tour of the trains, for many of them had never seen nobility before. Two courteous Japanese gentlemen fresh from courses at Queen's University fretted over the delay; their ship waited at dock in Vancouver.

For two days the passengers ate at the expense of the CPR in two of the best restaurants in the country, the dining cars "Frogmore" and "St. Cloud," famous for their excellent cuisine. Even the fussy Americans were delighted to find that the bill of fare continued to be exceptional, and in one aspect at least it improved:

> An indefatiguable Detroiter, who wandered up prairie trails ever searching for information, discovered mushrooms, of that large luscious, shell pink variety that only come from wild stretches of field and that have a flavour far more delicate and appetizing than those found in the city markets. Buckets, baskets, and even hats were requisitioned, and we supplied the dining car for every meal with those delicacies. The Detroiter gave us impromptu lectures on edible fungi. He was a man of most extensive information, had travelled the world over and kept his eyes open, but he told us he had never seen such quantities of mushrooms together as these. We gathered bushels of them daily. I hardly think the Indians eat these fungi, or else the enormous camp of Blackfoots would have been up betimes and secured our breakfasts while we yet dozed in comfortable berths, for their teepees arose smoke-tipped and conical, not five hundred yards from the siding where we lay.

The Indians made a good thing out of the C.P.R. mishap, for the tourists hired horses from them at a dollar a ride, and even the tenderfoot would vault into the Mexican saddle and ride away across the prairie. The sturdy shaggy inappi, laying back his ears, lopes away with the long, clean, rocking motion never seen except in the prairie bred animal. Only one lamentable accident occurred in the evening when we had baseball and horse races. In the latter, a fine grey pony, the property of a splendidly handsome blanket-and-buckskin clad Blackfoot, plunged into a badger hole, fell and instantly expired with a broken neck. . . . A goodly collection was taken up for the owner, which reward he deserved, as his steed had expired in making "a white man's holiday. . . ."[18]

Many of the whites on board predicted that the Indians would eat the horse since "Indians will eat anything, animals that die of disease, unclean portions of meat, etc.,"[19] but they did not. In fact, they were astonished that anyone had expected them to eat it. Pauline was proud of these "colour cousins of the prairie"[20] and even prouder when she joined some people who visited the camp:

> . . . a group of some dozen teepees, neat, orderly, and picturesque, were bunched against the southern rim of the prairie. Great herds of fat cattle and excellent ponies grazed nearby, for the Blackfoot is a thrifty person, and his wife is a marvel of dexterity in needlework. . . . The interior of the teepees was a delight. A fire burned in the centre, the smoke ascending through the apex of the canvas. Beautiful beadwork, buckskin garments, fringed and ornamented elaborately, hung about in profusion. Well-blanketed women cared for tiny children whose painted cheeks glowed vermilion and yellow in the fire and sunshine. . . .[21]

While they were still at the Blackfoot camp, the engineer sounded a long series of whistles; the holiday was over. Once again the three trains moved westward, only to stop at the edge of the Bow River. Ahead was a bridge so shattered that it would never be used again. In the meantime a footbridge had been built above its remains, and here the divisional superintendent of the CPR stood by to hand each passenger across while an army of porters came after them with their luggage. On the other side another train waited to take them into Calgary where they joined all the stranded passengers from the west.

The little town was hardly prepared for this influx of nearly twelve hundred extra bodies, and every hotel, boarding house and spare bedroom was commandeered to house the travellers. Even then, the CPR had to bed some of them down in the railyards in trains that had been in town when the bridges collapsed.

On her second day in town, Pauline went with McRaye in tow to see the collapsed bridge just nine miles west of the city. The bridge lay in the river, neatly broken in half. On the far side two trains waited surrounded by acres of luggage, mail and freight. As they stood watching, a new trestle to span the river was taking shape, one quarter of its pilings already pounded into place, sleepers laid, and tracks bolted. For Pauline this was a prime example of the "sturdy Canadian system" in which she took such pride.

Since her normal response to any large congregation of people was to see them as a potential audience, she soon began to look for an opportunity to give a recital. When the train had stood at Gleichen, this had been impossible, but in Calgary McRaye lost no time in finding a hall for hire and putting up posters around the town. With a captive audience they were naturally a resounding success, and they stayed on in Calgary until 19 July so that Pauline could write the story of their adventures for the *Toronto Globe,* where she would be billed as the paper's "special correspondent." This was one of the few catastrophes in her life that actually turned out well. In fact, she even made a profit.

The Johnson-McRaye partnership now headed for the Kootenay mining towns of southeastern British Columbia, lucrative territory for entertainers despite plenty of competition. A regular stream of travelling acts, most of them stock companies, came north from San Francisco, spending as much as four months at a time touring here and pocketing the miners' pay. Bad acts, however, did not last long, as the miners could afford to be choosy. They never threw things at the actors and they seldom caused an uproar; they simply walked out and demanded their money back.

For entertainers, travel was relatively easy in that period. The American companies could enter the country from Spokane on the Great Northern Railway and then travel on one of the ore-carrying branch lines of the GN or the CPR to the various mining towns. In fact, Nelson, though scarcely established, had a daily train to Spokane and three trains a day to Rossland. Even little Sandon, isolated in the mountains between Kootenay Lake and the Slocan Valley, had two trains a day. Wherever track had not yet been laid, stage lines provided transportation. Stageline companies such as Meyerhoffs worked four-horse coaches between Midway and Camp McKinney every second day, and the Palace Exchange Stage rattled up and down the mountainside between Greenwood and Phoenix twice a day. Plying the Slocan, Arrow and Kootenay lakes were the S.S. *Nakusp* and the *Trail,* and the stern-wheeler *Moyie* hailed from the shore from time to time to pick up some prospector or put off supplies.

Hotels were numerous in these towns—though not as numerous as saloons—but the quality was somewhat dubious. Most were simply glorified boarding houses with shared rooms or even dormitories. Meals were served in dining rooms that boasted one long table to accommodate all the diners and a single-item menu. A bath in these places was a rare luxury.

Performing space was sometimes makeshift, but most of the bigger towns had "opera houses" of fairly good proportions. Nelson's Opera House seated seven hundred people and had a stage 25 by 50 by 38 feet. Pauline, however, preferred to leave the opera houses to the stock companies and play in the more intimate atmosphere of church halls; besides, the rent was considerably lower. Luckily, the Methodists and Presbyterians among the mining brotherhood had been almost as busy building as the saloonkeepers, so she had plenty of choice in church halls.

Although most of these towns were close to the American border, the majority of the miners had come directly from the "Old Country" (usually Wales, Cornwall, northern England and northern Ireland) and they left their wives and children behind. Few ever saved enough to bring their families to join them; most looked upon their mining careers as a temporary money-making expedition in the colonies. The miners' union, the Western Federation of Miners, therefore became their family. The union took care of medical needs, fought for better wages, battled the employers for safety equipment in the mines, hired entertainment to play in the "Miners' Halls," and sent home the miners' final pay cheques and personal effects to their widows after a cave-in.

In the two years before Pauline and McRaye toured the area,

these towns had seen epidemics, fires, cave-ins and strikes. Sandon, caught in the path of a forest fire, had been burned to the ground on 4 May 1900. The timber buildings had roared into the midnight sky; in the morning several charred bodies had been found among the ashes. Typhoid, always a threat in these makeshift towns, became an epidemic in Fernie in the summer of 1902. And at Coal Creek, just four miles from Fernie, 151 men died when coal dust in Slopes 2 and 3 exploded one evening. There was no sprinkling equipment in the mine, though the miners had been pressing for it. The next day, Victoria Day, the miners' union held funerals instead of the parade that they had planned.

When Pauline and McRaye arrived in the little town of Rossland that same summer, it was still recovering from a disastrous strike at the LeRoi Mine, the town's sole reason for existence. Though the LeRoi was the richest gold mine in the west, the owners had suddenly laid off the union miners and brought in cheaper scab labour from the states. The union countered by having the government enforce the Canadian Alien Labour Law; then the union men rounded up the scabs and bundled them back over the border. Next the owners brought in thugs to beat up the union leaders; the miners ran them out of town, too. Finally, on 11 July 1901, the miners went on strike. Once again the company brought in scabs, and this time the government refused to authorize a deportation order. At this point some of the company directors arrived on the scene to investigate and began to smell a rat, and when they returned to London, the company president was arrested for embezzlement. He had forced the strike on the miners as a screen to cover his own activities. The strike, however, continued until 24 January 1902 and left the townspeople bitter and hostile to management.

It was into this tough, no-nonsense town that Pauline and McRaye carried their poetry recital, and they were delighted to find a full house in the Methodist church hall. Many of the miners, of course, came for the privilege of seeing a real lady. Not that Rossland had no women; it just had very few ladies. There was a small number of wives—those hardy souls who braved the awful living conditions to be with their men—and there were the "ladies of commercial virtue" who had migrated from the American mining towns. Pauline brought a touch of glamour and civilization that had little to do with her poetry. (In other settlements, she was sometimes not only the sole lady in the place but also the only woman, and in tiny Girard—or Gerrard—on Trout Lake, she was the first woman the miners had seen in months.)

The morning after their Rossland concert, Pauline and McRaye climbed the long hill to the LeRoi Mine where they had been promised a tour by the mine superintendent and the foreman. Pauline made a rather bulky figure with her skirts tucked into the overalls provided for her and a miner's coat dwarfing her small frame, but she gamely followed the superintendent to the black hole in the ground that was the mine entrance. Although a bucket transported ore to the surface, the miners and their guests were required to climb down a narrow, dark shaft while at intervals the loaded bucket clanged past them on its cables. At the first landing stage, they were given candles and shown how to hang on to them and the rungs of the ladder at the same time. They stopped at the three-hundred-foot level, and here a couple of the miners who had seen their show the night before presented them with pieces of gold ore from the rock face.

The reporter for the *Rossland Miner* tells the rest of the story with tongue firmly in cheek:

> Messrs. C. C. Woodhouse Junior and A. B. Clabon accompanied the lady and explained the difference between chalcopyrite and gabbro to her. She seemed to be deeply impressed with everything she saw, though she looked puzzled sometimes when Mr. Woodhouse told her some of the scientific facts concerning mining in technical language. For instance, Mr. Woodhouse said to the young lady, "In amphorous minerals there is no trace of crystalline form or special characteristics of structure due to individual crystals, although intermittent deposition of the mass composing the mineral may give an occasional difference of hardness or texture. The majority of the solid amphorous minerals are the result of the gradual change from a gelatinous state or the rapid cooling from the melted condition, and the majority of them are the result of the alteration of pre-existing materials." To which the fair poetess smiled and remarked, "I guess so." And thus science, speculation, and poetry walked hand in hand, as it were, through the dark galleries of the mines![22]

In Nelson, they entertained the miners of the Enterprise Mine and stayed at the Hume Hotel, which McRaye thereafter placed on his list of "fine establishments." They rode the *Moyie* to Kaslo, entertaining there, then boarded again for Ainsworth, gave a show, then steamed north to the Lardeau and up to Ferguson on Trout Lake. One night they found themselves stranded at the settlement of Kuskanook just north of present-day Creston with the next Great Northern train not due till morning. No more than a couple of hundred people were living there, but among them were six good Methodists who wanted to build a church. When they heard that Pauline would be there overnight, they asked her to give a benefit performance for them. Pauline agreed. She had never seen a place more in need of a church, she said. They sent a boy around the village ringing a bell and announcing "Concert to-night! Gus Fraser's got up a concert with Pauline Johnson! Concert to-night!"

By eight o'clock the Methodists had turned one of the saloons into a concert hall. A billiard table had been set across one corner as a stage, some Hudson's Bay blankets had been hung up for a dressing room, and a soap box served to connect dressing room and stage. It was one of the more memorable Johnson-McRaye recitals.

On 9 August they arrived in the rebuilt town of Sandon where the Ivanhoe and Star Mine flourished. A huge crowd awaited the train's arrival, but it was not there to greet Pauline. The miners had come out to welcome back Billy McAdam, the editor of the *Sandon Paystreak*. He had just narrowly escaped the malice of the judiciary after he had criticized two judges of the British Columbia court system. It was his opinion, he editorialized, that their drinking habits had a marked effect on their dispensation of justice. Billy was arrested and taken to Nelson, but in the end the charges were laughed out of court. Now the miners were at the train to let him know that he was a hero, though the celebrations had begun long before he stepped down from the train. As a result, not many people made it as far as the concert hall that night, so Pauline and McRaye closed up early and accepted Billy's invitation to join his party. The next day Billy, who had not seen their show, gave the performers a generous review: "Miss E. Pauline Johnson is a right up-to-date entertainer, while Mr. McRaye in his Dr. Drummond habitant characters was there with the goods!"[23] About a week later they were brought down to earth by the *Slocan Drill:* "Pauline Johnson and her partner gave a talking entertainment in the Music Hall Friday night before a small audience.

These two horse shows travelling the country are becoming most monotonous and tiresome."[24] The *Drill* was not in the habit of encouraging the entertainments that hit the Slocan Valley.

In Phoenix, they gave a benefit performance under the auspices of Snowshoe Lodge No. 46 of the IOOF for two miners, Syrsted and McClusky, who had been blinded in two separate mine explosions. There was a fair audience but not enough to provide the unlucky miners with any security, and Pauline left there knowing they had accomplished little for them.

The reporter for the *Boundary Creek Times* in Greenwood loved Pauline and "the clever way in which she interspersed descriptions of the humourous incidents in her public career. . . . Miss Johnson is really a dangerous person to be abroad. Nothing apparently escapes her Mohawk eye and in each town she finds materials for entertaining in the next. . . ."[25] The comic bits were the sugar coating on the culture pill and Pauline knew it, but she had decided that this was the only way to educate people to enjoy serious poetry. And even if she sometimes still felt a little like a traitor for descending from the lofty heights of pure poetry, she knew her audiences did not see her as one. They were simply grateful that this gifted and humorous woman had come to brighten up their dreary lives.

From Greenwood, Pauline and McRaye took the stagecoach to Camp McKinney. There were only a handful of people in the camp at that time, but they all brought out and arranged nail kegs and planks as benches and then paid a dollar each to sit on them.

The next morning McRaye hired a springboard wagon belonging to an irascible individual who demanded twenty-five dollars for the twenty-mile trip to Fairview, located in the hills just west of present-day Oliver and serving the Morning Star and Stemwinder mines. McRaye wheedled and stormed but the wagon owner was firm: "Young man, if ye're calculating to get from here to Fairview, that's what it's going to cost ye!" McRaye paid and they jolted off down the trail.[26]

In late August Pauline's first mining country tour came to an end in Vernon. Though she had played a few of the same towns on previous visits, she had never risked a full-scale tour because she had been travelling alone. But with McRaye as her partner, she could travel as freely as she had with Smily. She was absolutely delighted by the financial returns from the trip but was even more exhilarated by the spirit of the frontier which she had found. She now saw this raw country as the real essence of Canada and these working men as the romantic protagonists of a pioneer drama. She had not stopped yearning for the sophistication that she had found in London; she still craved beautiful ball gowns. But she no longer needed a salon full of sophisticated people applauding her. One or two cultured listeners in a hall full of ordinary folks would suffice, and in the Kootenays, just as in other parts of the country, these cultured people turned up in every crowd. Many of the men who worked the mines or tramped the hills prospecting had come from good families in England. One young fellow came to her with tears in his eyes after she finished reciting to say that he had not seen a woman in an evening gown since his mother and sisters used to dress for dinner every evening back home in England.

Before Pauline's first tour of the west in 1894, she had been firmly tied to Ontario by her mother's English upbringing; it was her father's heritage that had lured her beyond that little patch of civilization, and she had been migrating westward emotionally ever since. Her affair with Drayton, who had epitomized the better class of gentleman on the frontier, had drawn her as far as Winnipeg; her mother's death had shut the door on Brantford. Drayton's betrayal had thrust her from Winnipeg again without a home. Now with McRaye she forged westward once more, and by 1902 British Columbia's wilderness began to look like home.

But there was another force driving her westward: competition. When she had first begun touring she had been unique. Not that she had been the only elocutionist on the circuit, but she was the only Indian "princess" reciting her own poems on stage. For this act, she found a willing audience in the early years, but as time went by there were fewer and fewer Canadians in the southern strip of the country who had not had an opportunity to see and hear her. She had become a beloved institution, but when, year after year, she arrived in town with the same old poems to recite, it became easier and easier to say "I'll catch her next time" or "I've already seen her." There were plenty of brand new shows to see. Every large city in southern Ontario had been on the big American show circuits since the 1880s. James O'Neill and Robert Mantell brought their stock companies to Hamilton; Sarah Bernhardt appeared in Toronto; Oscar Wilde played both towns and even gave his lecture in little Brantford, which also hosted the touring company of the elaborate *Ben Hur* production. In the nineties Winnipeg was firmly established on the circuits as well. Even Regina and Calgary saw a few of the medium-sized companies by the end of the century. By 1900 it was estimated that there were nearly one thousand theatrical companies touring North America.[27] With competition like that, it was impossible for an elocutionist to outsell every other show in town, as Pauline had done in the winter of 1897-98 in Winnipeg. In fact, it was becoming difficult to find a hall to rent in the big cities.

Conditions were better in the west. The competition was not as tough. The San Francisco-based companies never ranked with those coming out of New York because they were smaller and poorer and had no real headliners. In this pioneer country it was still possible for Pauline to draw a bigger house than any of them.

Johnson and McRaye closed their summer 1902 tour in Vancouver on 9 September, and though Pauline's fans packed City Hall to hear her, "Fadladeen" of the *Vancouver Province* was critical of the performance. She wrote that she was "impressed with the marked change which two or three years have brought about in her stage manner, her pose, and even her delivery. Not that she has depreciated in any of these points but there is an air in all of them that is more professional and perhaps less charmingly ingenuous. This is doubtless a matter of taste, however. . . ."[28]

It is the fate of those rising to fame from obscure beginnings to be constantly examined by their public for signs of change. They are expected to remain unaltered even though the most pedestrian personality within the common mass is allowed to lose innocence and become hardened and moulded by the stresses of life. But a celebrity is the victim of the I-knew-her-when game, and it always turns out that she was a nicer individual when they knew her.

By 1902 Pauline had changed. Emotionally, she was not the person who had recited from the stage of the Academy of Music in 1892. T. S. H. Shearman, who had known her in her Brantford days, regretted that she had ever set foot on the stage after he saw her performing in Vancouver around 1908, bartering her "divine gifts for a wretched mess of pottage." He much preferred "the beautiful, timid Pauline Johnson of 1885"[29] to the accomplished artist he now saw. Peggy Webling, who had first met her in 1890, wrote of knowing her when she was "young and as yet unspoilt by flattery and success."[30]

At forty-one years of age Pauline was unquestionably a star in her own country, but there had been a price tag on stardom. She had become tougher, more calculating. She made use of influential people to advance her career. She developed a certain cynicism so that compromise came more easily to her. She learned onstage techniques to conserve energy: how to rely on tricks of voice and stage business to get effect rather than exhausting herself with an emotional performance every night. She learned that humour on stage cost her less energy than serious drama, and that it was no use bludgeoning the boondocks audiences with serious poetry. They would not thank her for the effort.

Offstage she had learned to keep her own emotional wellsprings untouched even while she convinced her fans that she was personally involved with them. She could sit through press conferences and interviews, answer the same old questions in town after town when she was already exhausted from a long train ride and from the show the prevous night, and still send reporters away impressed with her charm and her graciousness. And the next day when she read their reviews, she had learned not to bleed over them. If all these new traits made her "less charmingly ingenuous," they also made it possible for her to continue her career on the road.

Pauline was very aware of the criticism. In a letter written in 1900 she condemned the "carping voices" which told her that she was "not a bit like [the] old simple self"[31] she had been as a child. But even as a child, she had been petted and pampered and admired. She had always got her own way charmingly but determinedly. From girlhood she had understood how to gauge what she could get from people and how to manipulate them in order to get it. Pauline had never really had a "simple self." While it was true that flattery and success were important elements in what she became, the seeds had always been there.

She was not, however, an insensitive woman. Underneath the professional exterior, she was vulnerable to the needs of others. On a crowded early morning train out of Regina she had held the youngest of three small screaming children on her lap to give their aunt a little respite. After the others had been quieted with candy, which she bought for them, she learned that they had been recently orphaned and were being taken to their aunt and uncle's subsistence farm to begin a new life. Through the years Pauline kept track of the children, sending clothes and money especially for the baby whom the foster parents had named Pauline. To those as vulnerable as she had once been she was especially responsive. Bertha Jean Thompson, her protégé in the final years of her life, said, "For me the mask worn for the public melted from her face. . . . A woman of the world, she taught me in many ways, steering me clear of some things that could have been pitfalls to a girl alone in a big city. . . ."[32]

On their way east in mid-September, the Johnson and McRaye team ran neck and neck with the political circus being run by Robert Borden. As McRaye tells the story:

> Borden . . . in those days . . . was leader of a forlorn hope party in opposition. He was making his first trip across Canada; it was August and no one was particularly interested in politics. In such towns as Greenwood, Fernie, Nelson and Kamloops, we shared the excitement with him and won out, as his meetings were so small they often shut up shop and came to hear us.

Borden had assumed the party leadership only the previous year and was making this coast-to-coast junket in his effort to consolidate party support. He was much more successful than McRaye's recollections would indicate, for he spoke to large crowds wherever he appeared (which did *not* include Greenwood or Fernie or Nelson or Kamloops). In Vancouver, the only place Borden and the Johnson-McRaye team did play on the same night, Borden's audience was overflow and the entertainers played to over six hundred people.

In October, Pauline and McRaye played the prairie towns and travelled the beautiful Battleford Trail by stagecoach out of Saskatoon:

> Never were there such turquoise skies, such golden brown acres of prairie billowing away to the four points of the compass. The crisp October air caught us with the first hint of autumn as we emerged from the comfortable warmth of a drowsy sleeping car, and stepped on

to the station platform at Saskatoon where the lordly Saskatchewan river rolls away northwards. . . . We breakfasted and got our luggage into shape for the long drive into the interior, and then there was the clatter of horses and wheels outside. The crack of the "blacksnake" whip, a dash, then a halt, and "All aboard for Battleford" rang out the driver's voice, and the stage with His Majesty's Mails aboard was at the door.

The crowd "bunched" up to wish us bon voyage, rough looking western men with kindly hearts and open hands, speculators, ranchers, grain buyers, land seekers, one and all wished us "Good Luck" as the sturdy little roadsters Dan and Fox lifted their noses, wheeled up into the wind, and "hit the trail" for Battleford. The early morning sun was yellow and gleaming, the October sky was cloudless, the whole world was large and limitless, at last this was the mighty unbroken West, with the town and railroad dropping behind us and one hundred miles of prairie between us and the little historic romance-crowned settlement of Battleford. The wild breath of the Great West got into our blood. We felt in touch with Buffalo Bill, Kit Carson, Captain Crawford all the wild border adventurers. . . .[34]

When she learned that the stagecoach driver's name was George Wilson, she promptly rechristened him. Thereafter he was known as Alkali Pete. A prosaic name like George Wilson would never do in the romantic "Great West."

By mid-November they had played southern Manitoba and stopped briefly again in Winnipeg. A hectic year, it had begun with Pauline's almost fatal illness, then carried the two of them right to the Pacific and back again. Fortunately, they had done well enough financially to allow for a two-week rest over Christmas. McRaye went off to visit his mother in Brockville; Pauline spent the time with her brother Allen and her cousin Kate Washington in Hamilton.

In spite of her illness and the relentless pace of their tours, Pauline had returned to her writing in earnest in 1902 and had begun to prepare the manuscript of a long-postponed second book of poetry. Since 1897 she had been promising her public another book "soon," but the vicissitudes of her private life had intervened. Now at last, with her love affairs all sadly past, with a lucrative year of touring underway, and little Walter McRaye carrying the luggage and arranging for halls and hotels, she had the leisure to prepare it.

Although a book would not provide much direct income—Walter McRaye estimated that she made no more than five hundred dollars from her poems in her entire life—Pauline knew from experience that it would contribute to her literary stature and thereby enhance her stage image. Eight years earlier she had experienced a great surge of popularity following the release of *The White Wampum,* but the book had sold out within a year and there had been no reissue. Since then her new poems had appeared in newspapers and periodicals, but these media provided limited exposure. In order to really jog the public consciousness, she would have to produce a new book.

The collection she finally chose for publication included only thirty-one poems, five less than in *The White Wampum.* Of these, at least ten had been composed before the first book was published, which means they had been among those that John Davidson rejected. "Beyond the Blue," which found a place in the new book, had been written before she went on stage in 1892 and was one of her most popular recital pieces, leaving her audience in tears as it told the story of Ben who had gone "beyond the blue," leaving his brother and his dog Rover to mourn for him. It is not good poetry, but it was great stuff for the platform. "Through Time and Bitter Distance," inspired by Charles G. D. Roberts's poem "Rain," had been published in a periodical in 1892. "Little Lady Icicle" apparently predates both of these, and might even have been written during her Chiefswood days. In an interview about her early attempts at poetry, she told Isabel Ecclestone MacKay:

> It was always such a joy to write, I can remember the thrill of expectation and delight when one cold winter morning I awoke to see the window covered with frost and ringed with icicles and felt with breathless pleasure that I could write about it in verse. Before breakfast I had written "Little Lady Icicle". The glow of it stayed with me all day. . . .[35]

Many of the poems in this collection are from the Smily-Johnson piece called "There and Back"—"Where Leaps the Ste. Marie," "Harvest Time" (originally called "Summer"), "Silhouette" (originally called "Silhouetted"), "At Crow's Nest Pass," and "Fire-flowers." Others had never been previously published though she used most of them in recital. None of the love poems written during her engagement to Drayton and her affair with Wurz appeared in the new book.

If she excluded them through a sense of delicacy, considering them too personal for public exposure, she was being unnecessarily modest; her unpublished poems which have been tentatively assigned to this period are all rather chaste. However, there is the possibility that the more passionate pieces were destroyed by her sister after her death.

Occasional poems such as "The Coronation Ode" were also left out of this new volume, as were those which might most kindly be classed as "commercial." In 1896 she had won first prize in a Canada-wide contest for the best campaign song for the Dominion General Election. Her entry was called "The Good Old N.P." in honour of the National Policy League which advocated tariff protection for Canadian manufactured goods. In 1902 she kept the Summerland (B.C.) Development Company happy with a poem which took its title from the company's slogan: "Canada for the Canadians"; the company sold its plots of ground to Anglo-Saxons only. For the Manufacturers Association banquet in Brantford in 1903, she wrote "Made in Canada."

Pauline's public did not sneer at these poems, nor accuse her of "bartering her divine gifts for a wretched mess of pottage." Pauline herself was certainly not ashamed of them. She seems to have regarded them as patriotic messages, expressions of her confidence in the Canadian way of life. However, she must have considered them to be in a class apart from her other poems since she did not include them in any collection of her work.

The title poem in the volume, "Canadian Born," had been written sometime before April 1899 when the first Boer "outrages" were taking place, and it remained popular with her audiences even after the war ended in May of 1902. With all the subtlety of a sledgehammer blow, the poem expresses Pauline's entirely British vision for Canada's future. It caused no outcry from the East European immigrants who had been pouring into Canada for at least fifty years, because poetry in the English language was entirely foreign to them. And even if they had understood what Pauline was saying, they would not have been concerned. They heard the same sentiments every day from their British neighbours. Meanwhile, Pauline's audiences, composed entirely of people of British stock, were pleased to applaud the poem enthusiastically.

There are two facts which suggest that Pauline probably had to subsidize *Canadian Born.* In the first place, the book was published by George Morang Publishing of Toronto, an educational publishing house which frequently produced subsidized books. Pauline appears to have made her own choice of poems; if Morang did any editing it certainly was not comparable to that done by John Davidson. Pauline makes no mention of an editor in any of her personal accounts of the publishing process. In the second place, the book's appearance coincided with her first share of the Chiefswood rental in three years. The amount was seventy-five dollars, enough in those days to have paid the writer's share of a joint publishing contract of this size.

Canadian Born contained only sixty-seven pages. Bound in pale blue with gold lettering, it contained a portrait of Pauline in Indian costume, and the following dedication:

> Let him who is Canadian born regard these poems as written to himself whether he be my paleface compatriot, who has given me his right hand of good fellowship in the years I have appealed to him by pen and platform, or whether he be that dear Red brother of whatsoever tribe or province, it matters not— White race and Red are one if they are but Canadian Born.

The book was not well received. Pauline told Harry O'Brien:

> The Toronto "Globe" and "Saturday Night" gave it a most scathing roast. But the "News" and the Montreal "Star" gave me such splendid reviews.
>
> Lady Laurier wrote me such a kind letter about the book. And Sir Lawrence Alma Tadema, whose art I have inscribed a poem to, has also written me very cordially. . . . The "Globe" says this poem on the Art of Alma Tadema is the only good thing in the book. Poor book! And half the poems it contains were accepted by Harper's and brought me some excellent notice.
>
> Well, I must try a novel now, and get criticized.

What the *Globe* had actually said was: "We had looked to see the level of her work sustained if not heightened by the passing years and I must confess to a feeling of disappointment. The collection at hand gives so little evidence of her finer imaginative vision and more cultivated poetic diction."[37]

For very similar reasons, later critics have also been dissatisfied with the collection. There is a distinct feeling of anticlimax in these poems; they lack content and energy. The reader keeps turning the pages looking for a major poem, the passionate creation of a mature poet, but this is entirely missing. Paradoxically, the more disappointments and tragedies Pauline had faced in her life, the shallower her poems had become. Now her writing politely skimmed the surface of emotion. On the other hand, these same poems were very successful on the recital platform, simply underlining the fact that Pauline, though she still believed herself a poet, had really become a performer who wrote her own material.

Although the book had a positive effect on box office receipts over the next two years, Pauline was aware that it had damaged her literary reputation. She could not afford such a gesture again. Fortunately, at about this time she began to receive encouragement to write in a different format. Marjorie Pickthall, writing in the *Globe* on 13 June 1903, lamented the lack of Canadian stories for children. She concluded her article:

> It is a pity I imagine that Pauline Johnson does not turn her attention to fiction. Some sketches written by her have appeared in newspapers and magazines, sketches which might be classed as fiction—but nothing beyond this. And the wide field of Indian lore and legend remains practically untouched at any rate in Canada though in the States they are awakening to the fact that the aforesaid field presents almost unrivalled possibilities to the writer of tales.[38]

That summer Pauline began her first experiments in children's literature when she went camping with McRaye and her brother Allen in Ontario's Kawartha Lakes district. Allen had forgotten nothing of what he had learned as a youth of "the art and science of living in the woods. He knew where the bass would be biting, and where the deer were most likely to drink. He needed only a canoe and the shadow of a rock to be at home in the wilderness."[39] Walter McRaye, however, had been a city kid and knew little of life beyond the footlights. Allen had grown quieter as the years went by, using words sparingly and choosing them with infinite care; McRaye was seldom silent.

The holiday was not a success, and when Pauline and McRaye departed for a fall tour of Michigan and Illinois, they left Allen vowing never to associate with McRaye again. In Michigan the box office was poor and the audiences hard to control. Only a month into the tour, Pauline was anxious to be "home" again. She found the people of that state to be *"very* uncultured, very ignorant, very illiterate."[40]

By the end of 1903 Pauline's marvellous optimism had bubbled up again and she was busy planning another overseas tour. Following her usual plan of action, she sent out letters to beg introductions to the high and the mighty. Sir Wilfrid Laurier was at the top of her list. "About two years ago you were kind enough to tell me you would give me letters of presentation to Lord Brassey and the Prime Minister should I decide to visit Australia. I have now changed my plans and intend visiting England instead, sailing in May next. . . ."[41]

This was wishful thinking. She had yet to raise the money for the trip, and sales of *Canadian Born* would not be providing any of that sum. At the end of January 1904 Johnson and McRaye headed west once more, stopping at Saskatoon en route. The town had mushroomed in the eighteen months since they had last played there, and now instead of one flimsy hotel "centrally heated" with one small coal stove out in the corridor between the rooms, there was a score of hotels. They chose Dad Flanagan's place as the best and set out for a recital at Cairn's Hall. The good people of Saskatoon filled the hall to capacity, and once more Pauline could feel that warm western glow take possession of her.

A month later they were in Vancouver bedding down in the Hotel Vancouver, the finest hostelry in the city. Spring was early that year; pussy willows were out and daffodils were breaking into bloom. It was the first time Pauline had seen spring on the coast and she was spellbound. With McRaye she took a carriage around Stanley Park and, stopping near Siwash Rock, she pointed out the Lions to him. That night, Vancouverites packed the aisles of the old Pender Auditorium for a YWCA-sponsored concert to raise money for a new ladies hostel in the city. There were bouquets of flowers before the recital and more flowers afterwards from the "thrilled" audience. There was nothing whatsoever new in the program. She was still doing "Ojistoh" and "The Legend of Qu'Appelle," but Vancouverites had not heard them as often as the east had. Besides, there was a freshness and vivacity about Pauline on this occasion that had been missing for a long time. Vancouver responded with enthusiasm and the next afternoon a crowd of well-wishers saw the entertainers off to Nanaimo on the steamer *Joan*.

They spent the next six months in British Columbia, first playing the settlements of the Fraser Valley and then the Fraser Canyon. But before they left Vancouver, Pauline dined with her old friends, the George Edwards family. At dinner, five-year-old Lucy Edwards listened attentively while Pauline explained her Fraser Valley itinerary which was to end in Chilliwack where she planned to try out some new material. At this point, to her parents' horror, young Lucy said solemnly, "God help Chilliwack!" After a moment of shock, Pauline burst into laughter.[42] The show in Chilliwack was a great success, but it is not recorded whether or not God helped.

In Edmonton on 23 May the last patches of snow still littered the streets when Pauline and McRaye watched an exhausted dog train struggling into town, its sled runners grinding on bare ground more often than on snow. Later that day Pauline showed McRaye the rough version of a new poem which would be called "Train Dogs." A few days later, the same incident became the basis of her short story "The Haunting Thaw."

Their recital audience was very small because most of the town had gone to Fort Saskatchewan for a sports day, so on the twenty-fifth, Pauline and McRaye also set off for the fort and there they met Inspector Charles Constantine of the Royal North West Mounted Police and his wife. Pauline was captivated by the Constantines and by the entire Mounted Police garrison. The compliment was returned, and the two performers were invited to remain at the post for a week's holiday.

For Pauline, it was a chance to bolster her stock of rugged redcoat tales. Constantine himself supplied her with material for many of her later stories. He had served with the Red River expedition, been head of Manitoba's police force, served with the militia during the second Riel Rebellion and then entered the Mounted Police as an inspector. In 1894 he had been sent to the Yukon to establish the jurisdiction of the police force, and had been in command when the discovery of gold on Bonanza Creek brought the big rush of 1898.

Mrs. Constantine had never been far behind her husband, even following him to his spartan lodgings in the Yukon, and she was beloved by the junior ranks in the force because she mothered them. For Pauline, she became the model for the heroine in the short story "Mother o' the Men" as well as for many of the idealized mothers and wives who populate her later stories.

Early in June Pauline and McRaye returned to British Columbia, working their way southwestward through the Kootenay mining towns again, then up the Okanagan Valley and on towards Kamloops in the heavy dry heat of midsummer. Then at last in the little town of Ashcroft on 25 July, the real adventure of this tour began. Pauline had always wanted to travel the Cariboo Road to Barkerville, the settlement that had become famous thirty years earlier as the site of British Columbia's largest gold strike. Unfortunately, getting there involved a four hundred-mile trip by horse and buggy and Pauline had hesitated to make it alone, but once she found McRaye willing to go, she made up her mind to take the trip that summer. The story of this busman's holiday over the Cariboo Road became Pauline's best-known travel piece. It appeared first on 13 October 1906 in *Toronto Saturday Night,* and reappeared in innumerable newspapers across the country over the next year. Five years later she rewrote it to incorporate some of the personal material she had hesitated to include for *Saturday Night.* That version appeared posthumously in *Canadian Magazine* in February 1914 as "Coaching on the Cariboo Trail."

For Pauline, the entire trip was a marvellously happy adventure. The weather was hot and dry, the air heavy with the scent of sagebrush. She loved the little hired canopy-topped surrey, and even became lyrical over the freight wagons they met along the trail. When the driver provided by the BX (British Columbia Express) Company arrived with the surrey—"a tall, sun-tanned Westerner with a cowboy hat, fringed gauntlets and a knotted scarlet handkerchief at his throat"[43]—she fell in love with him, too, and immediately rechristened him "Cariboo Billy," though he had been getting by as "Buckskin Billy" Holton until that time.

The scenery was breathtaking: sheer-edged canyons through which the Fraser River wound to the ocean, rolling hills, dense timberland and great mountains. The people of the Cariboo overwhelmed her with their friendliness and generosity. After twelve years of sleeping in incredibly bad hotels from coast to coast, she could not believe the reality of the log "mile-houses" which catered to the traveller so expansively and the enormous meals served at all hours of the day and night. Pauline "slept like a baby, laughed like a child, and ate like a lumberjack."[44]

Of course, there was business mixed in with the enjoyment because the trip had to pay for itself. McRaye had mailed posters ahead to each village along the route, with a note asking the postmaster to put them up and letting him know that he would give twenty per cent of the take for the use of a hall. Since very few entertainers ever ventured north of Ashcroft, the pair were welcomed enthusiastically wherever they stopped to give a concert. At Barkerville, they stepped down in front of Kelly's Hotel and promptly came under the proprietor's personal care. When he heard how much they were offering for a hall, he was indignant. "Far too much," he said, and negotiated with the theatre manager for two nights for $4. The first night they had 210 people in the audience, and the next night about 75. This gave them a sizable take, for though they had started out asking a dollar a seat in the settlements closest to Ashcroft, they had been scaling the price up until now the seats were $2.50 each. Thanks to the hotel proprietor, most of this money went into the Johnson-McRaye coffers. In gratitude, McRaye invited all the men in Barkerville into Kelly's bar after the last show to drink the proprietor's good health, but health came at an exorbitant price in a town that far from the railway. Each glass of whisky cost 25 cents and McRaye had a bill of $67 to pay before he left town.[45]

Heading south once more, they played wherever they could find an audience. At Soda Creek there was no hall available, but a rancher volunteered his new barn for the evening. Pauline's dressing room was a curtained-off oat bin.

At Lac la Hache a huge, empty, cedar shake shed near the lake was available for a show, but there was no more than a handful of people at the townsite. "Don't worry," the performers were reassured. "You just set up and they'll come!" Two men rode off on horseback and within an hour the audience started to trickle in "ranchers, Indians, miners, half-breeds, and farmers."[46] Cariboo Billy stood by the door taking the cash; whites, $1, Indians, 50 cents. One man objected to this scale. He told the doorman that he was half-white and half-Indian. "Seventy-five cents," said Billy. The man paid happily.

Just as the recital was about to begin, there was a commotion outside and two men dressed in city clothes stood in the doorway.

One had a shock of perfectly groomed, prematurely grey hair. Handsome, physically trim, and just thirty-two years old, he had been the premier of British Columbia for more than a year. His name was Richard McBride, but he was better known as "Glad Hand Dick" or "Handsome Dick." His partner was Charlie Wilson, the premier's boon companion and adviser. The two were out canvassing votes for Archie McDonald in a by-election which McBride had been forced to call in Lillooet. McDonald, the former provincial roads superintendent for Lillooet, had won a seat in the general election in 1903, but his election had been voided the following February for "the merest technicality"—it was said that some of the ballot boxes had not been sealed!

McBride badly needed the Lillooet seat; he held only twenty-two seats in the forty-two-seat house. Therefore, with his pal Wilson in tow, he had set out on 11 August from Lillooet townsite to visit the major settlements in the riding and drum up support for McDonald. When they arrived in Lac la Hache, they found Pauline and McRaye had already captured the audience and the only hall. McBride, though not a brilliant man, was an astute politician. Could he stay for Miss Johnson's performance? he asked. And then perhaps these good folks would stick around to listen to him for a bit and afterwards have a dance or two! The good folks certainly would and did.

Pauline and McRaye began their show at eight, the premier took over at ten and harangued the audience until midnight. After that they all danced till daylight. To tunes bowed on Mike McCarthy's "voyalin," they waltzed and square danced and even danced good old-fashioned lancers. Pauline, in a brocade gown made for her in London ten years earlier, oats still clinging to it from the previous night in Soda Creek, was partnered with the premier for the "head set" of the lancers. He wore a tweed suit with a handkerchief tied around his neck to show that he was one of the folks. McRaye in evening clothes partnered a girl named Nettie who was nearly six feet tall. They shared the floor with men in chaps and overalls, and women in gowns long out of city fashion. And how they danced!

At six in the morning, Cariboo Billy was waiting beside the surrey, one-handedly rolling a cigarette, impatient to leave. Neither Pauline nor McRaye had had any sleep, but off they went, bouncing over the roads.

They arrived in Ashcroft on 14 August. They had been gone

twenty days and been jolted up and down in that tiny surrey for 850 miles, but Pauline was amazed to find she had not been "carriage stiff" or really tired during the entire trip.

Cariboo Billy Holton died in 1908, and Pauline was sadly moved by his death. He had been a special part of her Cariboo adventure. She wrote:

> The Great Dramatist was gracious to Billy. He did not cast him for a principal on the British Columbia stage but assigned him a bit of character work which had it been omitted would have left the mountain scenes of his day woefully lacking in human interest. But the bit Billy played got across. . . . Furthermore the Master of Stagecraft permitted Billy to make his exit in the very scene that saw the romance of the play on the wane.[47]

And though this had been offered as a tribute to Billy, it was also a comment on her Cariboo travels. Even Pauline the Romantic recognized that what she had enjoyed most about the Cariboo had been that part which was doomed. For her it had been the last frontier, the last glimpse of the real pioneer country which she had seen vanish from Winnipeg and then from the prairies. She would have to be content with a much tamer frontier from now on.

Their west coast tour ended officially in Vancouver's city hall on 30 August, but as they headed east on the CPR, they stopped off along the way to pick up towns that they had missed. One of these was Revelstoke where their concert coincided with a visit by William Randolph Hearst and his wife who were on holiday in the Kootenays. They happened to stay at the same hotel—"Sandy MacDonald's hotel with its smooth grassy terrace"—and were introduced by the proprietor. McRaye, always impressed by wealth and position, was entranced by the Hearsts and recorded the meeting in his memoirs. Pauline, who always attracted prestigious people, did not even mention the incident in her collection of anecdotes.

They opened their fall season in Minnedosa, Manitoba, and closed just before Christmas in Regina, once more under the patronage of Lieutenant Governor and Madame Forget. But though 1904 had been a happy year for the partners, it had been disappointing financially. They were still unable to finance an overseas tour.

Pauline's poetry output had diminished in favour of prose in the last year, but her writing was tighter in construction and more economical in language. In December her new poem "Train Dogs" had been published in *Rod and Gun*. They paid seventy-five cents for the privilege; she sent the money back to them, telling them that it was obvious they needed it more than she did. Earlier she had submitted the same poem to *Outing Magazine,* but assistant editor Lloyd Roberts, the son of her old friend Charles G. D. Roberts, had sent it back with a note pencilled in the margin saying he thought she could do better. Having known him since his childhood, she had been particularly offended by his condescension. (In March 1908 *Outing* magazine featured the poem on its cover page, attributing it to Owen E. McGillicuddy. Rumour had it that McGillicuddy was paid twenty-five dollars for it. Pauline's fans were outraged, but the hoax had actually been perpetrated by her good friend Bob Edwards, the publisher of the *Eye Opener,* who had been killing two birds with Pauline's poem. By his little trick, he proved that Roberts had discriminated against her in 1904 and he also dealt a blow to his hated rival, Daniel McGillicuddy, the publisher of the *Calgary Daily News.* Backed by Clifford Sifton's money, McGillicuddy had set up the *News* in March 1907 and launched a campaign to discredit Edwards who was one of Sifton's severest critics. When the *Outing* incident occurred, Edwards used it to imply that all McGillicuddys were frauds and cheats. Subsequently, McGillicuddy published a savage and unwarranted attack on Edwards, and Edwards sued him for defamatory libel and won. If the bogus McGillicuddy did receive twenty-five dollars for the poem from *Outing,* Pauline probably shared it with the bibulous Edwards.)

Encouraged by Marjorie Pickthall's remarks, Pauline had begun to tap a new market, that of the boys' magazines and annuals. They were happy to accept her stories of brave Mounties, trappers and cowboys battling blizzards, raging torrents, and ravening beasts in the Canadian wilderness; these were just the stuff to tempt the youth of America to heroic deeds. Her primary market was *The Boys' World* of Elgin, Illinois, which accepted stories such as "Maurice of His Majesty's Mail" and "The Hero's Sacrifice." None of these pieces ran more than three thousand words, and since the pay was only six dollars per thousand, the cheques did not add appreciably to the funds she was collecting for her trip to London. But it was a start in a new direction which Pauline would follow in the future.

In January 1905 the partners launched a new tour of Ontario

beginning in Aurora, north of Toronto, playing every hamlet that could offer a stage. They had little time for the big cities where the competition was too intense. They crossed the border to play New York State, then moved into New Brunswick. By July they were back in Ontario, touring the settlements in the north. In September they were on the prairies to help the newly formed provinces of Alberta and Saskatchewan celebrate their birthdays. November and December found them in Manitoba.

Early in the year Pauline's disappointment at having to postpone the London trip again had been evident in her performances, but as the months wore on and it became apparent that the partners would be able to finance the trip in 1906, she began to perform with more enthusiasm than she had shown since 1900. On stage she became wittier than she had ever been; she sparkled as she recited her lyrics, and terrified old ladies and timid shop clerks with her bloodcurdling Indian tales. And she thoroughly enjoyed herself.

Pauline and McRaye celebrated Christmas of 1905 in the lumbering town of Rainy River close to the American border. The proprietor of the little hotel laid on a Christmas dinner that surpassed anything they had ever seen. He served deer, bear, beaver, partridge, grouse and chicken as well as the customary turkey, and almost everybody in the settlement sat down to dinner with them. Afterwards, Pauline told Indian stories to the children while the adults played old-time parlour games; then everyone danced until the fiddler could no longer hold up his bow.

In the morning the whole town came out to see Pauline and McRaye off, and they left feeling richly contented. They were leaving behind a public that adored them and going forward into a new year which would include the long-planned trip to England.

Chief John Smoke Johnson,
"Sakayengwaraton" (*Brant County Museum*)

Chief George Henry Martin
Johnson, "Teyonnhehkewea"
(*Brant County Museum*)

Emily Susanna Howells (*left*, November 1847; *below,* April 1894) (*Brant County Museum*)

Chiefswood with members of the Johnson family and the pony Marengo
(*Brant County Museum*)

The Johnson children, January 1878. In a handwritten note on the reverse, dated 1882, Pauline wrote: "I cut Eva's head out as she did not wish me to keep it and she would not let me show it." (*Brant County Museum*)

Allen Johnson (*Brant County Museum*)

Henry Beverly Johnson
(*Brant County Musuem*)

Photographs taken
of Pauline in the
Chiefswood and
Brantford years,
c. 1876-1891
(*Brant County Museum*)

Pauline paddling her canoe "Wildcat" (*Brant County Museum*)

The duplex at No. 7 Napoleon Street (*Brant County Museum*)

Pauline's first theatrical costume, created in the fall of 1892 (*Vancouver Public Library*)

Frank Yeigh (*Brantford Expositor*)

Pauline in her first "English dinner dress" made at Barkers, High Street, Kensington S.W., June 1894 (*Brant County Museum*)

Almost 37 years old when this photograph was taken at Christmas, 1897, Pauline was preparing to marry Charles Robert Lumley Drayton (*Brant County Museum*)

Charles R. L. Drayton (*Provincial Archives of British Columbia*)

J. Walter McRaye in a
photograph taken for the 1906
English tour (*McMaster University*)

Photographs taken in the winter
of 1902-3 with Pauline's hair
unfashionably short

Pauline Johnson and Walter McRaye with the novelist Opie Reed on the Chautauqua circuit of 1907 (*Saturday Night*)

Indian delegation in London, August 1906. *From left to right*: Interpreter Simon Pierre; Chief Charlie Filpaynem; Chief Joe Capilano; Chief Basil (*McMaster University*)

Pauline in 1906 (*right*) and 1907 (*below*);
Essen of Preston, Ontario, took the
photograph in costume for a 1907
Chautauqua program (*Brant County Museum*)

Lucy Webling on her
wedding day, Vancouver,
August 1908 (*Mrs. Florence
Pratt*)

Lionel Waterloo Makovski
and wife, about 1911 (*Eric
Makovski*)

Walter and Lucy McRaye with Pauline, Vancouver, May 1912 *(Mrs. Florence Pratt)*

Dr. Thomas Ransom Biggar Nelles, about 1927 (*A. Arkell*)

Pauline in 1912 (*Mrs. Florence Pratt*)

Chiefswood today (*B. W. Switzer, photographer*)

Pauline Johnson memorial, Stanley Park (*Chris Keller, photographer*)

Chapter Nine

London Again

PAULINE AND McRAYE arrived in England aboard the Canadian Pacific liner *Lake Champlain* in the third week of April. Pauline was high-spirited and confident. They had spent the early months of the year in a triumphant swing through Ontario; one night in Peterborough they drew the largest audience that had ever turned out for a performance in the history of the town. Every seat was taken and people had to be turned away at the door. Pauline was riding the crest again.

In early April she and McRaye had crossed the international border to perform at Johnstown, New York, then had gone on to New York City to visit Eva who had been working there for a year. The visit was a mistake. Eva had been relatively diplomatic about her dislike for McRaye up until this time, but when she realized that he was going to London as Pauline's partner, she was shocked and angry. He was not a man of culture or refinement, she stormed.[1] What would people think? And when Pauline remained firm, Eva declared that McRaye had bullied her into taking him. He was getting a free ride to London on Pauline's money and her petticoats!

Pauline could hardly deny McRaye the right to accompany her to London since he had earned it. As for his suitability as a partner, he would be no more and no less suitable in England than he had been in North America. Pauline was certainly not going to leave him behind and be forced to look for a new partner when she got back. In the four and a half years he had been with her he had become an asset. He had developed poise on stage, improved his timing, and learned how to handle every kind of audience. Offstage, he juggled railroad time-tables, concert schedules and hotel bills with ease. McRaye had considerable value.

There had been many battles between Eva and Pauline in the past, but this was the worst. For Pauline the decision to take McRaye to London was purely a business matter; to Eva it was a matter of family honour and her sister's reputation. Neither woman would budge an inch from her stand, and when Pauline left New York her face was set in cold and lasting anger.

In London, Pauline and McRaye settled into an apartment in an elegant four-storeyed house at 53 St. James Square, an eminently fashionable address. Fifty years earlier, No. 53 had been transformed from a single-family residence into four luxury flats without disturbing its façade or the fine sensibilities of the other residents of the square. Through friends, Pauline leased the third-floor apartment complete with staff. She chose the front sitting room and adjoining bedroom for her own use because they looked out over a square to the beautiful Church of St. James Norland. For the first time in twelve years, she was "in residence"; she could bring out the porcupine quill mats, the deer skins and tomahawks, and surround herself with the mementos of her family and her father's people.

The social life of London's upper classes had subtly altered since Pauline's last visit. There was no longer the same desperate competition for drawing room entertainers. Parties tended to be smaller and more intimate, and bridge whist had become society's latest craze. Dinner invitations often included the prospect of going out later to dance, and supper invitations meant the theatre first. More and more hostesses were choosing their guests for their entertainment value— "Do invite Reggie, my dear, he simply makes any party!" Under these circumstances it was becoming extremely difficult for professional entertainers to find drawing room employment.

Pauline had no book to publish on this trip; her only reason for being in London was to perform. She could not, therefore, allow the changed conditions to upset her plans; she and McRaye had to have steady employment or they would run out of money. Consequently, they registered with the Keith Prowse Entertainment Agency, which advertised them in the newspapers under the heading "American and Colonial Artists," especially suitable for garden party entertainments. They had the advantage of being the freshest talent on the London scene.

Next, armed with Laurier's letter of introduction, Pauline descended on Lord and Lady Strathcona. As Donald A. Smith, he had been a prize example of the humble Scotsman who made good in the colonies. By 1906 he had become the Canadian high commissioner in London and had enjoyed nine years as a peer of the realm. His climb to this lofty perch, however, had started with an apprenticeship in the Hudson's Bay Company, which he parlayed into the governorship of the company. He had made and unmade John A. Macdonald's governments, dealt in railways and the Canadian economy with a cavalier hand, and earned himself the privilege of driving the last spike of the CPR at Craigellachie. When he was sent to London in 1896 to look after Canada's interests, he set himself up in Grosvenor Square and bought the beautiful estate of Knebworth out of his railway earnings. When Pauline came to call, he was eighty-six years of age and still looking for the next adventure.

Pauline had chosen his lordship and her ladyship to be her patrons for this visit just as she had chosen the Ripons in 1894. The Strathconas were delighted with the arrangement; they had never entertained an Indian in their drawing room before.

On Pauline's last visit to London she had performed only in private salons; on this trip she was determined to hold at least one public recital in order to introduce herself and McRaye to a wider audience and stimulate interest among wealthy patrons. Her intention had been to arrange this public recital for early June, but she had to settle for a reservation at Steinway Hall for 16 July.

While she was inspecting various halls and making rental arrangements, McRaye was savouring the delights of the city. Ten years earlier, when he had been a penniless stage-struck kid, New York's Broadway had been his career goal, the place where ultimate theatrical success was recognized. Now he realized he had been wrong. London was the greater challenge, the pinnacle of success. And Walter McRaye was standing in the wings waiting for his cue. So in order to play his part as he knew it must be played, he drove to the J. R. Dale Company in Westbourne Grove and paid ten pounds for a new dress suit. Then, as an afterthought, he bought a second suit for six pounds.

Even though the Steinway Hall concert had been delayed, the partners soon had a number of society entertainments booked, and each performance added to their reputation. Whenever they were not entertaining, Pauline took her partner to see the sights of the city or to visit friends she had made on her last trip to London. Though she did not include him in her visits to Lady Ripon or her dear friend Lady Blake, she decided quite correctly that he would enjoy a visit with the Webling family whom she had known long ago in Brantford. It turned out to be a most fortunate occasion for J. Walter McRaye, for out of it would come a meeting with his future wife.

There were six talented and handsome Webling daughters. Their father was a silversmith. Their mother, who had raised them to be young ladies of propriety, realized that they must make a living for themselves and had thrust them into the world of platform entertainment. The two eldest escaped to other careers, but the next three, Rosalind, Josephine and Peggy, became a recital team when the youngest, Peggy, was just ten years old. Their repertoire was culled mostly from Shakespeare's plays.

At eighteen, Rosalind, the handsomest of the sisters, became engaged and left the stage. This would have disturbed the family act had not seven-year-old Lucy Betty Webling been ready to make her debut. The audiences adored her. With long, dark wavy hair, brown eyes and a gentle, loving disposition, Lucy was an exquisite child, who could have become quite insufferable but who accepted the attentions of the public with unvarying politeness and no signs of temperament. Offstage, she wrote little poems for family and friends.

The sisters retired from the platform when nine-year-old Lucy was selected to be the first road company "Little Lord Fauntleroy"; she travelled in the part for more than a year in England, then Ireland and Scotland. Peggy played the shoeblack, and Mother Webling went along as a chaperone. At the conclusion of the run, the play's author decided to capitalize on its success by writing a second vehicle for Lucy. The Weblings backed it with all their savings, but the play was dismal and they lost everything. So Mother Webling packed up Josephine and Peggy and sent them to stay with an aunt and uncle in Brantford, Ontario.

They arrived in the summer of 1890 and, because their uncle was a prominent Brantfordite, were quickly admitted into the best circles. In this way, they met Pauline and became members of her group of intimates. One afternoon, while a group of them were lounging on the banks of the river, Pauline cut a strip of birch bark and began writing carefully on it. The next morning it was delivered to Peggy with these neatly inscribed verses:

> Dear little girl from far
>   Beyond the seas,
> From lands where roses are
>   You come to these—
>
> These where the birch tree flings
>   His ragged coat,
> These where the wild pine sings
>   With dreamful note—
>
> Ah! Little guest of ours,
>   The suns and snows
> Greet, mid their wilder flowers,
>   An English rose.

When winter came there were dances, euchre parties, parlour parties, suppers and "sociables." In return for all this hospitality, the English rose and her sister willingly recited the poems they had learned in their platform days. Inevitably, their performances in Brantford and their anecdotes about their years on the stage must have had an effect on Pauline's decision a year later to become a recitalist, while the Weblings' decorum must have helped convince the Johnsons that there was little danger in such a career.

Meanwhile, Josephine Webling walked off with one of Pauline's beaux, Alfred Watt, and they announced their engagement in the spring of 1891. That fall, Mrs. Webling, Rosalind (whose engagement had been cancelled) and Lucy arrived in New York with plans to tour America as recitalists. Peggy and Josephine joined them and for eight months they sought work unsuccessfully in New York. Finally, before they departed for England once more, all the Webling women went to Brantford for Josephine's wedding. It was an enormous summertime affair; afterwards they stayed on for several weeks and young Lucy captivated Brantford with her recitations. This was the summer of 1892, and Pauline had been launched on her platform career for six months. However, at the time of the wedding of her old beau, she was apparently vacationing at Rosseau Lake.

Now there were three: the beautiful Rosalind, the aspiring

writer Peggy, and little Lucy. In 1894 when Pauline first visited London she went to call on the Weblings and, seeing that their theatrical efforts were going no better in London than they had in New York, she urged them to try once more, but this time in Canada. She even suggested a good agent for them in Toronto—Ernest Shipman. Lucy was the star of the Webling company, since she could outsing, outdance and outact the others. She was sixteen when they re-embarked for Canada in the spring of 1895.

For nearly three years these young women toured Canada and the northern states, following the same relentless pattern that Pauline had followed: five nights a week, a new town every night. Occasionally, they crossed Pauline's path, but since she was touring with Smily in those days, the sisters never met McRaye.

In 1898, after the Weblings had returned to England, Rosalind travelled alone to Vancouver and married the well-known city photographer George Edwards, of Edwards Brothers Studios. Although she was probably far more decorous than the average young woman on the streets of Vancouver, her new mother-in-law treated her with contempt and referred to her as a "stage actress."[2] Lonely and far from her family, Rosalind was delighted whenever Pauline played Vancouver and soon became her confidante. It was Rosalind's husband who now took Pauline's publicity photographs, and it was Rosalind's daughter who invoked God's help for Chilliwack.

At home in England, Peggy left the recital stage in favour of a writing career. Lucy, left alone, resolved to return to acting. Luckily she was "noticed" by George Alexander, the manager of the St. James Theatre, and for the next two years she danced in his shows. After that, she became "Mimi" in William Haviland's company of *The Only Way* and stayed for a long run.

In the spring of 1906, when Pauline and McRaye came calling on the Weblings, Peggy's first novel had just been published to generally good reviews. She and her mother were delighted to welcome their old friend, but later both of them agreed that Pauline was much changed by fame. Lucy was on tour so she missed their visit, but as soon as she returned to London she came to see them at St. James Square.

At twenty-six, Lucy was still as radiant as she had been as a child. Small and delicate in appearance, she glowed with a serenity and gentleness that overwhelmed McRaye. He had admired a number of ladies over the years, but since he began touring there had never been time for more than a kiss and a promise. This time things were different. Lucy was everything he needed in a partner. She was beautiful, she could sing and dance and act, she was tough enough to withstand touring, and she could write. Already, many of her poems and short stories had been published; McRaye must have figured that it would be only one more step for her to write material tailored to his talents. He decided that he was in love.

His newly awakened passion was helped along by the knowledge that Pauline's interest in touring was flagging. She was forty-five, and McRaye sensed that she wanted to put down roots. He would have to find a replacement within the next half dozen years. It would pay him to begin courting Lucy, for it was unlikely that a better candidate would come along.

Lucy had been on stage for nineteen of her twenty-six years and in certain ways she had attained the sophistication that one would expect of an actress. But she knew very little about men. All their lives the Webling sisters had been closely supervised by their devoted mother. When the Webling Sisters act toured Canada, the girls had chaperoned each other and kept an especially severe eye on Lucy, the baby. Even in George Alexander's company Lucy had been protected; Alexander was an old family friend and he made sure that she went home to her family every night.

The only men she knew were the actors in her shows and the motley parade who hung around the stage door, eager to take the young actresses out for supper and a little "fun." But Lucy, like all her sisters, was a romantic. She was waiting for love, and when McRaye came along with his Canadian accent to remind her of beautiful Ontario and the wide prairies, her heart responded happily.

For Pauline, watching this courtship must have been both a relief and an anxiety. Like a mother, she must have hovered, pleased that McRaye was at last showing some desire to marry, relieved that he had recognized the need to look for a replacement when she retired, delighted that his fancy had been taken by this gentle, talented and beautiful young woman. At the same time, she must have been apprehensive for Lucy because she was aware of McRaye's selfish and callous side. Not that he was ever unkind to Pauline, but she had seen him behave with unnecessary cruelty to others when his ego needed bolstering. She had another worry as well: what if he decided to quit the partnership before she was ready to retire? Privately, she realized that she was tiring on the road more easily than she used to, and that well-dressed matrons and their doily-laden parlours gave her real pangs of envy. But she was not ready to relinquish McRaye yet.

While the McRaye-Webling romance was unfolding, Pauline and McRaye were busy performing in the drawing rooms of Mayfair, and though these affairs were smaller in scope than those of 1894, the quality of the clientele was every bit as good. That clientele was enlarged considerably when Box and Cox stated in *Stage and Sport:* "One of the most thoroughly drawing room entertainments which is being presented in society room circles this season is undoubtedly the thrilling reading by Tekahionwake, the Mohawk Indian girl, of her own poems. . . ."[3] *M.A.P.* increased her fame even more by printing the results of an interview. After the usual outline of her heritage and her career, the article continues:

> Some of the towns they [Pauline and McRaye] have visited a dozen times, some they've only picked up in passing, in other words just arrived in time to send out a bill-boy to announce the show. Miss Johnson tells a good yarn of a certain little town in Newfoundland. Arriving on the day of the performance she was annoyed to find that the walls were very poorly billed. The local bill-poster was summoned and questioned. He indignantly protested that he had done his best and took Miss Johnson to the end of the main street. There he posted up a couple of bills and asked her to retreat for a little distance and after a while a herd of goats appeared on the scene and made straight for the posters, stripping them off the walls to lick the paste underneath.
>
> "Guess them goats want to digest your show," the bill-poster said.
>
> Of course, Tekahionwake wears moccasins when she appears in Indian dress. More than once they have proved a source of great curiosity and interest on this side of the Atlantic where we rarely see them. The other day a lady gravely asked when she was examining the redskin costume why Miss Johnson's two tobacco bags were decorated with such elaborate beadwork. On another occasion, when a friend's lady's maid was helping her to dress, Miss Johnson thought it better

to explain at once that her soft leather boot coverings were not to be worn on the hands like gloves or hanging from the belt like tobacco pouches.

"Oh no, ma'am, I quite understand," said the lady's maid. "I've often heard that Canadian ladies wear toboggans on their feet."[4]

One of the letters of introduction that Pauline carried to London was addressed to Sir Gilbert Parker, a Canadian, born and educated in Ontario, who had set sail for Australia and the South Seas at age twenty-one to make his living as a journalist. After twelve years of this life, he had moved to London to make his name and his fortune as a novelist. He had been knighted in 1902.

Parker and his wife were immediately receptive to Pauline's charm and willing to co-operate in the arrangements for the July sixteenth recital in Steinway Hall. Parker was on good terms with most of the editors and critics of the influential London dailies and literary magazines so he simply wrote to them all asking them to attend the show; his name on a letter was apparently enough to ensure their attention.

It was Parker who introduced Pauline and McRaye to Hamar Greenwood, who sat as the Senior Member of Parliament for York in the British House of Commons. Greenwood was nominally a Canadian, but he had gone to England to be educated when he was only fifteen and had remained there for a career in law and politics. He was well-known as a public speaker.

Greenwood invited the two entertainers to tea on 22 June on the terrace of the House of Commons. Their fellow guest on this occasion was the Honourable Colin H. Campbell, the attorney general for Manitoba, whom Pauline had known in her Winnipeg days. During tea a steady parade of politicians, newspapermen, and other men of influence stopped by and sometimes joined Greenwood's table. McRaye, impressed with the company they were keeping, memorized the names: John Burns, the one-time Labour leader who had just become a member of the Liberal Campbell-Bannerman cabinet; Lord Aberdeen, the former governor general of Canada; Edward Blake, the Canadian who sat in the British House of Commons as an Irish Nationalist; Charles Devlin, the man from Quebec who also sat as an Irish Nationalist. . . . (Unfortunately, the credibility of the picture is somewhat spoiled by McRaye's inclusion of Michael Davitt on this list: Davitt had been buried three weeks earlier.)

But Sir Gilbert Parker's most important contributions to Pauline's success in London were introductions to the right people in the literary world. At one of the soirées given by Lady Parker, Pauline was approached by a middle-aged gentleman who asked quietly if she was the Indian poetess Pauline Johnson. Then he explained that Parker had told him she might be available to write "something" for his newspaper. She asked his name.

"Pearson," he said. "I have some papers in the city."[5]

Sir Arthur Pearson in fact owned more than thirty newspapers, but his most prized possession was the *Daily Express,* the paper that he was asking Pauline to write for. A few days later, editor Malcolm Fraser invited her to come around to discuss the type of article that she would contribute.

It had been one of Pauline's prime objectives in coming to London to find new markets for her writing. Although she had investigated the American and Canadian markets and found that magazines such as *Harper's, Toronto Saturday Night* and *Canadian Magazine* were willing to accept her articles and poems, she still considered it more prestigious to be published in England. She must have seen proof of this in the relative success of her two books: *The White Wampum,* published in England, had been critically acclaimed; *Canadian Born,* published in Toronto, had reaped critical abuse. She must have reasoned, therefore, that if she could develop a demand for her work in England, the American and Canadian journals would come cap in hand to solicit her literary output.

That summer the *Daily Express* published three of her articles: "The Lodge of the Law-Makers," "The Silent News-Carrier" and "A Pagan in St. Paul's." Although all were well received, it was "A Pagan in St. Paul's" that caught the public's imagination for it told of a savage Indian an earlier incarnation of Pauline herself who is drawn into the midst of the worshippers in the great cathedral and, at the conclusion, finds there is no difference between his form of worship and theirs.

As a result of her acceptance by the *Express,* the journal *Canada* also published some of Pauline's work, but the editor was less venturesome than Fraser had been. In fact, he would have been quite willing to just reprint the articles from the *Express*.

As in 1894, Dominion Day was celebrated with enthusiasm by the Canadian exiles, but since July first was a Sunday, all the festivities took place the following day. There were balls, fetes, garden parties, picnics, dinners, suppers and luncheons. The celebrants entertained each other with tableaux vivants, songs, dances, recitations, speeches and more speeches. Pauline and McRaye attended Lord and Lady Strathcona's Dominion Day party at the Imperial Institute in South Kensington. Both were asked to recite; predictably Pauline gave "Canadian Born," and McRaye gave "When Albani Sang." McRaye then went on to the "Men Only" dinner being given by Lord Strathcona at the Hotel Cecil Strand.

The highlight of the exiles' summer, however, was the Strathconas' garden party at Knebworth Hall in Hertfordshire on 14 July. Fifteen hundred people attended, including almost every Canadian of social note to be found in Britain, and every Briton who had ever set foot in the colonies. Although many of the more affluent "motored" down from London, special trains left King's Cross at intervals all afternoon to accommodate the rest of the guests.

During the afternoon, the band of the Royal Artillery entertained from a specially constructed bandstand in the garden and, whenever they tired, the pipers of the Scots Guards marched among the rosebushes and the tea drinkers playing highland music. An army of white-gloved waiters served tea and cakes and sandwiches under striped marquees set up on the lawns.

The Duke of Argyll was there, and the Marchioness of Donegal who had entertained Pauline in 1894; the Countess of Worford and Lady Knightly of Fawsley came representing the Ladies Empire Club. Sir Duncan Campbell motored down, and Sir Frederick Young buttonholed people to discuss his book on "imperial federation." (He was firmly against both colonies and dominion status.) Sir Charles Tupper came from his retirement home at Bexley Heath to ogle the ladies, and all the parliamentary Canadians trotted out for the show. Pauline had attended enough posh affairs to be only moderately impressed with this collection, but it was a grand occasion to be seen, and every bit of public exposure was important. McRaye stored up the event for his memoirs.

Two days after the garden party, Pauline and McRaye faced a huge audience at Steinway Hall. There was nothing new in their program, but it was new to London. And those who were not swept off their feet by the content of the program were won by Pauline's charm and vitality. Lord and Lady Strathcona led the applause. Old Sir Charles Tupper attended and made a point of telling everyone how he had introduced her to society on her last visit. Sir Gilbert Parker also came, but Lady Parker was in Carlsbad for the cure. Hamar Greenwood and the rest of the noteworthy members of the Canadian colony filled the boxes.

Sir Gilbert was as good as his word in bringing out the representatives of the press. The show was reviewed by the *Daily Mirror*, the *Daily Express*, the *Morning Leader*, the *Evening Standard*, the *St. James Gazette*, the *Morning Post*, the *Daily Mail*, the *Crown*, the *Standard*, the *Pall Mall Gazette* and *M.A.P.* The reviews were all favourable.

After the show, Theodore Watts-Dunton arrived in Pauline's crowded dressing room to offer congratulations. Although he had reviewed Pauline's poems when they appeared in *Songs of the Great Dominion* and in *The White Wampum*, giving them lavish praise, he had never come face to face with her before. Pauline, who looked on critics such as Watts-Dunton and Clement Scott as minor gods, was overwhelmed. Calling for silence in the dressing room, she told the rest of her well-wishers that this was the man to whom she owed most of her literary success. There were tears in her eyes as she pressed his hand. Her audience was very impressed, and so was Watts-Dunton.

Before they parted that night, Pauline had earned an invitation to dine at Watts-Dunton's home, The Pines, Putney Hill. Here she was to meet the great Algernon Swinburne whose poetry had inspired her since childhood. Swinburne had lived at The Pines for almost thirty years, ever since the day he had collapsed from alcoholism. Watts-Dunton had taken charge of him and acted as his guardian and friend, carefully supervising his diet and rationing him to one pint of ale per day. Under this regimen, Swinburne had prospered physically, and in time he turned out another twenty-three volumes of work. But when Pauline met him in 1906, he was hardly a romantic figure. He was then only three years away from his death. Tiny, with wispy moustache and goatee, bald except for a fringe of reddish-grey hair, he peered at his visitor through disconcertingly bright blue eyes.

Neither Pauline nor McRaye recorded this visit to The Pines, but Charles G. D. Roberts confirms that she made quite an impression on Swinburne. When Roberts visited him in 1908, they talked of Canadian poets and poetry, and Swinburne praised the works of Lampman and Bliss Carman. Watts-Dunton had interrupted, "Now, Algernon, don't forget our dear Pauline!" Replied Swinburne with feeling, "I could never forget her!"[6] And the conversation settled on her delightful poetry and her charming personage.

After the performance at Steinway Hall, Pauline and McRaye went on vacation to a country house in Kintbury, Berkshire, where Pauline completed her articles for the *Daily Express* and prepared material for submission to other newspapers and journals. There was little hope of drawing room engagements in August and even the garden party circuit had slowed down.

On 3 August "A Pagan in St. Paul's" appeared in the *Express* and, by a strange coincidence, two days later three more "savages" arrived in London, though their eyes were turned to Buckingham Palace, not St. Paul's. They were Chief Joe Capilano of the Squamish band, Chief Charlie Filpaynem of the Cowichans and Chief Basil of the Bonapartes. Since none of them spoke English very well, they had brought along an interpreter whose name was either Simon Pierre or August of the Coquitlams, depending on whose version of the story is believed.

In Vancouver, Chiefs Joe and Charlie had entrained together third class, since their tribes were paying their way. It was the hottest day of the summer, but Chief Joe wore his full chieftain's regalia: ready-made trousers and a fringed buckskin shirt, over these a tanned deer skin and a woven cedar root blanket that covered him from shoulders to knees, on his head a fox fur hat nearly a foot tall with its tail hanging down his back. Chief Charlie's regalia was the same, except that his hat was made of sea otter pelts.

Chief Joe acted as spokesman and, with the help of the interpreter, told the crowd at the train:

> I go to see the king in England. I will speak to him of what his Indian subjects want. I will tell them when I come back what he says. I will shake his hand in loyalty for you. He is the king of the Indians and the white men. Under him they are all one big family. When I see the king I will tell him that his subjects are all faithful in British Columbia. I will tell you all what the king says when I get back.[7]

There were a lot of smiles and a good deal of laughter in the crowd as the chiefs climbed aboard the train. Whoever heard of a monarch giving an audience to an Indian chief?

In Kamloops, Chief Basil joined them and the three settled down for the long journey. In Saint John, they embarked for Liverpool, carefully extending their funds by travelling steerage. They had no idea where to go once they got to London, but they knew what they planned to do. They were going to take their grievances to the king.

The Coast Indians had suffered in silence the encroachments on their traditional lands by settlers, fishermen, miners and railroad men. Now, new game laws had been enacted which denied the Indians the right to kill does and fawns between February and August. Restrictions had also been placed on fresh-water fishing. Since the Indians' food supply was made up primarily of game, especially deer, and fish caught in the rivers, the new laws would mean serious hardships for most tribes. Their protests had fallen on deaf ears in Victoria; obviously they had to find a higher authority.

When word of their imminent arrival hit London's newspaper offices, reporters scrambled madly for Euston Station. There had not been a novelty like this from the colonies in years! Bombarded with questions by the press, the three chiefs and their interpreter remained calm, but they must have been somewhat distressed by the reception. They were rescued by a functionary from Lord Strathcona's office, who had been notified of their arrival by a wire from officials in Vancouver. This gentleman found them accommodation and then notified the British secretary for the colonies that the next move was his.

The secretary hoped to satisfy them enough so that they would go home, but it quickly became apparent that the chiefs had no intention of leaving until they had seen the king. Legally they had no right to appeal directly to him; they should have been dealing with the provincial government. On the other hand, their tribes had never signed treaties with either the provincial or the federal government, so to whom could they appeal except the king? At length it was decided that they should be allowed to see him, but unfortunately their majesties were at Cowes for the annual regatta week. What should be done? The secretary took his problem back to the Cabinet, where it lay like some intangible football waiting to be put into play. And the chiefs sat in their hotel and waited.

In the meantime, Lord Strathcona appealed to Pauline for help. What was his staff to do with such responsibilities? The longer the chiefs waited, the lonelier and more homesick they became; and the more homesick they became, the more taciturn and difficult they were. Would Pauline speak to them and try to smooth their ruffled feathers? Indeed she would. There was only one problem: she did not speak any of the West Coast languages and the chiefs' English was definitely spotty. She did, however, know a little bit of Chinook, which was the hybrid tongue invented by the early traders on the West Coast in order to carry on trade with the Indians. Since it was all she had to offer, it would have to do.

She took the train to London and went calling on the chiefs, with reporters hard on her heels. They heard at least the beginning of the conversation before Strathcona's officials escorted them out.

"Klahowya Tillicum skookum," Pauline greeted the Indians, and their faces lit up in smiles of welcome.

The rest of the conversation was not recorded, but it would have been a linguistics expert's nightmare. Chief Joe, as spokesman for the group, did most of the talking. He habitually spoke a strange mixture of English and Chinook, which only the initiated understood with any degree of accuracy, but when he was under stress it was almost incomprehensible. How much worse it must have been on this occasion when faced with this beautiful and charming woman with her smattering of Chinook and such an obvious desire to help! There must have been a good deal of nodding and smiling and gesturing in that conversation. In any case, when Pauline left, though she was still somewhat unsure why the chiefs had come to London, she had acquired one very earnest admirer who would resurface in her life when she most needed a friend.

The day after the interview, Pauline was bombarded by requests from reporters who assumed that all Indians spoke the same language and had been looking for an interpreter to pave their way with the chiefs. Pauline was wise enough not to attempt the role of go-between.

The king and queen returned to London in due course and it was decided that they should receive the chiefs on 13 August. On the appointed day, the three were led into the royal presence at Buckingham Palace and presented to their majesties by Sir Montague

Ommaney, permanent undersecretary to the colonies. For the occasion, Chief Basil wore a blue-grey lounge suit and a flat-brimmed brown cowboy hat. Chiefs Joe and Charlie wore tweeds, but over them were draped their blankets, and on their heads were their ceremonial fur hats. In Chief Joe's arms were four cedar baskets.

The three of them walked miles of carpeted corridor, through rooms filled with people who stared and smiled in gentle condescension, under mirrored ceilings which frightened Chief Basil, and through massive doors to the throne room. At the farthest end stood the king and queen on a raised platform. The little party trudged up the long room, feeling more and more apprehensive until, when they were halfway there, the king stepped down and came to meet them, shaking Chief Joe's hand and leading them to the queen. At this point, lesser men would have been overwhelmed and tongue-tied, but Chief Joe recognized the gesture for what it was. Years later he told Pauline: "Now you see what great men do. Little man he stay on platform and make we chiefs walk up to him, but the Great White Chief he big man, the biggest man in the world. . . ."[8]

Comfortable now with the royal couple, Chief Joe gave the signal for the interpreter to read the speech which the Catholic priests on the reserve had helped him to prepare.

> May it please your Majesty. Perhaps we are among the most remote of your majesty's subjects but we will give place to none in our devotion to your majesty's person and to the British Crown. Our home is beyond the great Atlantic Ocean, beyond the Great Inland Seas of Canada, beyond the vast wheat-growing prairies of Manitoba, beyond the majestic Rocky Mountains, away on the shores of the Pacific Ocean. We bring greetings to your majesty from thousands of true and loyal hearts beating true beneath the red skins of our tribesmen. And it is because of our love to your majesty coupled with our desire to live in harmony with the white people who are filling up our country that we appeal to your majesty in person. Many years ago, Sir James Douglas came to our country and told us he had been sent by Her Majesty the late Queen Victoria whom we learned to love like a mother and whom we continue to mourn. Sir James told us that large numbers of white people would come to our country and in order to prevent trouble he designated large tracts of land for our use and told us that if any white people encroached on those lands he would remove them which he did, and we received remuneration for other lands

settled on by the white people. But when Sir James was no longer governor, the whites settled upon our lands and titles were issued to them by the British Columbia government. The Indians, being without votes, they can get no redress so they trust His Majesty's ears will be open to their cry. They point out that at one time the white people were glad to employ them but now Chinese and Japanese take their places in the labour market. We know how to work as well as the white man and why should we not have the same privileges as the white man? We ask the King to send some good men to British Columbia who will see and hear and take back a report to Your Majesty. We leave ourselves in Your Majesty's hands and trust we will be able to return to our people with good news.[9]

When he was finished, the chief held out the cedar baskets to the queen, explaining that his twelve-year-old daughter Emma had made them especially for her. One of the ladies-in-waiting stepped forward to intercept the gifts before they touched Her Majesty's hand, but the queen signalled her to step back and took them into her own arms. "The King," reported Chief Joe, "he is so pleased, he laugh when he see the baskets and he make me open them and show inside. Then I hand the great Queen picture of myself and my little girl and she laugh and thank me so pretty."[10] She told him that the next time she went for a picnic with her grandchildren she would pack their lunch in these baskets. Then she gathered them up, said good-bye to the chiefs, and left the room followed by her ladies. "Her dress," said Chief Joe, "when she walk it whistle like the wind in the fir trees on the mountains above my home."[11]

After the queen left the audience chamber, the king spent a further twenty minutes discussing the problems of the coast people and the distressing new game laws. At the end of the conversation, he shook hands with each of the chiefs and patted Chief Joe on the back. And then, according to Chief Joe, he said, "Chief, we see this matter right, but it may take a long time, five years maybe."[12]

Before the chiefs left London the next day, Pauline called once more to wish them a safe journey. This act cemented the special friendship that had sprung up between herself and the chief of the Squamish. On 15 August the three men and their interpreter embarked on the Canadian Pacific's *Lake Manitoba* as steerage passengers, but each of them carried something that most of the first-class passengers would have given much for: a gold medallion impressed with profiles of the king and queen presented by the king himself, and a clear and shining memory of a king's promise.

In early September Pauline and McRaye returned to the drawing room circuit, much in demand since their Steinway Hall appearance and the publicity surrounding Pauline's meeting with the chiefs. The days passed quickly, so that Pauline neglected to write to her brother and sister, and completely forgot Eva's birthday on September thirteenth, but Allen tactfully sent flowers for both of them.

Pauline loved London but, after six months' absence from Canada, found herself battling surges of homesickness. One night at a performance of Somerset Maugham's *The Land of Promise* at the Haymarket Theatre, McRaye looked over to find her lost in thought. The play was set in what Maugham and the play's designer believed a Manitoba homestead would look like and, although it was far from accurate, it had evoked home for Pauline. McRaye leaned towards her and whispered, "Not a bit like the real thing, is it? How would you like to be back on the old Cariboo Trail right now?" She smiled, but moments later was lost in thought again. When the intermission came, she sat quietly writing on the back of her program and, before the next curtain rose, she showed McRaye the first draft of the poem, "The Trail to Lillooet."[13]

Their last performances in London brought no financial gain but added to their prestige. On 2 November they performed aboard the Royal Mail Ship *Victorian* on a "programme of entertainment" in aid of the Liverpool Seamen's Orphan Institute. Pauline gave "Mrs. Stewart's Five O'Clock Tea," which seems to have made the trans-Atlantic crossing remarkably well. Pauline's last performance was given at the Green Park Club, 10 Grafton Street, Bond Street West. The manager, Luther Mundy, was famous for obtaining professional acts free of charge for the London clubs which he managed and, in time, it had become the mark of "having arrived" merely to be asked to perform by him. Almost all performers accepted his invitations; Pauline was no exception.

On this trip, establishing contact with people like Mundy and Pearson had actually been more valuable to Pauline than the rather fleeting successes of the concert platform. These men were capable of promoting both aspects of her career in the future. However, re-establishing herself with her old friends and contacts from 1894 had been very useful, too. "Whole-souled and Irish" Lady Helen Blake was back in London again after five years as the governor general's lady in Jamaica. Delighted to see Pauline, she had set the wheels in motion for her and McRaye to tour the British West Indies. It would be a lucrative trip. Jamaica's white population at that time was not very large—Kingston had only four thousand whites in a total population of fifty thousand—and the black inhabitants would be little interested in the program she offered. But the resident whites were augmented from December to March each year by tourists who had been coming there in increasing numbers for the last half century. Kingston was also becoming a prominent convention site. To cater to these transients, a vast organization of luxury hotels, restaurants and entertainments was developing. Pauline had her eye on this talent market but, in addition, she would carry letters of introduction from Sir Henry and Lady Helen Blake to their old friends among the island's plantation owners. They would be delighted to have her perform at soirées, especially since she came "direct from a London season." The Blakes had also secured the promise of the patronage of the present governor, Sir Alexander Swettenham.

Another old contact and friend, George Alexander, took them to meet the agent for the American Slayton Lyceum Society, which hired the partners to appear in the Midwestern states for the coming July and August. With bookings like this, 1907 promised to be a profitable year.

They arrived back in Halifax in late November but, on leaving England, there had been one sad note. Lucy Webling was not able to come with them; her career commitments were all in Britain, though McRaye had given her reason to believe that they would be partners in the future. With the whimsical sense of humour and the artistic talent typical of the Weblings, she commemorated the departure of her friends with a bon voyage card on which she drew four small elflike creatures, three of them seated on a maple leaf while the fourth is seated by himself in a rocking chair. The caption reads, "The one boy dreams of the three other boys."[14] Lucy had been admitted to the small "in-group" which had actually met The Boys, Felix and Jerusha and Baraboo Montelius, which indicated that her relationship with McRaye was really serious.

Chapter Ten

Chautauqua

PAULINE NEVER MADE her tour of the British West Indies. At 3:30 on the afternoon of Monday, 14 January 1907 an earthquake levelled more than ninety per cent of the city of Kingston, Jamaica. Nearly one thousand people died, including Britain's former postmaster general Sir James Ferguson who had arrived only the previous day to attend the Colonial Agricultural Conference. Hamar Greenwood, in Kingston to attend the Imperial Cotton Conference, escaped injury by running into the street as buildings crashed around him; while he stood watching the ruins burst into flames, he realized that he was wearing all he possessed and this did not include shoes.

In anticipation of the journey to Jamaica in mid-January, Pauline and McRaye had confined their performances since their return from England to the eastern provinces, mostly northern New Brunswick and the English-speaking pockets in Quebec. They had celebrated Christmas in Montreal to give themselves ample time to work their way back to Halifax for a mid-January embarkation. Now, with no prospects left for a sunny working vacation, they set off once more into the snow of the Maritimes.

At the beginning of March they returned to Ontario. McRaye made a scheduled visit to his mother in Brockville, while Pauline settled in with her cousin Kate Washington in Hamilton to rest and write. Though an occasional poem still came from her pen, the bulk of her output was now short stories and articles. She wrote one of these in a day or two at the most and even composed some of them to order. On 4 March Elizabeth Ansley, editor of *Mother's Magazine* of Elgin,

Illinois, wrote to her in care of her cousin Kate, pleading for a "Dominion Day Mother's Story" for its Canadian readers—"any tone or theme" not exceeding three thousand words but please, please could they have it a month from the date of pleading.[1] On 8 April Ansley mailed her a cheque for $17.64 for "Her Dominion."[2] On 7 April *The Boys' World* paid her $57.04 for three stories they had just received: "The Broken String," "Little Wolf-Willow," and "The Lieutenant Governor's Prize."

She also prepared an outline of articles she would write for the 1908 *Mother's Magazine* in response to Ansley's orders for articles about "outdoor sports, mother and child out-of-doors, health exercises, picnics, camping, etc., all written especially for the mother and her family."[4] The first of these appeared in January. It was an article called "Mothers of a Great Red Race," an idealization of the lives of the women of the Six Nations. (The following year she reworked the same material for the *Halifax Herald,* calling it "Iroquois Women of Canada," but in this later version the Iroquois women are portrayed somewhat more realistically.) In February 1908 *Mother's Magazine* published "Winter Indoor Life of the Indian Mother and Children," in June "How One Resourceful Mother Planned an Inexpensive Outing," in July "Outdoor Occupations of the Indian Mother and her Children," in September "Heroic Indian Mothers," and in November "Mother of the Motherless," the story of the three orphaned children and their aunt whom Pauline had met on the CPR train out of Regina in 1904. She had promised Ansley one more article—an "authentic instance of heroic but not dramatic motherhood: the Labrador Lighthouse Keeper"[5]—but this was not published in *Mother's Magazine;* instead, she sold it to the *Vancouver Province* in March 1912 as the "The Unfailing Lamp."

On 6 April 1907 Pauline took leave of her Hamilton cousins and went on to Brantford, checking in at the Kerby House as a guest of her brother. Then for one peaceful week, with no public engagements to interfere, these two spent long hours together as they had when they were children. They must have walked to their old haunts looking for signs of spring, gone to look at Chiefswood (tenanted by strangers now), and stood by the graves of their parents and brother. And they must have talked far into the night, reliving their childhood, worrying about Eva, mourning Chiefswood; Pauline must have talked of her travels, of her need for roots, and Allen must have talked of his wedding. At forty-nine, he was at last marrying Floretta Katherine Maracle, one of their father's people, a schoolteacher from Ohsweken. The wedding was to take place on 25 June.

Of all the family, only Allen was to marry. Although marriage had never been discussed among the Johnson children, all of them when young had fully intended to marry; but Beverly had felt that marriage was denied him by their mother, Eva denied herself that happiness, while Allen had drifted. In the social class that the Johnsons moved in it was easy to allow the years to accumulate waiting for the financially correct moment and socially correct mate, until at last the single state appeared to be the natural one. Allen had finally been saved by a lady who refused to allow him his comfortable bachelorhood; as a result, he was the only one of the three to escape the "waifs and strays" fate that Beverly had predicted.

For Pauline, however, spinsterhood had never seemed natural, and she must have left Brantford with her pleasure in her brother's happiness undermined by pangs of envy. Before she left, a reporter from the *Brantford Expositor* managed to glean the information that she was returning to Hamilton, but this was only partially true. She returned there only long enough to collect her trunk and continue east. On 27 April she sailed aboard the *Lake Erie* from Saint John, New Brunswick. Her destination was Liverpool.

Back in London, she returned to No. 53 St. James Square and installed her collection of Indian artifacts, reindeer hides and photographs. Only two documents still exist to give a glimpse of her activities on this third London visit. One is a souvenir program for the visit of the king and queen of Denmark to London. King Frederick VIII was the brother of Queen Alexandra and had been crowned only fifteen months before he and his queen arrived on this state visit on 8 June 1907. Most of the events of the next four days were official luncheons, military reviews, state dinners and balls, but the royal guests were also taken to the opera, horse shows and the Royal Academy of Art. At one of these latter events Pauline was present and acquired the souvenir program.

The second surviving document is a telegram from the news editor of the *Daily Express*. Apparently they had wanted her opinion on some development in the news, but before they had been able to locate her, the story had gone dead.

Pauline never discussed this trip or her reasons for making it. One biographer speculated that it had been a holiday, but since she had already been off the recital circuit for a month visiting her cousins in Hamilton and an additional week with her brother, this seems unlikely. Her limited finances had never allowed for protracted holidays; three weeks was usually the maximum. If she had gone with only a holiday in mind she must have been disappointed. England was excessively wet that spring, and May and June were chillier than usual. The theatrical season was singularly dull; Madame Melba sang at Covent Garden, Violet Vanbrugh starred in *The Duel* at the Garrick, and the Americans Julia Marlowe and E. H. Sothern brought the season to a close at the Waldorf to less than enthusiastic reviews. Luther Mundy retired from the Green Park Club on 7 June, and George Alexander stood him to a benefit matinee at the St. James in which half of London's stars performed. Pauline probably attended for old times' sake.

She made no public appearances on this trip, and did not even advertise her services as an entertainer. In any case, since she had left McRaye behind she would have had to perform solo or else pick up the British equivalent of "local talent." She had not come to look for a publisher. Although she had completed many more short stories than she had ten years earlier when she had talked of publishing a book, she made no effort to publish them on this trip.

She might have gone to London for a romantic rendezvous, perhaps arranged the previous autumn. However, this is very doubtful. By 1907 Pauline was no longer a romantic figure. Since her desperate illness five years earlier, she had been remarkably healthy, seldom missing a recital. But five years of improved health plus her always substantial appetite had changed her shape considerably. At forty-six, she had become a matronly figure with a noticeable double chin. (For photographs she kept her chin raised to minimize it.) In addition, she despaired of ever marrying and now did little to make herself attractive. Her body no longer followed the elegant lines that had drawn such passionate response from her male admirers; the body that had prompted critics to refer to her as the "Mohawk girl" until she was past forty had disappeared. And on her face were etched lines of fatigue and disappointment.

What Pauline probably hoped to find in London was not a lover but an alternative to her career as a platform entertainer. She had been thirty-one when she launched her platform career. In the fifteen years since she had toured to the Pacific Coast at least seven times, played the Maritimes nine times, catered to the "vulgar" Americans of the north central states four times, been booked into cities on the eastern seaboard five times, and done two London seasons. She had published two books and at least twenty-five articles and short stories. She had had numerous sore throats and attacks of strep throat, survived two bouts of rheumatic fever and a disastrous erysipelas infection. She had lost her brother, her mother, her fiancé and her lover, and had gone through three managers and two partners.

She was tired. It was an effort of will now to put on her buckskins and mount the stage each night. The reserves of energy she had taken for granted fifteen years earlier were gone. For weeks at a time she was too tired from performing to write, and when she curtailed her tour itinerary to buy time for writing, she knew she was being unfair to McRaye. The 1906 London season had affected her like a tonic. Briefly the old energy and enthusiasm had come back and she had swept onto the stage radiating her old magnetism, but she had felt her enthusiasm seeping away long before she headed back to Canada.

The answer to her problem was to reverse the course that Yeigh had set for her in 1892. She must leave the stage and become a writer once more. Not just a poet this time, but a writer of stories and articles with poetry as a sideline, a private luxury. She had proved by her sales to *Mother's Magazine* and *The Boys' World* in April and May that it was possible to write enough each month to support herself. But because the work she was turning out had a limited appeal, she could only count on sales to women's and religious magazines, boys' annuals, and the periodicals that printed Canadian travel pieces. By 1907 her work had been published by only three or four of these publications and she needed a wider acceptance or she would soon saturate her market.

While she was in London in 1906, her work had appeared in the prestigious *Daily Express* and in *Canada,* and as a result it became more highly prized by Canadian and American journals. Unfortunately, as soon as she returned to North America, her British markets had dried up. To Pauline the answer seemed obvious: establish a permanent base in London and make frequent trips to North America to keep her name in front of the public; then she could have the best of both worlds. Gilbert Parker had done this successfully and had even earned a knighthood out of it. Charles G. D. Roberts was more respected at home after he began living part of the time in London and part in New York. Ernest Thompson Seton made forays into his native Canada from his base in New York. Hamar Greenwood and Sir Charles Tupper and Charles Devlin had all happily transplanted themselves to the soil of the mother country and all had thrived.

But what Pauline had to offer had a restricted appeal; there was a limit to the number of articles and stories on North America's Indian population and Canada's beauty spots that the British periodical market could absorb. During her 1907 visit none of Pauline's work found its way into print in Britain, nor did any in the years that followed. The Mohawk Princess was already forgotten. Without regular sales in Britain, she could not afford to establish herself there.

She embarked from Southampton via Cherbourg as a cabin passenger on the United States Mail Steamer *St. Paul,* arriving in New York on 19 June to be in time for Allen's wedding and the beginning of the chautauqua tour on the first of July.

"Chautauqua" had originally been a campground evangelical institution. It started as a summertime program to educate Sunday school teachers and church workers, but by 1900 about four hundred imitations of it had sprung up across the United States. They were all called chautauquas after the name of the upstate New York town where the idea had originally developed, but they had become more secular in their programs. This change was partly the result of a melding with the older American institution called the lyceum, which had its origins in Massachusetts in 1826. The lyceums were dedicated to bringing lecturers and debaters into the smaller towns in a sort of adult education summer school. In time, professional organizers had taken over the lyceums, paying fees to the lecturers. The chautauquas soon took advantage of the organizers' services. The fee that was offered plus the eminent respectability of the lyceum/chautauqua drew speakers such as Ralph Waldo Emerson, Daniel

Webster and Nathaniel Hawthorne, as well as a whole army of evangelical preachers and platform entertainers to leaven the philosophical and evangelical mixture.

Although the chautauquas were permanent institutions, few of them ever established permanent buildings. Band shells to improve acoustics were the exception to the rule. Most lectures and entertainments were staged in large tents set up in the local park. Around them the audience pitched their own family tents, or rented chautauqua tents and camp cots, and settled in for a week or ten days of uplifting and mind-expanding talk. In the Midwest most of the audience consisted of farmers and their wives and families who had taken time off between planting and harvest, leaving one member behind to mind the livestock. This meant that a small but articulate portion of the audience—squalling babies and small boys with peanuts and rubber bands—were not one bit interested in all the uplifting talk. Those on stage had to have excellent projection and witty or mesmerizing delivery to be heard at all. One lecturer, seeking to get a laugh as well as to end the din, asked coyly from the stage, "Why is a crying baby like a good resolution? Because it is seldom carried out!"[6] The audience was not amused.

Entertainers on the circuit needed hardy constitutions since they were fed on campground meals, the ability to cat nap in odd corners since their schedules were often rearranged on short notice, and great reserves of sincerity since "uplift" is hard to fake. Chautauqua audiences expected their full money's worth even when entertainers arrived late after train delays, and even when, at the end of August, they had already given the same speech forty-seven times in as many towns and did not believe a word of it any more. When William Jennings Bryan travelled the circuit, he gave himself some relief by carrying a pair of three-hour-long speeches in his head and making the audience vote on the one they wanted to hear. But for most performers, their topics were established with the lyceum office at the time they were booked; to deviate would have brought down the wrath of the local chautauqua committee and the cancellation of further bookings.

Pauline and McRaye joined the Slayton Lyceum Bureau's circuit in Indiana at the beginning of July 1907. For most of their bookings, they spent one day travelling by rail and a day or a day and a half in the town. From time to time their arrangements coincided with that of another performer on the circuit, but for the most part they were as isolated from the regular stream of life as they had always been. And perhaps this was preferable considering their probable incompatibility with their audiences and with their fellow performers. Professor Pearson, the head of the school of oratory at Swarthmore College, gave a lecture-recital called "Some Favourite Hymns." Congressman Hobson of Alabama exhorted his listeners to understand America's "MIGHTY MISSION!" Governor Bob Taylor was unsurpassed (or so said his publicity) in "amusing, entertaining, and instructing an audience" with his "unique and unsurpassed lecture 'The Fiddle and the Bow.'" Miss Elma B. Smith, "the delightful child impersonator and bird warbler," staged a "Grand Concert of Impersonations and Warblings" all by herself. Two and a half hours of it. The Orphean Male Quartet sang everything from opera to popular songs, but they were outdone by the Cleveland Ladies Orchestra who "surpassed expectations" with their cornet and trombone solos. Governor Henry A. Buchtel of Colorado, who just happened to be a preacher as well as a politician, was famous for having won the governorship by outtalking his opponents. His chautauqua speech was three and a half hours long. Opie Read, the playwright and novelist, was hired to give readings from his books, and the "famous" humourist Strickland Gilliland did a standup comic routine while he peddled his latest best seller, *Off Agin, On Agin, Gone Agin, Finnegan*.

The Johnson-McRaye bookings took them from Indiana to Michigan, and then to Iowa, Nebraska, Colorado, Kansas, Missouri and Illinois. In Indiana, Pauline was billed as an American Indian, McRaye as a French-Canadian *habitant*, probably in an effort to make them seem less foreign to the local farmers. In Illinois it rained so hard that roads and bridges were washed out and the trains ran late. The chautauqua grounds were a sea of brown water and soupy mud dotted with collapsed tents, but the show went on.

In Missouri there was a wreck on the Wabash Railroad outside St. Joseph where they were supposed to perform; it was four in the morning before they arrived in town to find all the hotels occupied by an Elks convention. They were travelling with William Jennings Bryan on this leg of the tour, and the three of them now sat discussing American politics till breakfast time in a little park outside the hotel where they were to have spent the night. Bryan was philosophical about the wreck on the Wabash line; it was the third time that particular railroad had inconvenienced him in this way. When the local paper came out, the day's cartoon showed Bryan sitting in the midst of a smashup with the Wabash line on one side and another rail line marked "White House" on the other. Bryan is saying, "Three times on this line and twice on this!"—a reference to his two attempts to become president. McRaye asked him to autograph a copy of the cartoon and, good-naturedly, Bryan wrote: "Not hurt yet. William J. Bryan."[7] McRaye did not confess that he had earned his bread and butter back in 1899 on the west coast by doing a parody of Bryan's famous "Cross of Gold" speech.

Pauline never wrote about the chautauquas in later years and seldom referred to the tour during interviews. On the other hand, McRaye wrote volumes about his own experiences. Pauline's silence does not signify a lack of success, because the available reviews are full of praise. McRaye's memoirs confirm this. Her unhappiness with the chautauqua tour seems to have stemmed from the reaction she received from the Midwesterners. The states she toured had been frontier country not more than seventy years earlier. At mid-century the "Indian Wars" still raged, and only forty years before Pauline arrived, the Union general Philip Sheridan, setting out to annihilate the savages in the Indian Territory, had issued his often-quoted line, "The only good Indians I ever saw were dead." The reaction of Midwesterners to Indians had not changed much since then, except that they now allowed Indians to be either dead or captive. They rather enjoyed seeing one now and then in a side show or a circus, because it gave them an opportunity to show their children what the enemy looked like. They treated Pauline as if she too were a circus freak, though they were a bit awed by her obvious refinement and talent.

In early September Pauline and McRaye left the circuit in Illinois and headed east. At midmonth they played Boston, and Pauline gave a special recital before the Massachusetts Indian Association at the Vendome. The reception she was given afterwards helped to soothe the wounds of her Midwest encounters, for Boston's "bright literary set" competed for the honour of entertaining her. In the midst of all this lionizing, she gave an interview to a reporter from the *Boston*

Herald. Like most of her interviewers, he was dazzled and charmed by her wit and brilliant conversation. Then something misfired. Pauline had been talking about her poetry when something she said caused the reporter to give her a skeptical glance. That was all she needed.

"Ah, I understand that look," she told him. "You're going to say I'm not like other Indians, that I'm not representative. That's not strange. Cultivate an Indian, let him show his aptness and you Americans say he is an exception. Let a bad quality crop out and you stamp him as an Indian immediately."[8]

She smiled her beautiful white-toothed smile all the time she was speaking, but there was no mistaking the anger behind the words. The reporter, poor soul, had simply raised an eyebrow, but he must have been the scapegoat for all those who had acted condescendingly towards her in the past two months, the people who had marvelled that an Indian could write real poems and behave with company manners just like a white person.

Pauline and McRaye spent the final week of September at the Roycroft Hotel in East Aurora, New York. The Roycroft settlement had been founded about a dozen years earlier around a printing business which had been set up by the author and philosopher Elbert Hubbard. From this base he had published a series of booklets called "Little Journeys" and a magazine called *The Philistine* which contained rambling essays of comment and satire. Of these, only "A Message to Garcia" was of lasting interest. When the printing establishment proved successful, Hubbard opened furniture and leather workshops, a smithy, and an art school to turn out the fine handcrafted articles that were being supplanted by machine-made goods. He added a hotel to the settlement to cater to the visitors who came to look at his industries. Pauline was very impressed by Roycroft and felt that in many ways the workers there lived ideal lives. Hubbard was apparently not a slave driver, and they were free to move about and talk on the job—real innovations at that time.

The hotel was unusual in many respects. Instead of numbers, the rooms were given the names of great painters, writers, musicians or philosophers, and in each one the visitor found an example of the work created by the individual to whom the room was dedicated. But it was the hotel library that attracted Pauline. It was filled with Hubbard's personal collection of rare and valuable books, "some of them worth hundreds of dollars."[9] The library was open to all guests who were free to take books to any part of the building without signing for them. When Pauline asked Hubbard about theft, he assured her that very few books ever went astray. Hubbard capitalized on the fact that his clientele were mostly writers, actors, philosophers and artists by not importing talent to entertain his guests, but encouraging them to provide entertainment for each other.

McRaye, when he wrote of Roycroft in his memoirs, stated that Hubbard was more interested in his own Drummond recitations than in Pauline's work. This is very probably the case since Hubbard's taste ran to hearty homespun philosophy and there was a strong moralistic strain running through his work. Indians did not really interest him.

On 5 October Pauline and McRaye stopped briefly in Winnipeg to give interviews and prepare for a tour of the west. They made up a list of towns that would be expecting to see them again, checked the railway schedules, and mailed out new posters and handbills. It was two years since they had travelled the prairies and three since they had seen the coast; it was country ripe for the picking.

They headed northwest towards Prince Albert and Saskatoon, confident of a welcome in every town along the way. On 4 November they took a day off in Edmonton to greet one of Pauline's old friends, Ernest Thompson Seton. They had not met face to face since 1903, but when Pauline learned he was expected shortly in Edmonton from his six-month research expedition north of Athabaska Landing, she decided to surprise him. Their visit was brief since he had promised to speak to the Canadian Club of Edmonton before catching his train for New York, and Pauline had a performance schedule to keep, but it was long enough to renew the bond of mutual admiration.

On the sixth Pauline and McRaye were off by train for Vernon, and by the twenty-third they had performed their way to Trail in the Kootenays. At this point, instead of continuing westward as they had planned so they could enjoy the mild winter at the coast, they caught the eastbound train for Battleford. The coast would have to wait, because an old friend was getting married.

Pauline had met the Finlayson family of Battleford in the winter of 1898-99, and since then she had been "entertained" in their home every time she came to town. She was fond of the entire family but loved Billy, the youngest member, best, because he made her laugh.

Now Billy was about to get married, and the letter which had reached Pauline in Trail implied that it would not be a real wedding unless she were there. So the trunks were packed, letters were sent cancelling dates, and Pauline and McRaye set off for the celebration.

They could afford this trip because Pauline had just received two cheques from *The Boys' World,* one for $23.23 for "A Night with North Eagle,"[10] which was based on her adventures near Gleichen in 1902, and one for $13.95 for an article called "Winter Indoor Life."[11] The *American Boy* was also showing interest in her work, but since it paid only $5 per thousand words, she decided to stay with the higher paying *The Boys' World.*

They played out the remainder of the year and the early months of 1908 on the prairies, then again climbed aboard the eastbound train for the Maritimes. April was devoted to New Brunswick, and even if the financial returns were not always what the performers hoped for, Pauline received tremendous moral support from her women fans. The church ladies group that had sponsored her in Saint John sent their cheque late, as so often happened, because "the returns from the ticket committee were [not] all in," but they sent along an extra gift of ten dollars for Pauline as "tangible proof of the interest we women take in you, Miss Johnson, and in all women who strive for name and place in this Canada of ours."[12]

In the middle of June, after they had played their way across Nova Scotia and Prince Edward Island, Pauline begged for time off. Once again the partners headed west, but this time Pauline left McRaye in Ontario to arrange their fall tour while she carried on across the continent to Vancouver. On 29 June she checked into the Hotel Vancouver for a month's rest.

Four years had passed since she had been in Vancouver, and in that time the raucous, self-important little town had grown appreciably. Almost a hundred thousand people were settled there, but it still bore the signs of a frontier boom town. There were more real estate companies than grocery stores, and most of the business district still had wooden sidewalks. In the West End there were gingerbread mansions, boxwood hedges and Chinese houseboys, while just over the water in Point Grey were stumps and bush and salmon spawning streams. Society's children were dressed in Little Lord Fauntleroy suits and learned to play the piano. Matrons joined the Browning

Club, while their husbands speculated in two-acre lots in Richmond, and they all drove to Stanley Park on Sunday to have their pictures taken beside the Hollow Tree.

When Pauline arrived at the end of June, the new Empress Theatre was just nearing completion, Minnie Maddern Fiske and her Manhattan Company were playing the Imperial Theatre, and Will Rogers and Buck McKee were starring as "lariat throwers" on the Orpheum's vaudeville bill. But Pauline had not come for this kind of entertainment. Instead, she sent a note to Chief Joe Capilano asking if she could visit him. His reply was to send his son Mathias in a canoe, and the two paddled to the North Shore together. There, Pauline was given the use of a light canoe for the duration of her stay; she spent the next month paddling along the shoreline of Burrard Inlet and English Bay. One of her favourite haunts was Coal Harbour.

It was a perfect July, rainless and cloudless, as Pauline allowed her canoe to drift along the shores. The only real annoyance was the tide which often left the upper reaches of Coal Harbour high and dry. For just that reason the Squamish people had named this end of the harbour "Chulk Walsch," which means "the bay that goes dry at low tide." Pauline renamed it "Lost Lagoon" "to please [her] own fancy."[13] Many years later, after this part of the harbour had been dammed off to form a true lagoon, it was officially given the name she had selected for it.

She used her holiday to prepare her contributions to *Mother's Magazine* for 1909, and based the first of them on a legend told to her by Chief Joe Capilano's wife. "The Legend of the Two Sisters" was first published in January 1909. For February she provided "Mother o' the Men," a story about Mrs. Constantine, and for March "The Envoy Extraordinary," a tale of family misunderstandings. Next she began work on the four-part serial, "My Mother," which she maintained was the true story of her mother's life. Finally, for December she wrote an article on inexpensive Christmas ideas for the family called "The Christmas Heart."

The reason for Pauline's visit to Vancouver was the same as for her London visit the previous year: she was looking for a place to retire and write. On 29 June she had told the *Vancouver World*'s reporter that she had come for the summer, then added mysteriously, "maybe longer. . . . There is no place in Canada that has a warmer spot in my heart than Vancouver."[14] Obviously, she had arrived in the city with her mind half made up.

In 1908 Vancouver had three newspapers which could supplement her income from her American markets and give her time to re-establish her market in the journals of eastern Canada. Vancouver had three well-attended theatres which catered to a wide variety of audience tastes, and there was a growing interest in cultural events. Pauline had always drawn good audiences here, and she now planned to use the city as a base for short tours into the Fraser Valley or even farther afield. She had already been introduced to a suitable recital partner, Eileen Maguire, an Irish contralto who gave a recital at the Hotel Vancouver on 6 July. Maguire preferred to stay close to her family in Vancouver, but she welcomed the idea of partnering Pauline on short tours about the lower mainland.

When she left Vancouver on 14 August, Pauline's mind was made up. This was where she would retire. The only question must have been how soon. She would need a "stake" to allow herself time to get organized in a new home and way of life. And McRaye would need time to organize his career without her.

McRaye's reaction must have been a curious mixture of pleasure, sadness and fear. Although he had been expecting this decision for a long time, it would still have come as a shock of sorts. Two years had passed since he had reached an understanding with Lucy that they would marry as soon as the time was right, and now suddenly that time seemed to have arrived. He was to marry and get a new partner all at the same time. But would Lucy be able to cancel her commitments just now? She had a good role in a successful tour; how would marriage weigh against that? McRaye was confident that their partnership would be a sensation since he was always confident of everything he undertook, but surely he felt a little shaken at the thought of starting afresh without Pauline. Although he had been touring for twelve years, only the six and a half years with Pauline had been successful. He knew he had improved, but he did not know whether he had improved enough to headline a show. Would the public come to see McRaye without Johnson? After long discussions and telegrams and letters across the Atlantic, it was decided that Pauline would delay her retirement one more year. Vancouver would have to wait.

She did not announce a farewell tour, probably because she wished to give McRaye the benefit of receptive sponsors on his first tour with Lucy. But the decision also had a lot to do with her loathing of ostentatious emotional displays. She could not have endured two hundred farewell bouquets, or the halting speeches of mayors, or presidents of the Ladies Auxiliary wishing her a tearful Godspeed, or audiences sobbing when she had come to entertain. In the old stage tradition, she preferred to leave them laughing.

While Pauline was in Vancouver, McRaye had arranged a tour that blanketed Ontario, then dipped over the border for dates in Cleveland and Pittsburg. Pauline celebrated Christmas in Hamilton with the Washingtons and afterwards went to tell Allen about her plans for retirement. In January the partners were off across the prairies for three and a half months of one-night stands. And all the way Pauline said her silent good-byes, taking a last look at this small town with its quiet streets, and that one with its gentle people. This bend in the river which had inspired a poem, this street corner which had inspired a story. For her devoted admirers her smiles were unchanged, but to a very few friends, those close and dear to her, she confided her news. Although they cried in sincere regret at losing her, they were happy that she had found a home. And probably in good time, they told each other. She did not look well this year. Her colouring, perhaps. Or maybe it was the dark shadows beneath her eyes. But the Pacific air would do her good!

On 6 May, in Vancouver's Pender Auditorium, Pauline announced her intention of settling in Vancouver. Her audience was overjoyed. The city's first captive poet!

There was one more tour to make while they waited for Lucy to arrive from England. Pauline and McRaye played the Fraser Valley, the Okanagan, and up the Nicola Valley to Kamloops where they held their final joint concert. On 23 August 1909 they arrived home in Vancouver.

The following day Walter and Lucy were married. Despite the fact that both bride and groom were of the smart theatrical set, the wedding was very traditional. It took place in the city's most fashionable church, Christ Church Cathedral at Georgia and Burrard, the Reverend C. C. Owen officiating. Lucy had brought her wedding dress from London—a simply styled empire gown of ivory silk Mechlin lace with a yoke and high collar of finely tucked net. On her handsome head was a large white hat swathed in clouds of white chiffon and trailing long white plumes. She carried roses and carnations. Her attendants were her young niece Lucy Edwards and Evelyn Eveleigh, the daughter of family friends.

At the altar McRaye waited with his best man, Jeremy Howard, a character actor with the D. E. Lawrence Stock Company, which had been playing the city ever since the Empress Theatre opened the year before. In McRaye's pocket were telegrams of congratulations from Lucy's friends Ellen Terry, Lewis Waller and George Alexander.

While they signed the register, Eileen Maguire sang. And Pauline sat misty-eyed; another wedding, but not for her.

All the portents were right for a "happily-ever-afterwards" kind of marriage, and George Edwards, who gave his sister-in-law away, was only trying to be amusing when he told her just before he escorted her up the aisle, "Cheer up, Lucy! The worst is yet to come!"[15]

Unfortunately, George Edwards had sized up Walter McRaye quite accurately.

The day after the wedding the McRayes left for a three-day honeymoon in Victoria. When they returned, Eileen Maguire joined them, and the three began the first "McRaye Company" tour. The high point of their program was a playlet specially written for the newlyweds by Peggy Webling.

Chapter Eleven

Vancouver

PAULINE WAS ALONE, but it was a comfortable solitude of her own making. Her performing career was now officially over, and from this day onward she would write just as she had done in the days before Frank Yeigh had thrust her onto the stage in 1892. However, this time she would have certain advantages as a writer that she had not enjoyed in her youth. She would not be writing from obscurity: everything she wrote would be enhanced by the prestige and glamour of her name. Her work would be given priority by editors, and she could expect the occasional commissioned article or story as well. On the other hand, editors would demand a higher standard of workmanship from her now than they had expected when she was an unknown Mohawk girl and this situation would have financial implications. Although well-crafted writing takes more time, it does not necessarily bring in more money.

In the old days, there had been no insurmountable financial worries. When her work did not sell, her family provided for her. Now her writing must pay the rent and provide all her comforts. She could not count on Allen or Eva for help. There would not even be much in the way of extras from the family estate since most of the rent cheques were eaten up now by repairs on the old house. Its timber frame was still sound, but twenty-five years of tenants had left the place in deplorable condition.

These were all facts that she must have considered carefully while making her decision to retire from the recital stage and turn to writing full time. Now she quietly reorganized her life to fit her new circumstances. She had always stayed at the Hotel Vancouver when she visited the city in the past and though its rates were reasonable—sixty dollars a month for a room and all meals—it was far too expensive for a working writer. As soon as the McRayes left town, she moved into an apartment at No. 1117 Howe Street in the West End of the city. The building had only been completed that year and all four of its suites had been rented immediately because it was in a prime location, just a few blocks to the downtown shops and within walking distance of Stanley Park. Fortunately, the occupant of Suite 2 moved out just at the time Pauline required a home. She arranged for her Saratoga trunk and her valise to be sent to her new address, and then happily sent off messages to Allen and to her cousin Kate asking them to ship the trunks and crates she had left in their care. She could at last surround herself with all the things that meant home.

Pauline always reacted to gifts and surprises like a child, and the day her possessions arrived from Brantford was just like Christmas. Some of her things had been packed away since her mother died eleven years earlier so that she had actually forgotten them entirely, but she must have searched eagerly through the straw for other remembered possessions as she unpacked the crates. There was the round Mission oak table and chair that had come from Chiefswood, and the green china tea set she had intended for her hope chest, and her mother's cut glass decanter and sherry glasses, and all the silver-ware and bonbon dishes and teapots. Then there were the mementos gathered over the years of touring: a reindeer pelt, a beaded Indian "couee" stick, a silver sugar and cream that had been souvenirs of New Brunswick, the pearl brooch from Lady Blake, autographed books and photographs from her fellow writers, and her father's pictures of Napoleon. Everything would need a place in her new home.

The apartment was not large, but it was adequate for one person. There was a sitting room which provided enough space for a couch, the round oak table, and a couple of chairs. There was a place in the kitchen for another smaller table and two chairs, and it was here that Pauline ate most of her meals. There were two small bedrooms; the slightly smaller one, which she called "the steamer state-room," was for the steady parade of friends who came to visit.

Her days quickly developed a pattern: writing, walking, entertaining, and then more writing. Every day, no matter what the weather was like, she went walking, usually to Stanley Park, stopping to rest at Siwash Rock, then marching home again. Many days she arrived back with her skirts clinging soddenly to her legs but with her spirits refreshed. "It's the only way to chase the glooms away—go out, no matter what the weather,"[1] she told a young friend.

She plunged into the writing that had been neglected during the summer tours and the wedding preparations. She had to hurry to fulfil her commitments to *Mother's Magazine* and *The Boys' World* for their 1910 editions. But she had become so used to writing on trains, in hotel rooms, and even backstage at the theatre that this sudden permanence seemed alien. For the first time in seventeen years she could sit at her own desk in her own room to write. She could even leave her work spread out on the table when she retired for the day. There were no trains to catch, no sponsors to appease. There were no costumes to mend where the braid had caught on scenery stacked in the wings or a hem had ripped on a steep backstage staircase. She did not even have to curl her bangs any more.

She worked swiftly on the boys' stories. She had promised eight of them plus a four-part article on the silvercraft of the Mohawks. The inspiration for the silvercraft series had come while she was putting away her Indian costume with its silver badges around the neckline. For the article she simply made sketches of those designs and beneath each one explained its symbolism and how the craftsmen achieved the design in silver. Under "the sun of friendship" badge she wrote:

> Stronger than his hate, stronger than his revenge, stronger than his love, stronger than death itself, is the friendship of a red Indian. Friendship is the power of heat, of light, of strength. Without the sun of friendship the Mohawk holds that the heart of mankind would be the bleached, colourless, bloodless thing that a plant is when grown in the dark.[2]

Pauline could not survive in the dark. She needed to be surrounded by friends wherever she went. And she never lacked for them. She had travelled across a continent to make a home far from the town where she grew up and yet she was still surrounded by friends. Some were people who had come from Brantford to Vancouver (in 1909, there were very few Vancouverites who had not come from someplace else), and many were people she had met in her travels, but many more were the people who naturally gathered around her wherever she went. Even in retirement she radiated the glamour of the stage, and her faithful fans still paid homage. And though she had long since lost most of the innocent, ingenuous quality which had woven such a spell in her early years on the stage, and had substituted expediency for idealism, she still had a charisma that enchanted everyone she met.

At teatime her friends came in droves. Rosalind Edwards was now living close by on Thurlow Street; sometimes she arrived with her three children, but often she came alone just to gossip, and Pauline loved joining the Edwards family for supper. Many of the ladies from the committees that had sponsored the Johnson-McRaye concerts in past years now came calling on their captive celebrity. Pauline, thoroughly enjoying her chance to play hostess at last, welcomed them with her charming smile. One of them, Mrs. Frederick Cope, had come backstage in 1904 and taken Pauline home to be royally "entertained." Now she enjoyed fussing over her and mothering her, and Pauline welcomed the attention.

A young acquaintance from a camping holiday in Ontario paid a call, desperately lonely for the sight of "down-home-folks." This was Bertha Jean Thompson, an elocution teacher now living in New Westminster. Pauline, having lost McRaye, was in need of a new protégé, a new interest, and she opened her arms to this unhappy young woman. She nicknamed her "Tommy" and referred to herself as "Johnlums," and she would sit listening to Tommy's troubles "quietly with a funny look in her eyes," and then say: "Tommy, you're a source of continual amusement to me!"[3]

Tommy brought with her an imaginary friend whom she had dreamed up several years earlier. The creation was a young woman named "Belty," "dressed in a shirtwaist and cloth skirt, a leather belt, and strong cowhide boots." Pauline enjoyed hearing about Belty's adventures but apparently had no respect for the creature. She herself had taken full possession of Felix Joggins and "The Boys" when she parted from McRaye, and now she informed Tommy that Felix did not like Belty. Tommy suspected it was the heavy boots that put him off.

Chief Joe Capilano came to visit. He would sit in one of the straight-back chairs in Pauline's little parlour for an hour or so, then leave without having said more than a half dozen words. Pauline knew enough not to impose on his silence and sat patiently in his company, as wordless as he was. Her reward would come when, after many such visits, he would suddenly say, "You would like to know this?" and then launch into a "wondrous tale, full of strange wild poetry—the kind of folklore which soon will be heard no longer."[4] These tales were the legends of his people.

Although Chief Joe's birth date had never been recorded, he must have been close to sixty at this time and already dying of tuberculosis. During that fall of 1909, both he and his listener must have felt the urgency of the passing days: she to hear the whole range of the Capilano legends, he to deposit them in a receptive ear.

In his mixture of Chinook and English, he told her the stories that were the backbone of his people's history and their customs. And sometimes, when there were other guests for tea in the little parlour, the old man could be persuaded to recount his adventures in London and his reception by the king and queen. Then he would laugh again, remembering Chief Basil's face when he had been frightened by his own upside-down image in the mirrored ceiling of the royal reception hall, and he would smile as he heard the echo of the queen's silk taffeta gown whispering like the wind blowing through the trees.

In October of 1909 Eileen Maguire returned to the city, having left the McRaye tour in Alberta. Pauline was happy to have her company once more since she had the same "whole-souled and Irish" qualities that had drawn her to Lady Blake. She was also the one person to whom Pauline felt she could talk about personal matters.

For some time, probably as much as two or even three years, there had been a lump growing in Pauline's right breast. She had not gone to a doctor. Her mother's instructions about men were partly to blame for this, but also she was disenchanted with doctors. There had been too many of them in her life already. She had been poked and prodded by them during all her bouts of rheumatic fever and erysipelas and strep throat, and none of them had done one bit of good. But since her last terrible illness in the winter of 1901-1902, she had remained reasonably healthy. There had been the odd cold and a touch of laryngitis from time to time, but nothing that required the attentions of a doctor. When the lump first appeared, she had probably considered going for advice, but in her peripatetic existence she would have found it difficult to locate a doctor with whom she felt comfortable.

Subconsciously she must have known what the lump was, but that knowledge might have worked against her seeking help. Every woman at the time knew that the only "cure" for breast cancer was the radical mastectomy. Unfortunately, they also knew that this operation was usually only a delaying tactic since it seldom removed the entire cancer; surgical procedures were not sufficiently refined for that degree of success. By 1900 radium had been used experimentally on cancers in Europe, and in America by 1904, but the first use of radium on human tumours was not attempted until 1914. Pauline must have known what the options were.

Maguire was horrified by Pauline's condition though she had suspected as soon as she saw her again that something was wrong. Pauline was losing her matronly figure. At first, Maguire put this down to her daily walks and the fact that she was doing her own cooking, but there was a shadowed look about her eyes that suggested ill health. After Pauline confessed her problem, Maguire hurried off to make an appointment for her with a doctor, and Pauline, still half-heartedly resisting, finally allowed herself to be taken to see him. His name was Thomas Ransom Biggar Nelles and though he was only twenty-six years of age, he was the most qualified doctor in the city to take on Pauline's case. He had taken his medical degree at McGill, served two years as houseman at the Montreal General, and then gone for further study to the New York Skin and Cancer Hospital. In Vancouver he was registered as a general practitioner specializing in dermatology, but because he was the only doctor with any training in the treatment of cancer, most of the city's cancer cases were in due course referred to him.

Whereas all these qualifications must have recommended him highly to Pauline, there was one other that mattered more. Tom Nelles came from Brantford. He was the son of Thomas Ransom Nelles and the beautiful Georgina Biggar who had been a favourite of Pauline's parents. The Nelles were descended from William Henry Nelles who had fought side by side with Joseph Brant in the Revolutionary War and been given lands for himself and his five sons out of the Six Nations grant. Because of this feeling of kinship she put her entire faith in young Tom Nelles.

But there was nothing Tom Nelles could do for Pauline except deal with her pain. Her condition was already beyond the operable stage.

She took the news stoically, perhaps relieved that there would be no surgery. If there were tears, only Tom Nelles saw them and he never told. From that day until the day of her death she did not shed a tear for anyone to see. She was always cheerful, always witty and gracious and charming. She was touchingly grateful for every kindness, no matter how small. She was thoughtful of others, making sure of their comfort, striving to make them happy. She never complained or lamented her fate or lingered over long recitations of her symptoms. She was at once the epitome of the stoical heroes of her father's people and the stiff-upper-lipped Englishmen of her white ancestors.

But there was no one to record how she behaved when she was alone. There were clues—a few tear-stains on the pages of a letter, an outburst to her sister—but they tell very little of the long hours she spent alone in the little rooms on Howe Street.

All her life Pauline had fought to do exactly what she wanted and had stubbornly refused to do the things others had pressed on her. She had become a writer, then, having been denied the stage, she had taken the next best thing, the concert platform. She had travelled and seen the world, and been accepted by the highest society. She had done all these things while defiantly proclaiming her Indian-ness. But she had regrets. She had looked for love so many times, found it twice and lost it again. Her imagination held half a lifetime of stories and poems still waiting to be born. There were the places she had never reached—Australia, Jamaica. There were the streams where she had never paddled her little light canoe . . . But if she mourned these things, it was in secret.

She wrote at a furious pace now to complete her commitments and earn her living. Work had always been her salvation in time of grief. She refused to allow Maguire to tell anyone else of her plight; she needed to be strong now and sympathy would have weakened her spirit.

Sometime before Christmas 1909 she conceived the idea of putting Chief Joe's legends into written story form. She knew that they were special and should command a good readership, but she also recognized the difficulty in finding the right market for them. They would have to be published in some West Coast journal because of their local appeal. To test the market, in February 1910 she got out the manuscript of "The Legend of the Two Sisters" which she had written for *Mother's Magazine* and took it to the office of Walter C. Nichol, owner of the *Vancouver Province,* whom she had met socially some years earlier. An astute businessman, Nichol was impressed with the idea of being the first newspaper to run a Pauline Johnson series, and he called his magazine editor, Lionel Makovski, into his office.

"This is Princess Tekahionwake whom you probably know as Pauline Johnson of Canada's theatrical trails," he said.

Makovski smiled incredulously. "Not 'A Pagan in St. Paul's'?" he asked.

Her face lit up. "The same," she said. "That was the best piece of prose I ever wrote! How do you know it?"

Then he explained that he had heard it quoted the evening after it was published in the *Daily Express.* He had been listening to a critic goad a young writer when the young man had turned on his tormentor and, to prove a point he was trying to make, had read out the article in full. Makovski never forgot it.

At this point, Nichol broke into the conversation to explain that Pauline had a story that seemed suitable for the *Province,* after which he excused himself and left the office. For a few minutes more they spoke of London, then abruptly Pauline returned to business.

"But I'm taking up your time. I'll leave this story with you. If you can use it, I can follow it up with others."

He looked at the title.

She read the question on his face. "White people call them The Lions but the Indians call them The Two Sisters. I have written their story as Chief Joe Capilano told it to me."

She turned to go. "I am living on Howe Street; the number is on the manuscript. I'm very pleased to have met you." And she walked out.[5]

Makovski was dazzled.

He had come to Vancouver from England three years earlier. After an education at Marlborough College and Heidelburg University, he had entered the newspaper business in Liverpool, writing drama reviews for the *Daily Post*. From there he had returned to London, worked on several papers, and finally headed for Canada looking for a more exciting career. At thirty-five years of age he had been the *Province*'s magazine editor for only a few months when he met Pauline. Suddenly, he had his hands on one of the most promising series an editor could hope for, written by an enchanting lady. He decided to give it first-class treatment and went off to look for the best photographer in the city to illustrate it. He chose George Edwards.

The stories as they appeared in the *Province* were not exactly as Chief Joe had told them to Pauline, nor were they the same as any version his people had ever known. J. N. J. Brown, who was superintendent of the Squamish people at that time, complained that Pauline simply did not fully understand the chief's mixture of Chinook and English which had been thinly stretched to provide words to explain the symbolism and subtle meanings in the legends. The mistakes, he suggested, were in the passage from the teller to the recorder.[6] Perhaps to a certain extent this is true, but even if Pauline had understood every word and every nuance of meaning, they would probably have turned out roughly the same. Pauline *never* retold events exactly as she heard or saw them. She sifted them through her vivid imagination and they emerged on paper transformed. It was not deliberate falsification on her part; she simply could not give a direct translation because she reacted mainly to the dramatic parts of any tale. These parts she bolstered with bits and pieces of drama from her mental storehouse until they were in a form which suited her. She had done exactly this with her grandfather's stories and her embellishments had been excused—even by her family—as poetic licence. Fortunately, these legends were also recorded by others with a keener eye for accuracy, and thus they have been preserved in spite of Pauline.

The *Province*'s readers loved the stories and, not realizing that they had been transformed, accepted them as the authentic legends of the area's aboriginal inhabitants. And, in spite of the transformation of their legends, the Capilano Reserve Indians made no protest and continued to regard Pauline as their friend, probably because in oral traditions it is quite acceptable for each storyteller to add his own embellishments. It is also possible that the Indians did not read the *Province* newspaper.

On 10 March 1910 Chief Joe Capilano died in his sleep. Seven days later, at the little church on the reserve in North Vancouver, two ceremonies took place: the installation of the new chief and the burial of the old one. The women came to mourn first and knelt around the coffin to pray and chant. When they had gone, the elders responsible for selecting the new chief remained in the church with Chief Joe's son Mathias. The young man's sixteen-year-old sister Emma, clutching a picture of the queen who had so graciously accepted the baskets that she had woven, stayed close beside him. The elders took Chief Joe's untanned deer hide from the coffin and draped it over Mathias's shoulders, then bound the old man's multicoloured belt around his son's waist. On his chest they pinned the medals bestowed by the king. Then, as if with reluctance, Mathias slowly wrapped himself in his father's blanket and placed the tall fur hat upon his own head.

When this ceremony was over, the coffin was carried from the church to the graveside in a procession led by the Indian Mission band. There the final service was read and hymns were sung as whites and Indians stood side by side to pay their last respects. The coffin was lowered into the ground, carrying with it a spray of white lilies. Pauline, the representative of the Mohawks, had chosen the flower that to her people signifies peace and power.

Her eyes were dry as she stood by the grave. Then as the people slowly dispersed, Makovski, who was standing by her side, heard her speaking softly and leaned closer to hear.

"I'm coming," she said. "I'm coming. I hear dem angels calling . . . poor old Joe. . . ." Then seeing that Makovski had overheard, she added, "Well, it's the one thing we're all certain of, isn't it?"[7]

Gently, he took her arm and led her from the graveyard.

In those early months of their friendship, Makovski was not told of Pauline's cancer, though he must have sensed that something was wrong. She was having shooting pains in her right arm by this time and often had to cancel appointments or miss functions which she had been expected to attend. Perhaps she still hoped to keep their relationship separate from this thing that was devouring her, because she desperately needed Makovski's admiration and his kind attendance on her: she may have feared that if he knew the truth, the admiration would turn to pity.

But during the summer of 1910, the pain in her right arm came more and more frequently, preventing her from writing for days and then weeks at a time. At last she was forced to tell Makovski of the cancer and explain that she could not complete her series of legends for the *Province.*

Makovski knew perfectly well that she could not afford to give up the series, even though each story paid a mere six or seven dollars. She had little other income at this point. He announced therefore that he would transcribe the stories as she dictated them. So during the evenings of August and September, he sat writing in the little parlour on Howe Street while Pauline lay on the couch and dictated. In this way the legends continued to reach the newspaper regularly throughout the summer. That fall, however, Pauline had nearly two months of remission in which she was able to do her own writing again, turning out a spate of new work. The last of the legends, "The Grey Archway," was completed just before Christmas and appeared in the *Province* on 7 January 1911.

Earlier in the year, through Makovski, Pauline had met Isabel McLean who wrote for the women's page of the *Province* under the pen name "Alexandra." The daughter of Vancouver's first mayor, Alexandra was eminently respectable and travelled in the upper strata of Vancouver's social elite. Through her, Pauline became a member of the newly formed Canadian Women's Press Club, which was eager for members as there were no more than a handful of newspaperwomen in the city. Now, as soon as the news of Pauline's affliction spread, this little group of newswomen began making quiet efforts to help her.

From the summer of 1910, people who came to call on Pauline never knew whether they would find her lying on her couch incapacitated with pain or out shopping and enjoying the sunshine. The attacks, or "spasms" as she called them, came and went unpredictably; she could suffer for weeks or hours. But rain or shine, unless she was totally prostrate with agony or with Tom Nelles's morphine injections, she went walking in the West End, even as far as Stanley Park when she could muster the strength. Her walk had become more Indian-like now, "a flat placing of the foot in front with a straight, almost toeing-in step." She had at last acquired "the Indian Trail"[8] of her father's people.

A number of times, when she was too ill to go any distance, she hired an open carriage to drive around the park, stopping the driver from time to time so that she could walk a little among the trees. One evening in the late summer, when Makovski had been unable to keep their appointment to work on the legends, she was approaching the park by carriage when she overtook a man and a youth out for an after-dinner stroll. Hearing the clip-clopping of horses' hooves in the silent evening, the strollers turned and she recognized two old friends from Brantford: Harry Weir and his son Harold. She had often visited with the Weirs in Brantford, and had enchanted the boy "not only because of the melodious beauty of her voice but because of her extraordinary charm."[9]

Pauline called out, "Why, Harry!" and the two men, recognizing her voice immediately, came over to the carriage. She had not known that they had moved to Vancouver or that Harry Weir was now a partner in a grocery business close by her apartment on Granville Street. The two clambered up to sit on either side of her, and she held each by the hand as they drove around the park.

For fourteen-year-old Harold, who would one day become a columnist for the *Vancouver Sun,* this was a memorable occasion.

> Knowing my father so well and so long, she recited snatches of her lilting verse as the shadows lengthened and the sun prepared to sink in the western sea. As we parted from her, my father kissed her, whereupon I was overwhelmed with hobbledehoy embarrassment. I never saw her again in this life. On that evening she was only forty-nine, but the marks of fatal illness were on her.[10]

She still attempted to give recitals from time to time to augment her income. Eileen Maguire joined her on most of these occasions since there was little hope of Pauline carrying a full program, but she cut down on her outlay of energy still further by reading her prose selections, especially the Capilano legends, instead of reciting poetry. On other occasions, she gave "informal talks" on the legends and traditions of the Mohawk people. For these, she sat down. As time went by, however, she accepted fewer invitations to talk or recite and often had to cancel out at the last minute. But though she was almost always in pain, she remained cheerful in front of her public. Just as she had impressed reviewers and audiences in the past with her charm, she now impressed admirers with her courage and optimism.

Her callers increased steadily in number. Besides Maguire and Tommy and the Edwards family and Makovski, Alexandra made

Pauline her special concern, and installed her young writer-protégé, Annie Ross, as a boarder with the family upstairs in Pauline's building. Presumably the young woman was expected to keep an eye on Pauline from above. In October another dear face appeared in Pauline's doorway; Lucy McRaye had returned to Vancouver to await the birth of her baby. Pauline must have looked upon this coming child almost as a grandchild.

The baby was born at Christmas and was greeted enthusiastically by everyone, especially the Edwards children. Florence (the youngest) was given the task of warming his tiny clothes in front of the stove before he was dressed. However, no amount of love and care could save the little thing's life, for he had a defective heart and his skin was tinged blue with cyanosis. Medical science had not yet tackled this circulatory problem and the child died at six weeks of age. Walter McRaye was on tour in the Kootenays and never saw his son, but when he finally received word of the child's death he wrote a brief note to his wife consoling her, then advised her to go out and buy a new hat. He enclosed a five-dollar bill. [11]

From time to time, young Chief Mathias came to call on Pauline as his father had done, and in the spring of 1911 she helped him plan a trip to Ottawa to confront the federal government with his people's problems. To add prestige to his trip, Pauline wrote to Sir Wilfrid Laurier asking him to receive Mathias. When this was granted the young man was overwhelmed and repeatedly assured Pauline that his greatest desire was to "shake the hand of the government"[12] and to tell Laurier personally that he was loyal to King George V. Mathias's visit to Ottawa was just in the nick of time for later that year Laurier went down to defeat, and though Pauline had crossed paths with his successor, Borden, in 1904, she had never met him.

In June 1911 Pauline promised to give a recital in Hammond, a farming community in the Fraser Valley, but a few days prior to the event she had to beg off. This was her last attempt to make a public appearance. Understanding her plight, the two young women who had arranged the Hammond event substituted a program of local talent, then brought Pauline the profits. They had changed the money into gold pieces and presented it to her in a box of strawberries, the first of the season. She was so deeply affected by their kindness that she could not speak to thank them.

The money was all the more welcome because her funds had come to an end. Writing was impossible—some days because the pain prevented the use of her arm and the rest of the time because the morphine dulled her creativity. She had considered sending to her sister and brother for help, but she had changed her mind; they would only tell her to come back to Brantford. Even the meagre returns from Chiefswood had dried up: the last tenants had moved out and new ones had not been found. She watched for contests in the newspapers and tried to write acrostics, but the effort was too much. At last she decided to sell some of her family heirlooms, knowing that in a boom town like Vancouver there would be plenty of buyers.

Before she could carry out this plan, her friends tactfully intervened. However, they knew that donations were only a temporary solution since Pauline stubbornly resisted charity. Alexandra, being an extremely forthright and determined young woman, took the matter in hand and began investigating ways to provide Pauline with an income without making it look like charity. She knew that the Musson Book Company had been interested in publishing *The White Wampum* as part of their Canadian Masterpiece series. Pauline had rejected the offer because it would have paid very little in royalties, but Alexandra sensed that there was another way to use this idea. She began to gather the nucleus of a committee about her to tackle the problem.

On 2 August 1911 Pauline's protégé, Tommy, was married in Christ Church Cathedral, Vancouver, to Harry Stevenson. Pauline was one of the witnesses. She looked pale and drawn, and her clothes hung loosely on her body, but she smiled radiantly for the sake of the bride. Late that night, she sat alone at the round table in her sitting room and in great pain wrote these words:

Dearest little Tommy,

It is only a little note, darling, but I want you to know that I am thinking of you very lovingly, that I am hoping for you all that is good, and happy, and inspiring, and noble, and above all, humanizing. Love is hard to ensnare, hard to appropriate as one's own. I am so sure H. will make you happy if you will only leave yourself gently and sweetly in his hands. You looked so well today, so effectual. I was very proud of my little campmate of years ago, and someway or another I had a certain pride in H. too. He is very real, Tommy dear, very manly

and devoted. Try to make him happy as well as yourself. It is a poor
rule that does not swing both ways. Good night dear old girl, and may
all the happiness go forth to you that your first girlish idealization
longed or wished for—and for my part—this—[13]

Her signature was blurred with tears. It was the closest she would
ever come to expressing her regrets and her longings. For a brief
moment she had let down the barriers, probably because of the
occasion. She had always been the bridesmaid, never the bride.
Though she had become famous from coast to coast as an entertainer
and a poet, though she had shared tables with nobility and confi-
dences with the great men and women of her time, though she was
always surrounded by people who loved her, she had wanted one
thing more than she had wanted any of this: she had wanted to be
married.

When she told Tommy that "love is hard to ensnare, hard to
appropriate as one's own," she must have been seeing the faces of
Drayton and Wurz again. And they must have been in her mind when
she had written playfully to Tommy on an earlier occasion: "The Bug
says 'John, males is false, very false—don't you trust 'em,' and the Bug
knows."[14]

Oddly enough, though the false Wurz was a continent away, the
false Drayton was right there in Vancouver. He had come to the city
in 1904 to head up the western division of his company, and then four
years later had formed a new company, the Vancouver Financial
Corporation. He and his wife lived in the West End just six blocks
away from Pauline's apartment and they were part of Alexandra's
social set.

In September 1911 Alexandra finally assembled her forces at the
home of the mayor, Charles Manley Douglas. Present were the
members of the Women's Press Club, the Women's Canadian Club,
Lionel Makovski and Bernard McEvoy of the *Province*, and Sir Charles
Hibbert Tupper. The committee had decided that the legends of the
Capilanos should be published in book form with the profits to be
paid into a trust fund to provide Pauline with an income for her
remaining months. In order to finance the project, the Women's
Canadian Club held a recital in the Pender Auditorium with Mrs.
Blanche Holt Murison giving a "sketch" of Pauline's life and Isabel
Ecclestone MacKay reading from her poems. The profits from the

recital along with some private contributions enabled the fund organizers to order Sunset Publishing to print the first thousand copies of the book. Over Pauline's repeated objections, it was called *Legends of Vancouver* rather than *Legends of the Capilanos*—which Pauline had chosen to honour her old friend, Chief Joe—because it was believed that it would sell better. This first edition was improperly proofed and bound only in paper covers, but even with very little publicity, it sold out almost immediately through Vancouver bookstores.

The fund organizers were now ready to launch the ambitious part of the project. With the proceeds from the first edition, they ordered another thousand copies and began advertising in earnest. At this point, Walter McRaye returned to Vancouver and volunteered his services. He persuaded Pauline to autograph the books to add to their value and as a result he was able to sell them easily at two dollars apiece, an exorbitant sum for a book of short stories. Autographing the books also helped Pauline to feel part of the project and now, whenever her arm allowed, she inscribed her name in copy after copy. McRaye then began a letter-writing campaign, contacting everyone they had ever met on their travels: tycoons and hotel-keepers, theatre owners and leading ladies, poets and politicians. He told them simply of Pauline's plight, described the book, and asked them to send two dollars for an autographed copy. But he warned them above all not to make it look like charity and not to dwell on her illness in letters to her.

All this took time and in December, long before any profits had accrued, Pauline's funds were once again completely exhausted. Luckily, an old friend in Brantford, Mrs. A. Hardy, learned of her need and went out canvassing among some of the more affluent citizens of the city. By calling on eminent men like Alexander Robinson, Harry Cockshutt, A. J. Wilkes and E. L. Goold, she collected five hundred dollars in the space of a few hours. This gift arrived in time for Pauline's Christmas and provided her with necessities until well into the spring. By this time the book fund was able to support her.

In February of 1912 Pauline's condition became suddenly worse and by the end of the month it was believed that she had only weeks to live. Once again Alexandra organized her forces. Money was coming in at a steady pace, thanks to the group's advertising campaign and

McRaye's efforts, so it was decided that all the resources of the fund should be used immediately to provide Pauline with better medical care. Dr. Nelles agreed that she needed round-the-clock nursing.

A private hospital had just been opened on the northeast corner of Bute and Robson streets. It was a porticoed three-storey structure, the former home of a fashionable doctor, but it had been converted into an up-to-date nursing home by Mrs. G. W. Moran. Alexandra and her committee looked it over and found it suitable, then enlisted Tom Nelles's help in persuading Pauline to be admitted. She was given a sunny private room on the second floor and her friends decorated it with her favourite possessions. Then everyone sat back and waited for the end.

But Pauline did not die. Instead, as spring advanced she began to gain strength. By early June she was able to write again. One of her first letters was to her old friend Yeigh to thank him for a recent gift of money. Her close encounter with death had not diminished her mental acuity or her joy of living.

> My dear good Yeigh-man,
>
> Once again I have another evidence of your splendid old-time loyalty and friendship for me. What am I to say? How am I to thank you for this cheque that shows so unchanged an interest in me, so much of effort and work on your part to give me less worry, more comfort in this long, long, tedious, irksome illness? It seems so little for me to write that I appreciate it, and you, and your ever sincere good fellowship, and thought of me. You have always been the same old friend, but this unexpected proof of it has swept me off my feet with gratitude and I can only express my thanks, by using this money as I know you and the good old Brantfordites would desire me to—to give myself what care and comfort my illness demands with some little fresh air pleasure thrown in now and again while our beautiful summer lasts.
>
> I am in hospital, but just now I am very well. I go out walking daily, and can take many little enjoyments when I am not suffering pain. My splendid young doctor is in the East for a much needed rest and I promised him to remain in Hospital until his return, although I have not had a heart "spasm" for seven weeks, and my arm is in good working order as you can see by my writing. . . .
>
> Dr. Nelles is about thirty-two or three years of age I should guess, and without doubt the most skillful medical man I ever had attend

me. He has pulled me up on my feet time and again, over and over, when the whole city thought I should never be seen again walking its lovely thoroughfares. I have true and loyal, and many friends here but none who I regard more highly than this clever, kind young doctor. He has given me hours and hours of attention when he has been rushed with work, and wearied with anxiety, and his skill in my case amazes both my friends and myself. I have just come through two months of being in bed, much of the time in extreme pain, but I am able to walk down town and in Stanley Park and by English Bay, able to shop and sew and write, and laugh and enjoy life for a little while before another of the inevitable spells catch me, and for all this I thank my good doctor and all my good friends who have put their hands deep into their pockets in Brantford and in Vancouver that I may have comforts and pleasures, when I am too ill to wield a pen to earn my own "Muck-a-Muck" as the Chinook tongue hath it. And now comes this gift from Toronto—I want you to thank every contributor to it, thank them personally, one and all, for me. In my public life I must have builded better than I knew, my good old Yeigh-man, that my old townsmen should so regard and remember me. . . .[15]

So Pauline went back into the world again, frail and thin, but still alive. During one of her shopping expeditions on Granville Street the novelist Ethel Wilson saw her. The street was crowded and Pauline walked very slowly, lost in "sombre thought." In spite of the ravages of her illness, Wilson recognized her easily because as an eleven-year-old she had met her at the close of a recital in the Homer Street Methodist Church. Propelled forward by relatives to shake Pauline's hand she had heard her say, "You may come to see me if you like." Wilson had not gone, too self-conscious, too overwhelmed by adolescent inadequacies to risk such a visit. Now, as she watched Pauline thread her way slowly through the crowd, she felt somehow responsible, as if this thing that had attacked her had been the result of Wilson's withheld love.[16]

Pauline now embarked on a new project which she had had in mind for a long time: the preparation of a collected edition of her poems. It would contain all the poems in *The White Wampum* and *Canadian Born* plus a selection of those she had written since. Many of this last group had never been published or recited in public and required reworking before they could be included. A number of them, such as "Brandon," "The Trail to Lillooet," "The Lost Lagoon," and "Calgary of the Plains," reflect her years of travel. "In Grey Days" and " 'And He Said Fight On' " are quite specifically about her illness and approaching death; "Day Dawn," and "The King's Consort" are laments for lost love, though they contain such resignation that the poignancy is blunted. The publishing committee now added this new volume to their project, but this time they agreed that Pauline's title, *Flint and Feather,* was quite suitable.

At the same time, the ladies of the Press Club began preparing some of Pauline's other prose selections for two books. The first was composed of the boys' stories that she had submitted to *The Boys' World* since 1906, and was to be called *The Shagginappi* after the title of one of the stories. The second volume were stories that had been submitted to *Mother's Magazine* and included her four-part story, "My Mother." This book was called *The Moccasin Maker.* Both were published posthumously in 1913.

Ever since they had been invited to take part in the original publishing venture, the ladies of the Women's Canadian Club had taken a proprietary interest in Pauline, gradually stepping up their efforts to minister to her. At the same time, the Daughters of the Empire began yet another campaign of aid, designating their local chapter "The Pauline Johnson Chapter." Both groups placed Pauline high on their "shut-ins visitation" lists, but she also received regular visits from the presidents, Elizabeth (Mrs. Jonathan) Rogers of the Canadian Club, and Lady Tupper of the Daughters. Both women were efficient, hard-headed and aggressive. They would have succeeded brilliantly in the world of business, but instead they lived their lives as consorts to minor tycoons, channelling their talents into organizing ladies clubs, fund drives, and cultural events. Pauline was therefore ideal for their purposes: she represented culture, and she needed funds. Although both women were determined to look after her, it was the less aggressive of the pair, Elizabeth Rogers, whom Pauline gradually allowed to take over the management of her personal affairs.

In mid-August Pauline's spasms began again and Tom Nelles stepped up the morphine injections. Although she continued to walk in the West End whenever possible and even occasionally went as far as Stanley Park, she was a barely recognizable shadow. The gaunt outlines of her face emphasized the features of her father's race more than ever before. But she seemed somehow happier, as if at last reconciled to her death and appreciative that in her reprieve she had been given time to muster her forces to depart from life more gracefully.

Some of the credit for her new peacefulness may have been due to the efforts of Reverend Owen of Christ Church Cathedral who paid regular calls and offered her communion. Pauline had done nothing over the years to indicate that she shared her parents' and her grandfather's view of Christianity, and had even of late taken to referring to God as "The Great Tyee," but since she was still nominally an Anglican, the Reverend Owen persisted. She never rebuffed him, but neither did she seek out his ministrations. After a time she allowed him to administer communion to her and seemed to be content that he had agreed to conduct her burial.

It was at this point that McRaye did something so ill-conceived that it almost outweighed the good he had done Pauline in acting as salesman for *Legends of Vancouver*: he wrote Eva Johnson inviting her to come to her sister's bedside. He seems to have been convinced that sisters should be reconciled at such a time and that Pauline needed to have family beside her at the end. She had long since given up on both Eva and Allen. She had written them of her illness but had received little comment from either. Then in June, after she entered the Bute Street Hospital, she received a short letter from Allen enclosing a clipping from an eastern newspaper. It quoted a Vancouver source as saying that Pauline was in actual want and would never write again. Furious, she wrote him a letter to illustrate that she could still write. It was a bit late for Allen to be showing concern.

Eva was still living in New York when she received McRaye's letter and was understandably less than enthusiastic about quitting a perfectly good job, but, convinced that she was needed, resolutely packed her bags and set off for Vancouver. The two women had not set eyes on one another since the summer of 1907 when they had met at Allen's wedding. Eva's major concern then had been the repairs needed at Chiefswood. Pauline's thoughts had been on her own failure to find a place to retire. Now Eva's thoughts were still primarily on Chiefswood as she headed west to sit at her sister's bedside.

The reunion of Pauline and Eva followed a pattern quite predictable when estranged family members decide to patch up their relationships. They greeted one another with great warmth and affection, greater by far than anything they had shown one another since they were children. There were tears over Pauline's plight, and Pauline confessed to the anguish she had felt over the naming of her book. "Why didn't you fight them?" asked Eva. "I was too sick!"[17] Pauline told her and felt she had an ally at last who completely understood her.

But within days, the old antagonisms had arisen once more, and predictably the biggest battles were waged over Chiefswood. Eva wanted Pauline to sign her share of the house over to her before she died. Pauline insisted that she would will it to her, but this was not good enough for Eva. Pauline must have recognized that it made no difference whether she gave her share to Eva now or later, but she would not submit to her sister's bullying. So Eva continued to nag.

Then there was Eva's determination to take Pauline "home" to Brantford. Pauline was horrified; she had made up her mind to end her days in Vancouver and had even chosen her burial spot there. Left out of the preparation for her sister's death, Eva became a general menace. She renewed her battles with McRaye, and out of Pauline's sight and hearing McRaye vigorously held his own. She harassed Alexandra's committee, antagonized Elizabeth Rogers and Lady Tupper, and gnawed at Makovski like a dog with somebody else's bone.

Jean Stevenson blamed the differences between the two women on the fact that Eva "was chiefly English while Pauline was nearly all Indian. . . . She felt so responsible for Pauline though her responsibility took a form which offended 'John' to a cold lasting anger."[18] Eva had spent her whole life organizing people and events; she could not believe that Pauline had already organized her death to suit herself.

Although there was anger in Pauline's reaction to Eva, there was fear, too. She did not want to go east. She was well looked after in the little hospital, she had an excellent doctor, she was surrounded by people who loved her, and she had an income from *Legends of Vancouver* to provide for her needs. Threatened with being torn from all this, she summoned Makovski to her room and in front of all the nurses made him swear that on no account would he allow her to be taken east. Thus reassured, she left orders with Mrs. Moran that Eva should be admitted only at limited, stated times. Contrary to expectations, Eva did not leave town; she settled in to wait for the end. The problem of Chiefswood had not yet been resolved.

In September 1912 the Duke of Connaught, now governor general of Canada, came west to open the new Connaught Tunnel on the CPR just east of Revelstoke. Since his itinerary also included civic functions in Vancouver, he was prevailed upon to pay a visit to Pauline. Makovski later claimed that he had suggested the visit when he was covering the tunnel-opening for the *Province;*[19] Eva claimed the duke had come at the request of the Six Nations Council of Chiefs.[20] Fortunately, Pauline was left to believe that his visit had been his own idea and she prepared happily for it. The nurses helped her to dress in a new blue and gold kimono, and they dragged out the old red cloak she had worn with her Indian costume and draped it over the chair he was to sit on.

He arrived in a carriage on 20 September with his A.D.C.; a police escort preceded them. Mrs. Moran ushered them upstairs past beaming and conspicuous nurses in fresh uniforms eager for a close look at the important visitor. Then the door closed on Pauline's room and the spectators were left to speculate for half an hour as to what was going on. For a while the conversation dwelt on the duke's memories of Chiefswood and her family and of the historic ceremony that had taken place on the reserve so many years before. Then Pauline made a request. Would he allow her to dedicate her collected poems to him? He would be delighted.

Before the duke left the hospital, he asked Makovski if there was anything more he could do, and he was told there was. A month or so earlier, Clare McCartney Fitzgibbons of the Women's Press Club, who wrote under the pen name "Lally Bernard," had telephoned Elizabeth Rogers to suggest that since Pauline had expressed a desire to be buried in Stanley Park, perhaps Mrs. Rogers could use her influence to gratify this wish, her husband being the senior member of the Parks Commission. There was only one problem in arranging it: the park did not belong to the city. It was leased from the admiralty. Mrs. Rogers was not daunted by this setback, however, and embarked on the task by first obtaining Pauline's assurance that she really did wish to be buried there. Then she asked her husband to apply to the admiralty for permission. The admiralty duly considered the request. After noting that no one had been buried within the park since the coming of the white man, and cautioning against the setting of precedents, they finally gave permission on one condition: Pauline must be cremated. Mrs. Rogers took this answer to her. Pauline laughed. "Some people tell me I've got to be burnt anyway whether they bury me in a cemetery lot or not. Well, they can burn my body in this world to make certain of it! As for my spirit, that will be between the Great Tyee and myself."[21] Rogers returned her answer to Ottawa.

The negotiations had reached this stage when the Duke of Connaught arrived for his visit. Makovski's request was that the duke should speed up the formal approval since time was growing very short.

"I'll see what I can do directly I return to Ottawa,"[22] he said.

In December *Flint and Feather* was received from the printers. Pauline had been unable to proof it herself but had dictated the necessary changes to Elizabeth Rogers. She was very pleased with the result and now set about autographing every copy that was to go out for the Christmas trade though each signature caused her excruciating pain. The seventh edition of *Legends of Vancouver* was issued the same month, but by now Pauline only autographed those intended for personal orders.

Just before Christmas Charles Mair, whose *Tecumseh* Pauline had praised extravagantly, arrived in Vancouver for a visit. He was grief-stricken by the change he found in her. "The worn face, with its sad but welcoming smile, the wasted form, the hand of ice! Never can I forget the shock as my thoughts ran back to the beautiful and happy girl of former days."[23] When he left, she followed him to the head of the stairs. And as he reached the front door he heard her call out a last good-bye. She had used a Chinook word of farewell which if taken literally means "yellow weather," a fitting description of the months that remained to her.

Just before Christmas she decided to settle her differences with Eva, who had finally acquiesced in the matter of Chiefswood and allowed Pauline the right to settle it in her will. Now to Eva's complete consternation, Pauline graciously signed her share of the house over to her sister. She also returned to her several small tokens that Eva had given to her long ago and a number of family mementos that Eva had set her heart on. At the same time, she returned to McRaye his gifts.

Pauline had once told Tommy Stevenson that if she knew she was going to have a lingering death and be a burden to others she would end it quickly.[24] However, she continued the battle to survive even though she was little more than a skeleton, her right arm was useless and her lungs were affected. She clung to life with a terrible will, perhaps waiting for one more remission like those over the past three years that had renewed her battered life. Or perhaps she only clung because she had always refused to submit to bullying.

All through January and February of 1913 she stubbornly resisted death. Sometimes she even emerged defiantly to walk the streets of the West End. Several times, heavily sedated, she was able to spend an evening with friends. It was as if she had to live out the words of her own poem:

> Their ensign will not crown my battlements
>   While I can stand and fight.
> I fling defiance at them as I cry,
>   "Capitulate? Not I."

At the end of February Tom Nelles told her friends that she could not possibly live more than a few days, and Eva settled into the chair beside her bed to wait. McRaye came and went not knowing what to do with himself in the interminable vigil. Elizabeth Rogers came, held Pauline's hand, and departed. Makovski, for whom she had coined the private title of "Dearest of All Men," came, kissed her, and left.

Though drugged with morphine, Pauline was fully conscious. She watched them coming and going, and she consoled them. But she was past worrying about them. She had remained in Vancouver to the end as she had wished: the Women's Canadian Club had agreed to supervise her funeral exactly as prescribed and permission had been granted for her burial in Stanley Park. Everything was in order.

On the morning of Friday, 7 March, Eva finally gave in to fatigue and wandered into the adjoining room for a nap. Her place was taken by the nurse on duty, Jessie Leitch, who sat quietly reading, rising to check on her patient from time to time. At midmorning she heard Pauline sigh, and, leaning over the bed, she discovered that Pauline had at last been released from her suffering.

Nurse Leitch woke Eva gently and told her the news. She was somewhat startled by her reaction.

"Why wasn't I called in time?" she demanded.

Chapter Twelve

Purification By Fire

"WHY IS IT," Pauline once asked, "that we rejoice when a soul is born into this world of sorrow and mourn when one passes through to the Happy Hunting Grounds?"[1]

Nine days before she died, Pauline had signed the final version of her last will and testament in the presence of one of the junior partners in Sir Charles Hibbert Tupper's law firm. In it she described quite clearly and unambiguously her wishes in the matter of her burial and the conduct of her mourners.

> I hereby direct my trustees and request them and the officers of the Pauline Johnson Trust Fund to see that my body is not taken east after my death, but that the same is cremated either in the City of Vancouver or in the City of Seattle or the nearest possible point, and my ashes disposed of as near to the Pacific Ocean as possible.

> I particularly desire that neither my sister or brother wear black nor what is termed mourning for me, as I have always disliked such displays of personal feelings.

> I desire that no mourning notepaper or stationery be used by them, and that no tombstone or monument be raised in my memory, as I prefer to be remembered in the hearts of my people and my public.

> When dead, I desire to be dressed in my grey cloth evening cloak, with my small gold shield-shaped locket (containing the photograph of a young boy) fastened round my neck by my small gold chain. Also I desire to wear my gold ring of the design of two serpents and to have my silver and ebony crucifix placed in my hand.

The Vancouver chapter of the Women's Canadian Club to whom Pauline had entrusted her final disposal was little more than three years old, but there were already 750 enthusiastic patriotic ladies in the fold–Vancouver's social elite. Since their husbands comprised almost the entire industrial, business, trade, and political community of the city, among them the ladies commanded all the forces necessary to stage a minor revolution. They were, therefore, perfectly equal to the task that Pauline had assigned them. Her body would not get out of the city.

As directed, they dressed her in the garments and jewelry she had selected and prepared her for cremation. Apparently, neither the nurses nor the ladies in charge opened the locket that they placed about her neck. Elizabeth Rogers, however, had already seen what it contained; some weeks earlier Pauline had shown it to her. In 1945, at the request of Vancouver archivist Major J. S. Matthews, Rogers agreed to record her recollections of that occasion. "It was a photograph of a man," she told him, "but I refrained from asking who it was, and she did not inform me."[2]

Who was the person in the picture in the locket? In her will Pauline had called him "a young boy"; Rogers called him a man. Did Rogers assess his age incorrectly? Was he a teen-ager, and what teen-aged males did Pauline hold dear? Or was it a youthful picture of a man whom she had held dear?

And which of the males in her life did she hold so dear that she wished to take his picture with her to the fire? It could not have been Yeigh or Smily or McRaye or either of her brothers because none of these had inspired that kind of devotion. It might have been O'Brien, but that relationship seems to have cooled to a pleasant friendship by the turn of the century. If it had been a picture of Makovski or Nelles or Drayton, Rogers would have recognized him. If it was her father as a youth, why would she refer to him as "a young boy?"

Of all the men in her life, the only one who cannot be completely ruled out is Charles Wurz, partly because so little is known about him. He is the only one who could have still represented a romantic dream to her. It is irrelevant that he squandered her money and abandoned her to fend for herself; men have done far worse and still been adored by the women they have left behind.

There is one more peculiarity in the matter of the locket. Before she had shown the picture to Elizabeth Rogers, she explained to her very carefully that she wished it to remain a secret. Then she opened the locket and showed her what was in it, thereby contradicting her own directive. It was almost as if she really wanted her to ask the man's identity. But Rogers, well-bred lady that she was, did not ask such questions, and Pauline was left with a secret that she may have preferred to share.

In the course of her long illness, Pauline's face and body had become so emaciated that there was little trace left of the enchantingly beautiful woman she had been. Realizing that she now looked grotesque, she had told Rogers that she did not want anyone to see her after she was dead. But as soon as her body had been laid out in its grey velvet lined coffin in the hospital's reception room, a steady parade of friends and admirers and curiosity seekers trooped in to gaze at the sad face she had wanted to hide. The sculptor Charles Marega even arrived to take a death mask.

Rogers took her responsibilities seriously and immediately after Pauline's death tackled Mayor Baxter to have him declare a public half-holiday on the day of the funeral. The mayor huddled with several aldermen and returned with the pronouncement that such a holiday would be "more honoured in the breach than in the observance." Instead, he decreed that all city offices should be closed that day from two to three in the afternoon and that flags should be flown at half-mast.

Meanwhile, on Sunday, 9 March, in the Mohawk Church on the Six Nations Reserve near Brantford, a memorial service was held to mark her passing. Said Principal A. W. Burt of the Collegiate Institute of Brantford, "In the death of Miss Pauline Johnson we have lost one of the greatest, if not the greatest, of the women poets of Canada. Canada has sustained a great loss."[3]

On Monday, 10 March, the funeral cortège left the Bute Street Hospital at 1:30 for the three-block journey to Christ Church Cathedral. The carriage containing the coffin was flanked by the honorary pallbearers: Fred Cope, A. B. Clabon, G. S. Forsythe, J. J. Banfield, Capt. M. Moran and F. T. Maguire. They were followed by a long parade of the city's distinguished men and women in horse-drawn carriages, though a few at the end of the procession drove automobiles. Mayor Baxter represented the city with Aldermen

Mahon, Woodside, Hepburn and Crowe. The Parks Commission officially sent W. R. Owen, but Jonathan Rogers also attended with his wife. Lady Tupper led the Daughters of the Empire, and the Pauline Johnson Chapter of the Daughters sent Mrs. Townley. Mrs. Jonathan Rogers and Mrs. Fyfe-Smith marshalled the ladies of the Women's Canadian Club who had been advised by a notice in the newspaper that they were all expected to attend. The Canadian Club sent Ewing Buchan and Mrs. R. H. H. Alexander, and Isabel Eccleston MacKay joined the procession for the Women's Press Club. Behind her came representatives of almost every organization that had been formed in the young city. Near the very end of the procession walked Chief Mathias and Superintendent J. N. J. Brown with a large group of Indians from the Capilano Reserve.

Silence fell over the streets as the solemn parade moved up Robson Street and down Burrard to Georgia. The sidewalks were lined with people, their heads bowed, many of the men holding their hats in their hands. On every public building, flags had been lowered to half-mast. Long before two o'clock, Christ Church Cathedral was crowded and the street outside was jammed with those who could not be admitted. Quietly they parted as the hearse appeared and the pallbearers lifted the coffin to carry it into the church.

Through the stained-glass windows the afternoon sunlight fell across the coffin and the flowers banked around it. Pauline had loved flowers. Once when the three-year-old from the upstairs apartment on Howe Street had brought her a bunch of dandelions, she had placed them reverently in a vase. She had adored all the bouquets given her in the course of her career: the carnations at the unveiling of the Brant Monument, Kit's sad brown bouquet in Copper Cliff, the lieutenant governor's roses in Regina. But, believing that flowers were for the living not the dead, she had specifically requested that there should be no flowers at her funeral.

The Daughters of the Empire felt they were honouring her wish by working a pall in leaves only—simple ivy leaves. The Women's Canadian Club provided a wreath of laurel tied with a purple ribbon to be placed on the coffin. The Society of Fine Arts sent a wreath of oak leaves. The rest was flowers: wreaths of lily of the valley, hyacinths, roses and carnations, crosses of violets and daffodils, lyres of narcissus, sprays of orchids and palms, tribal badges made out of hyacinths and tulips, intertwined hearts of roses and baby's breath, and bouquets of lavender and primroses. Never in the short history of the city had so many flowers been ordered for one funeral.

To the chagrin of Rogers and her committee, the organ broke down so that "The Dead March" which should have begun the service had to be replaced by the choir's offering of "Peace, Perfect Peace." The Reverend Owen then gave a short funeral service omitting all references to Pauline's career since he could have added nothing to the congregation's knowledge of her. Reverend Vance read from the Bible, and the service ended with the choir singing "Crossing the Bar" as it led the way out of the church to the hearse.

Outside, the crowd had grown larger, waiting in silence for the end of the service. The coffin was placed in the hearse, the dignitaries returned to their carriages, and the procession set out once more, this time along Georgia Street between rows of "silent red men . . . who stood motionless as statues"[4] and men and women openly weeping. The coffin was at length deposited at Mountain View Cemetery for cremation.

On 13 March Rogers and Makovski were called to the funeral home to collect the ashes. Since there were no proper urns available, the ashes had been placed in a tin can, either a coffee or baking powder container, which had been painted brown and tied up with a white ribbon dangling the label "Pauline Johnson." One of the undertaker's clerks tried to open the tin to show them the ashes, but the lid fitted so snugly it would not come off. With great resourcefulness, he got a letter opener and began prying at it with renewed determination.

Rogers, fearing that the lid would suddenly fly off, stopped him. "Don't do that," she told him, "don't do that! Leave it alone. You'll spill Pauline Johnson all over the floor!"[5] He stopped, unsure what to do next, and Rogers reached out and took the can from him.

A small square concrete box had been prepared by the city works department and deposited at the funeral home along with two small cushions covered in white "China" silk. It was certainly not what Rogers had ordered, for it had been crudely executed, its only refinement being a lip to prevent the concrete lid from slipping off. However, it was too late to demand something better. She placed the tin can between the cushions and Makovski laid copies of *Flint and Feather* and *Legends of Vancouver* on either side. They replaced the lid and the assistant carried the box to the Rogers's automobile.

Their destination was Ferguson Point in Stanley Park, a spot that was still practically in the bush at that time. The Parks Commission had to send in workmen to hack out a clearing for a burial site in the angle between the new park drive and the old road leading steeply down to Siwash Rock. A small crowd was gathered at the foot of a birch tree when the two arrived with the box, and several of the men came forward to place it in the hole prepared by the parks crew. Reverend Owen read a short burial service and Walter McRaye recited "The Happy Hunting Grounds," one of Pauline's early poems. Afterwards, Mrs. J. J. Banfield, the president-elect of the Women's Canadian Club, gave the funeral oration. She told how Pauline's income had dwindled "until she was actually in want and decided to sell some of her precious possessions. Had it not been for certain true members of her own craft she would have died sooner than she did—" she paused for effect, "though not of cancer!"[6]

When the mourners had gone, the parks crew covered the concrete box with earth, then rolled into place a boulder on which one of them had chiselled out Pauline's name—a last tribute from an admirer. But inadvertently these kind men had done one more thing she had not wanted: they had given her a tombstone.

A few days later the contents of her will were made public. After designating her burial arrangements, she made a long list of bequests. Except in one important instance, they were not financial in nature. They were simply keepsakes which she wished to give to old friends, things to remember her by. Eva's name was not included in the list; she had already received her inheritance.

> I bequeath to the Museum of the City of Vancouver my Indian costume intact, and comprising the scalps, silver brooches and all other decorations, and including the skirt and bodice, moccasins, bear claw necklace, eagle crest, and the pair of bead and tooth bracelets given to me by Ernest Thompson Seton, also the scarlet broadcloth blanket used in the ceremony of making His Royal Highness, the Duke of Connaught, chief of the Six Nations Indians, also the single "baby" moccasin worn by my late father, also the wooden ladle left me by my Indian grandmother, also my "Ojisdoh" dagger which is the steel dagger with deerhorn handle which belonged to my father, also the personally autographed letters written me by Paul Bluett (Max O'Rell), Sir Frederick Leighton, John Greenleaf Whittier, and the Duke of Argyll.

I bequeath to my brother Allen W. Johnson my Cariboo gold nugget which I desire him to wear on his watch chain, my beaded buckskin "fire bag," my silk embroidered buckskin mitts and Indian ceremonial stones which will be found in a package marked with his name, also my walrus bladder tobacco pouch and two Squamish Indian cedar root caskets.

I bequeath to Mrs. Frederick Cope, wife of Frederick Cope, electrician, of the City of Vancouver, my cut glass decanter and cut glass sherry glasses, also the first gift she gave me of a Russian leather case containing scissors, also my gold brooch set with pearls given me by Lady Blake, wife of the Governor of Jamaica, also my large Wedgewood jug in the design of dancing girls.

I bequeath to Bert Cope, son of the said Mrs. Frederick Cope, my Mission oak table at which I have written my entire book, the *Legends of Vancouver* and my Mission oak chair, also my framed picture called "The Moose Call," also my solid silver salt spoons which were my mother's, and my hanging bowl of Damascus brass.

I bequeath to Frank Cope, eldest son of Mr. and Mrs. Frederick Cope above mentioned, my silver-mounted deer-horn handled set of carvers.

I bequeath to Doctor T. R. B. Nelles who has attended me with extreme kindness and skill through a long period of suffering and to whose friendship I owe whatever bravery I have been able to command, my green china dessert set consisting of six plates, two salad dishes, and one large centre dish, my "Onondaga" turtleshell medicine rattle, my reindeer pelt and one porcupine quill mat with my mother's writing on the back.

I bequeath to "my beloved" Eileen Maguire of Vancouver who is dear to me, all the plates, cups and saucers belonging to the teaset of my green china, my small Wedgewood jug, the turquoise ring presented to me by the City of Brantford, my ring containing five whole pearls, my Crown Derby cup and saucer, beaded Indian "couee" stick decorated with a tassel of bear claws, one porcupine quill mat with my mother's writing on the back, my silver sugar-tongs, cut glass vinegar cruet, and my pair of silk embroidered buckskin gloves, my New Brunswick souvenir sugar basin and cream jug, all my sterling silver coffee spoons, and my single Limoges plate.

I bequeath to my fellow artist and dear comrade of many years, Walter

McRaye, the following books, namely:—Poetical works of Byron, Works of Whittier, Works of Adelaide Proctor, Works of Owen Meredith, and the manuscript of Charles G. D. Roberts' book *Songs of the Common Day,* also the autographed copy of Sir Gilbert Parker's *Donovan Pasha,* also the photographs of and autographed by respectively, Sir Gilbert Parker, Ernest Thompson Seton, James Whitcombe Riley, Sir Charles Tupper, and Dr. Drummond. Also the faded half of my birch bark portfolio worked in moosehair which was a wedding gift to my mother from the Larette Indians, also my Cantonese cup and saucer, egg cup and bowl, the silver medal with the profile of Queen Victoria, the British coat-of-arms on the reverse side and engraved crest of the Prince of Wales, and dated 1860, also my tall brass candlestick which was my mother's, and any monies that may come to me from my books which he has been instrumental in selling.

I bequeath to Bertha Browning the wife of John Browning of 41 Palmerston Avenue, Brantford, Ontario, the set of three oxidized silver waist buttons in the design of Indian heads, the express charges from Vancouver to Brantford on package containing all the above to be prepaid out of whatever balance remains in the bank to my credit.

I bequeath to Mrs. J. J. Banfield, wife of John J. Banfield of the City of Vancouver, the unfaded side of my birch bark portfolio which is worked in moose hair and was a wedding gift to my mother from the Larette Indians.

I also bequeath to the said Walter McRaye my silver seal set with an amethyst; my silver tablets which will be found on a long silver chain, my cut-glass silver mounted vinagrette with the square-shaped end (the one with the bit of blue silk tied to it), my old Haida Indian silver bracelet (the one that clasps), and my picture (framed) of the Duke of Connaught autographed by His Royal Highness the Duke and dated by him "Vancouver, September 20, 1912."

I bequeath to Mrs. P. J. McKay [Isabel Eccleston MacKay] of Vancouver who is one of my executors, three of my smallest toilet pieces, videlicet: my shoe-horn, my nailfile, and my tooth-brush handle.

I bequeath to Mrs. Nellie McClung of Winnipeg, author of *Sowing Seeds in Danny,* three toilet pieces mounted in sterling silver, videlicet: clothes brush engraved with my name, my hat brush, and my comb. I wish to have her written to by either one of my executors and told how much I valued her loyal friendship, and that I wish her to keep these little things and prize them just because they were mine.

For Eva, Pauline's bequests were a cruel stab in the back. She could not understand why her sister had given family possessions away to strangers so far from their real home. Once she had returned to New York she began a letter-writing campaign asking those who had received bequests to give her the things that had belonged to their parents. In return, she promised to send them something else which had belonged to Pauline. They all refused. She was "heartbroken" about the soup ladle and the baby moccasin that had been left to the Vancouver Museum: "That baby moccasin should have remained in the east. It is about two or three inches long, perfect in make, and saved as a white woman saves her first baby's shoe."[7] But Eva's distress made no impression on the museum's administrators.

Just before she left Vancouver, Eva had cleaned out Pauline's apartment on Howe Street, packing up those items which were to be taken back to Brantford for her brother as well as the residue of articles that had not been assigned in the will. The task was painful because, in spite of all the quarrels, Eva had loved her younger sister very deeply. It must have hurt her as well to learn the details of her sister's private life only through the letters and notes she found after she had died. In a box beside Pauline's bed she found the manuscript copy of the poem " 'And He Said Fight On.' " It had been included in *Flint and Feather,* which had been published by Hodder and Stoughton, but Eva pocketed the manuscript and later sold it to the Musson Book Publishing Company for fifteen dollars. "But they stole the copyright," she later wrote angrily, "and I stopped the sale!"[7] However, she kept the money, giving half of it to the Brantford Historical Society. She intended the other half to go to Vancouver for a memorial to Pauline, but never sent it.

T. S. H. Shearman, an old friend from Brantford, found Eva in Pauline's apartment when he came to pay his respects. "I found her busy arranging and sorting over Pauline's papers and literary remains. It was early in the evening and she had been busy all day and seemed tired and weary."[9] When he learned she had not yet had her tea, he escorted her down Nelson to a little cafe around the corner on Granville Street. Eva was delighted to talk to someone from home in this alien city.

Because she could never bear to part with anything she had been given, Pauline had collected an enormous number of mementos and letters. She may have lost a few things over the years—there was, for example, a book belonging to O'Brien that she misplaced in 1903 and apparently never found. She may have left things behind in hotel rooms; though, as a result of her mother's dictum that one must not give unnecessary work to servants, she had always tidied up before she checked out. She may have thrown trivia away when she had accumulated more than she could carry, but judging by the theatre ticket stubs and the cleaning bills she did keep, that did not happen very often.

When Shearman interrupted Eva's labours, she had been sorting through this collection in a well-intentioned effort to protect her sister's good name. She had very efficiently burned all her personal correspondence, reserving only those letters that had come from famous people and innocuous letters from admirers. Everything that exposed Pauline's private life and loves—letters, pictures, clippings, tokens of love—she had destroyed. Thus, it was a very chaste collection indeed that she took back to Brantford where for the next fifteen years most of it remained packed in boxes in the attic of the sheriff's house. [10]

In spite of Pauline's orders, in the spring of 1914 the Women's Canadian Club began raising money to build a monument for her gravesite. Charles Marega was called on to design it, and he envisioned two units of sculpture, one of them to be a group of Indians and the other to depict Pauline seated facing them. The ladies approved the design because they felt it was aesthetic and because it allowed them to commission the statues separately as they could afford them. However, the First World War intervened and the fund drive for the monument had to be set aside for more pressing concerns.

Early in 1915 the editor of the *Vancouver World* received a cheque from Eva Johnson for $225, and in an accompanying letter she explained that it was half the amount that she had received as her share of the proceeds from the sale of *Legends of Vancouver*. [11] The other share, she said, had gone to Mr. McRaye. She asked the editor to use the money she had sent for the "artistic or literary life" of the city as she felt that she did not deserve it. But Pauline had not willed Eva a share of the proceeds from the sale of *The Legends*; she had willed it all to McRaye, probably because she knew that he would have a rough time on the circuit without her name, and because she knew that Eva had been saving for her old age from the time she earned her first penny. If Eva felt that she did not deserve *The Legends* proceeds, it was because she literally did not deserve them. How she came into possession of them is unknown.

In any case, the editor now held a sum which he felt was "too small an amount to do anything outstanding and yet considerable enough that it could not be treated with indifference."[12] Months went by and then his dilemma was resolved when dispatches from the front lines in France told how Canadian troops were suffering from a serious shortage of guns. The *World* launched a subscription fund to raise a thousand dollars to buy a gun to send to the 29th Battalion which had only recently been sent overseas; Eva's $225 was the seed money. Public response was enormous and in a short time the full amount was raised, the gun purchased through the minister of militia and sent on its way. On the gun barrel was inscribed the single word "Tekahion-wake." In 1920, after a determined battle with Ottawa's bureaucracy and with military officials, the *World* managed to have the gun returned to Vancouver and placed in the hands of the Duke of Connaught's Regiment which had assimilated the 29th Battalion. Battalion.

Eva sent a similar amount of money to the city of Brantford where it was used to establish a Pauline Johnson Memorial Room in the General Hospital. She was very pleased, saying that the money had "been put to far better use than I could otherwise have made of it."[13]

After the war the Women's Canadian Club resumed its efforts to build a monument to mark Pauline's grave. This time the ladies had to reject Marega's design entirely as they had only been able to raise $1200, even with the help of the Daughters of the Empire. However, the memorial which the club finally erected in 1922 raised a furor as soon as it was unveiled. On a large stone, a medallion showing Pauline's head in profile had been carved and bronzed, and on either end Mohawk motifs had been chiselled. In front of the stone, directly over the concrete burial box, a small pool and fountain had been built. Aesthetically, the monument was satisfactory, and it suited its quiet site in the woods. The quarrel was with the image of Pauline. For some reason, it is her right profile that is shown, so that she is forced to face forever into the trees instead of towards her beloved Siwash Rock. Furthermore, her hair is dressed in braids bound about her head, a style that she never wore, and to top it off, the face does not resemble Pauline Johnson. But when the complaints were voiced, it was too late; the monument had been built and dedicated and it would have to stand.

As the years went by, Eva's bitterness increased. As of old, her favourite target was McRaye. Before leaving Vancouver in 1913, Eva had enlisted his help in covering up the evidence of Pauline's love affairs. The problem years were 1898 to 1901, so Eva encouraged McRaye to lie about the date that he had become Pauline's partner. Since he had trouble with the truth at the best of times, he needed little encouragement. However, as usual, he forgot to quit when he was ahead and continued to sell his own shows on the strength of his former association with Pauline, his most offensive advertisement being the one in which he claimed he was "in collaboration with the late Pauline Johnson."[14]

Eva was afraid that if she attacked him openly, he might suddenly decide to remember some of the embarrassing information about Pauline that he had forgotten. She therefore confined herself to sniping at him in letters to friends. But when in the early 1920s he attempted to sell the items that Pauline had bequeathed to him, Eva launched a campaign of vicious denunciation in letters to anyone who would read them.[15] No matter what McRaye's reasons might be, Eva considered selling precious "relics" unforgivable.

Another source of bitterness for her was Vancouver's proprietary affection for Pauline. In 1924 she wrote:

> I do not like the way Vancouver seems to claim Pauline. Pauline lived all her life in the East with the exception of about four years which were passed in Vancouver where she died. To be sure, they have erected a memorial to her there, but as some of the North West papers pointed out, Pauline Johnson was distinctly of the East, and the memorial should be in the East. However, since Vancouver is erecting it, nothing can be said.[16]

She seems to have wanted a memorial to Pauline somewhere— even though she knew that Pauline had not wanted one—but she refused to contribute to the erection of one. In 1909 she had sent twenty-five dollars to W. D. J. Wright of London, Ontario, hoping it would form the nucleus of a fund to build a monument to Tecumseh. Subsequently, she had solicited funds from the important men who she felt would be interested in honouring Tecumseh, but for a variety of reasons they failed to contribute. In 1922 Wright tried to get her to transfer the money to the Vancouver monument fund. The answer was a firm "No!"

> Do you not think, Mr. Wright, that a memorial should be erected to the memory of this great warrior before one to Pauline? I do. . . . I have been such an admirer of Tecumseh, and my father was before me, that I still wish my contribution to remain the nucleus for a memorial and I believe my sister Pauline would be the first to wish him to be memorialized. If, however, the deposit is causing you any inconvenience I will endeavour to arrange to have you relieved."[17]

As for Chiefswood, the beloved home for whose possession she had bargained so passionately with Pauline, a succession of tenants and long periods of emptiness had caused its decay. The buildings needed repairs and paint, the farm had been neglected, and the forest had crept perceptibly closer. But for Eva, on her annual trips to Brantford, Chiefswood still represented home though she had not lived within its walls for forty years.

Allen Johnson died in 1923, and Eva arranged for his burial in the family plot in the Mohawk Cemetery. There were now two places left—her own and Pauline's.

In 1936, one year before her death at eighty-one, Eva was interviewed in Brantford by Mazie Mathews of the *Montreal Star*. They met on a bench near the Brant Monument. Almost totally blind, Eva was now a very little, tired old lady clutching a brown purse and a sturdy cane. She spoke eagerly of the upcoming Silver Jubilee of George V and recalled the royalty she had met in her youth, and the day the Duke of Connaught had been made chief of the Six Nations. She spoke with pride of her father's people and identified with them still, but she told the reporter:

> Indians can not yet compete with other folks and that is why I am going to fight against the movement to give the franchise to the Indians. We are not ready for it yet, nor can we be expected to be. It took the English hundreds of years to become what they are now, and you can not make a savage equal in one hundred years. There are, of

course, a few, but the majority are not advanced enough yet. It is slow work, and the best way is not to force or try to hurry them; let them awaken for themselves, as they will when they compare their way and means of living with the white folk.

Eva Johnson died on 10 June 1937 in the Willingdon Hospital in Ohsweken, Ontario. She was buried in the family plot in the Mohawk cemetery. Her death occurred one year before she would have been allowed to open the "time capsule" that Pauline had left in her care. This was a triple-sealed box which Pauline had prepared in the last months before her death, entrusting it to Eva with the rider that it was to remain unopened for twenty-five years. Anticipating the eventuality of her death before the expiry date, Eva willed the box to the Brantford chapter of the Daughters of the Empire. It was not until September 1943, however, that the chapter executive ventured to break open the three seals on the box and expose the items Pauline had hidden there.

Uppermost in the box were two large pictures of Napoleon, one from his younger days and the other depicting him on horseback on the battlefield. According to the enclosed instructions, these and a mater dolorosa were to be hung on the walls of Chiefswood. Beneath the pictures were letters, reviews, personal books, and a silk bag containing the animal teeth and claws that Charles Mair and his friends had collected for a necklace long ago. There was a lock of her mother's hair and her mother's tortoise-shell combs as well as a collection of snapshots of the Cariboo country and several of Chief Joe Capilano, some autumn-tinted maple leaves, and a single pressed rose.

What was the significance of the items? A record of the things she had loved perhaps, and the things that held value for her? Her mother's love, her father's heroes, the Cariboo country, wildlife, good friends, her years on the stage. Had she intended them to say more? Was there a code that the ladies overlooked which would have unlocked their significance?

Or was there originally more in the box? Did Eva remove the articles that she found offensive and reseal the box? She was a scrupulously honest woman, but she was almost obsessive in her attempts to protect her sister's reputation. It is just possible that the box originally contained the identity of the "young boy" in the locket, or that it contained love letters from Drayton or Wurz. If there were no secrets in it, why did Pauline use this elaborate device to conceal articles of such a prosaic nature? There is, of course, the possibility that she only did it to see if Eva could control her curiosity for that long. After all, Pauline did have a good sense of humour.

Eva willed her beloved Chiefswood to the Six Nations to be used as a home for the aged members of the tribe, but this proved to be unfeasible and the building was allowed to stand uninhabited until 1958. In that year it was decided that it should be restored as a national literary shrine and this was accomplished in time for the centenary of Pauline's birth, 1961. It was refurnished with authentic period furniture, and wherever possible the original Johnson furnishings were installed. An excellent collection of Pauline's personal belongings, her clothing, manuscripts of some of her poems, and copies of her books was given effective display. The old house became a fitting tribute to an exceptional Canadian.

In Vancouver, the monument that Pauline never wanted suffered the opposite fate of Chiefswood. After twenty-five years of annual pilgrimages by the Women's Canadian Club, the Daughters of the Empire, and assorted admirers on the anniversary of Pauline's birth and burial, the monument was badly neglected during the years of the Second World War. In fact, in March 1945 all the bronze was stripped from the sculpture by thieves and in June 1953 it suffered further desecration when vandals splashed red paint over it.

In March 1961, when the government issued a stamp in honour of Pauline's centenary, Don Stainsby of the *Vancouver Sun* made a private pilgrimage to her grave. In great disgust, he reported in his column "Books and Bookmen" that within the past year the pipe which carried water to the pool had sprung a leak so that water was spouting out the side of the monument between the stones. Since the pool had been constructed without a drain, whatever water still reached it overflowed onto the ground and did not drain off during the winter months. "The whole area is a stinking swamp!" said Stainsby. [17]

If the civic fathers heard they did not heed. In July of that year a group of Six Nations Indians paid a visit to the monument, then visited the newspapers to complain of its condition. There was no immediate reaction. The following year, however, the water intake was permanently disconnected because the works department decided that it would be prohibitively expensive to repair without tearing up the pool. This situation remained for the next twenty years. Finally in June 1981 workmen tore out the original pool, installed new plumbing and a proper drain, and then carefully rebuilt the pool.

Now water trickles down from a cleft in the front of the monument and is caught in a stone bowl before it overflows and runs into the pool below. Above the water, Pauline's sad image stares sightlessly off into the trees. Few people stop to pay their respects any more though the roads which flank the monument are both paved now and a bustling teahouse stands nearby. But occasionally on a fine spring morning an admirer will leave a handful of wildflowers in the stone bowl of water.

Epilogue

FRANK YEIGH left his post as private secretary to Ontario's premier in 1896 and concentrated on a career in lecturing and writing. He specialized in highly nationalistic talks on Canada's frontier country and accompanied them with lantern slide shows. In 1902 he began publishing an annual known as *Five Thousand Facts about Canada*. He also produced *Ontario's Parliament Buildings* (1893) and *Through the Heart of Canada* (1910).

Yeigh's first wife, Kate Westlake, died in 1906 and he married Annie Laird two years later. He had one son, Norman. Yeigh died in 1935.

HARRY O'BRIEN became the assistant law clerk for the House of Commons in 1896, and from 1908 to 1914 he served as law clerk and counsel to the speaker. He served in France in World War I and was invalided home in 1917. He married Miriam Knowlton of Saint John, New Brunswick, in 1918; they had one son, Murrough. O'Brien published a number of important legal tomes, among them digests of Canadian railway legislation and of the fish and game laws of Ontario and Quebec. An admirer of Thomas Chandler Haliburton, he published a short biography of the man and a bibliography of his work. He died in 1958.

CHARLES DRAYTON and his wife became prominent in Vancouver social circles during the years after Pauline's death, and Drayton's business affairs prospered. A few years after the war he left Vancouver to return to the east; his ultimate fate is unknown.

J. WALTER McRAYE returned to the recital circuit with his wife, Lucy, after Pauline's death, and early in 1914 decided to try his luck in England. He and Lucy were caught there at the beginning of World War I but managed to get passage on a steamer for Canada. Their only child, Louis Drummond McRaye, was born shortly before Christmas, 1914. McRaye then enlisted in the medical corps and was shipped to France. At the end of the war he returned to the circuit alone as his marriage to Lucy was virtually over by this time. She and her son returned to England in 1924, and McRaye never saw them again. About this time he began to make his home with a wealthy cousin who doted on him and he remained in her care with frequent forays onto the patriotic lecture circuit until the late thirties. He died in 1946.

Notes

CHAPTER ONE: HERITAGE

1. Ernest Thompson Seton, from the Introduction to *The Shagginappi* by E. Pauline Johnson (Toronto: William Briggs, 1913), p. 5.
2. Horatio Hale, ed. *The Iroquois Book of Rites,* Brinton's Library of Aboriginal American Literature (Philadelphia: D. G. Brinton Limited, 1883), p. 21.
3. Charles M. Johnston, *The Valley of the Six Nations: A Collection of Documents on the Indian Lands of the Grand River,* The Champlain Society (Toronto: University of Toronto Press, 1964), p. iv.
4. Ibid., p. xi
5. According to Eva Johnson, her father was the firstborn child, but Pauline called him the second born in her account of his chieftainship in "Mothers of a Great Red Race," *Mother's Magazine,* 3 Jan. 1908.
6. Dorothy Keen and Martha McKeon as told to Mollie Gillen, "The Story of Pauline Johnson, Canada's Passionate Poet," *Chatelaine,* March 1966, p. 97.
7. E. Pauline Johnson, "From the Child's Viewpoint," Chapter 1, *Mother's Magazine,* * May 1910, p. 30.
8. Item from the Brant County Museum collection, Brantford, Ont.

---

*Mother's Magazine was published by the David C. Cook Publishing Co., Elgin, Illinois.

9. E. Pauline Johnson, "From the Child's Viewpoint," Chapter 2, *Mother's Magazine,* June 1910, p. 60.
10. Keen and McKeon, "Story of Pauline Johnson," March, p. 96.
11. Keen and McKeon ("Story of Pauline Johnson," Feb., p. 42) state that there was still one more delay in the wedding plans because of the death from consumption of Mary Margaret Elliott, the last surviving Elliott child, who was to have been Emily's bridesmaid. Mary Margaret, however, died on 11 June 1854, a year after the wedding had taken place.
12. Keen and McKeon, "Story of Pauline Johnson," Feb., p. 42.
13. Letter from Evelyn (Eva) to J. S. Rowe, 27 May 1924, Brant County Museum. Eva wrote in 1924 that the moccasin was "about two or three inches long, perfect in make and saved as a white woman saves her first baby's shoes." She seems to have forgotten that Helen was half white.
14. Letter from Emily Johnson to George Johnson, Point Frederick, Kingston, 15 Aug. 1855, Brant County Museum.
15. This is one of two dates given for completion. A small item in the Brant County Museum records the event as happening when Beverly was nine months old, but Keen and McKeon, "The Story of Pauline Johnson," place the date as 1856. They corroborate this with a story concerning young Beverly as a toddler. Apparently during construction he was rescued from a beam on the unfinished second floor where he had climbed in search of his father. Presumably sister Eva was the source of this anecdote.

CHAPTER TWO: CHIEFSWOOD

1. Dorothy Keen and Martha McKeon as told to Mollie Gillen, "The Story of Pauline Johnson, Canada's Passionate Poet," *Chatelaine,* March 1966, p. 96.
2. E. Pauline Johnson, "From the Child's Viewpoint," Chapter 2, *Mother's Magazine,* June 1910, p. 60.
3. Ibid.
4. Johnson, "From the Child's Viewpoint," Chapter 1, *Mother's Magazine,* May 1910, p. 30.
5. Johnson, "Child's Viewpoint," Chapter 2, p. 60.
6. Keen and McKeon, "Story of Pauline Johnson," Feb. 1966, p. 44.
7. Johnson, "Child's Viewpoint," Chapter 1, p. 30.

8. Ibid.
9. Ibid., p. 31.
10. Ibid., pp. 30–31.
11. Interview from unspecified U.S. newspaper, c. 1897, McMaster University Library, Hamilton, Ontario.
12. Isabel Eccleston MacKay, "A Romance of Yesterday," *Toronto Globe,* 30 Nov. 1912, p. 3.
13. Peggy Webling, *Peggy: The Story of One Score Years and Ten* (London: Hutchinson and Co., 1924), p. 139.
14. Johnson, "Child's Viewpoint," Chapter 2, p. 60.
15. Ibid.
16. Jean H. Waldie, "Pauline Johnson," *Ontario History,* vol. 40, Ontario Historical Society, 1948, p. 66.
17. Johnson, "Child's Viewpoint," Chapter 1, p. 31.
18. Webling, *Peggy,* p. 149.
19. Jack Scott, "The Passionate Princess," *Maclean's*, 1 April 1952.
20. Unsigned review (probably Charles Wheeler), *Winnipeg Tribune,* 3 Sept. 1894.
21. Waldie, "Pauline Johnson."
22. Johnson, "Child's Viewpoint," Chapter 2, p. 61.
23. Ibid.

CHAPTER THREE: BRANTFORD

1. Peggy Webling, *Peggy: The Story of One Score Years and Ten* (London: Hutchinson and Co., 1924), p. 139.
2. *Brantford Expositor,* 14 Oct. 1886.
3. *Toronto World,* 14 Oct. 1886.
4. Pauline was approximately five foot three inches in height, which even in 1886 was not considered tall. She wore size eight gowns. Her hair, alas, was not black, but the other particulars seem to agree with existing descriptions.
5. Property of McMaster University Library, Hamilton, Ontario.
6. *Hamilton Spectator,* Oct. 1886.
7. Property of the Brant County Museum, Brantford, Ontario.
8. Webling, *One Score Years,* p. 149.
9. Ibid., p. 161.
10. "E. Pauline Johnson," *McMaster University Monthly,* 14 (1904) 104.
11. Dorothy Keen and Martha McKeon as told to Mollie Gillen,

"The Story of Pauline Johnson, Canada's Passionate Poet," *Chatelaine,* March 1966, p. 96.

12. Johnson Interview, p. 104.
13. Keen and McKeon, "Story of Pauline Johnson," March, p. 96.
14. Webling, *One Score Years,* p. 211.
15. Keen and McKeon, "Story of Pauline Johnson," March, p. 97.
16. Letter from E. Pauline Johnson to A. Harry O'Brien, 20 June 1894, Queens University Archives, Toronto, Ont.
17. "Around the Campfire," *New York Times,* Sunday, 20 Aug. 1893.
18. Johnson to O'Brien, 4 Feb. 1894, Queens University Archives.
19. E. M. Pomeroy, *Sir Charles G. D. Roberts* (Toronto: Ryerson Press, 1943), p. 126.
20. Johnson to O'Brien, 20 June 1894, Queens University Archives.

CHAPTER FOUR: LONDON

1. J. Lewis May, *John Lane and the Nineties* (London: John Lane, the Bodley Head, 1936), p. 37.
2. *Sketch,* London, 13 June 1894, p. 358.
3. May, *John Lane,* p. 37.
4. Letter from E. Pauline Johnson to A. Harry O'Brien, 20 June 1894, Queens University Archives, Toronto, Ont.
5. Ibid.
6. Mrs. W. Garland Foster, *The Mohawk Princess* (Vancouver: Lions' Gate Publishing, 1931), p. 49.
7. Letter from E. Pauline Johnson to L. W. Makovski, Christmas 1911. Property of Eric Makovski.
8. J. Walter McRaye, *Townhall To-Night* (Toronto: Ryerson Press, n.d.), p. 40.
9. Johnson to O'Brien, 20 June 1894.
10. Ibid.
11. "E. Pauline Johnson," *McMaster University Monthly,* 14 (1904) 104.
12. *Spectator* (London), 19 May 1894.
13. Hector Charlesworth, *Candid Chronicles,* vol. 1 (Toronto: Macmillan Co., 1925), p. 101.
14. May, *John Lane,* pp. 209–10. The account of the tea party is third hand. E. H. New recorded it in his diary; Harry Furniss

quoted the diary in his book *Paradise in Piccadilly;* J. Lewis May quoted Furniss. Unfortunately, Furniss gives the date of this party as 25 July 1895, when Pauline had already left London. New's diary no longer exists.

15. Undated clipping from Romike-Curtice Clipping Agency, McMaster University Library, Toronto, Ont.

CHAPTER FIVE: THERE AND BACK AGAIN

1. *Brantford Expositor,* 27 July 1894.
2. Letter from E. Pauline Johnson to A. Harry O'Brien, 23 Aug. 1894, Queens University Archives, Toronto, Ont.
3. Letter from Horatio Hale to E. Pauline Johnson, 13 July 1896, McMaster University Library, Hamilton, Ont.
4. Johnson to O'Brien, 25 Aug. 1894, Queen's University Archives.
5. The branch of the Canadian Pacific Railway running from Winnipeg to Morden, Manitoba. In 1894 there was one return trip each day.
6. Vancouver was incorporated as a city on 6 April 1886 and was almost totally destroyed by fire on 13 June of the same year.
7. Johnson to O'Brien, 21 Sept. 1894.
8. Peggy Webling, *Peggy: The Story of One Score Years and Ten* (London: Hutchinson and Co., 1924), p. 213.
9. E. Pauline Johnson, "From the Child's Viewpoint," Chapter 2, *Mother's Magazine,* June 1910, p. 61.
10. Ibid., p. 62.
11. "Pauline Johnson's Shy Sister Devoted Life to Her," *Vancouver Province,* 25 November 1939.
12. Jean Stephenson, "The Real, Lovable, Tender, Fun-Loving Pauline Johnson," *Vancouver Province,* 6 March 1932.
13. Dorothy Keen and Martha McKeon as told to Mollie Gillen, "The Story of Pauline Johnson, Canada's Passionate Poet," *Chatelaine,* March 1966, p. 101.
14. *The Week,* 1 Feb. 1895, p. 228.
15. Ibid., 22 Feb. 1895, p. 299.
16. Property of Mills Memorial Library, McMaster University.
17. Webling, *Peggy,* p. 214.
18. Mrs. W. Garland Foster, *The Mohawk Princess* (Vancouver: Lions' Gate Publishing, 1931), p. 63.

19. Johnson to O'Brien, 9 June 1895, Queens University Archives.

20. Ibid.

21. E. Pauline Johnson, "Trails of Old Tillicums," *Vancouver Province,* 31 Dec. 1910. J. Walter McRaye's account of this acquisition is contradictory; he says the event took place at Medicine Hat, that the tribe was not Blood but either Sarcee or Blackfoot, and the scalp was that of a Cree warrior. However, his first meeting with Pauline was three years after the event, so his description is the product of hearsay only.

22. Foster, *Mohawk Princess,* p. 73.

23. Charlesworth, *Candid Chronicles,* vol. 1 (Toronto: Macmillan Co., 1925), p. 103.

24. Article in *Toronto Saturday Night,* n.d., McMaster University Library.

25. *Sketch* (London), 13 June 1894.

26. Letter from E. Pauline Johnson to Sir Wilfrid Laurier, 18 Jan. 1907, Provincial Archives, British Columbia.

27. Ibid.

28. Johnson to O'Brien, 23 Aug. 1894, Queen's University Archives.

29. E. Pauline Johnson, *The Moccasin Maker* (Toronto: William Briggs, 1913), pp. 58, 60–63.

30. "Mothers of a Great Red Race," *Mother's Magazine,* Jan. 1908.

31. This American novelist (1831-1885) wrote *Ramona* in 1884. She also wrote *A Century of Dishonor* to expose her government's Indian Affairs policies.

32. *Wacousta* was written by the Canadian novelist John Richardson (1796-1852) in 1832; its sequel, *The Canadian Brothers,* was published in 1840.

33. Charles Mair was one of the founders of the "Canada First" Movement in 1898. Filled with naive idealism, he helped to foment the Red River Rebellion and was instrumental in goading Riel to act in 1869. For his pains, he was captured by Riel who sentenced him to death, but he escaped. In 1885 he served in the force that was sent to quell the second Riel Rebellion. In 1898, at the age of sixty, he joined the immigration service, serving in Alberta and B.C. until he retired to Victoria at the age of eighty-three. He wrote *Dreamland and Other Poems* and the drama *Tecumseh.* Pauline met him in 1899 or 1900.

34. Henry Rowe Schoolcraft (1793-1864) specialized in the study of the Ojibway Indians of the Lake Superior Region. His six-

volume work is entitled *Historical and Statistical Information Respecting the History, Condition, and Prospects of the Indian Tribes of the United States;* Frances Parkman (1823-1893) studied the primitive Sioux of the American plains. His work is incorporated into *The History of the Conspiracy of Pontiac, The Jesuits in North America, and LaSalle and the Discovery of the Great West;* George Catten (1796-1872) painted more than five hundred paintings and sketches of Indian life, and published the two-volume *Letters and Notes on the Manners, Customs and Condition of North American Indians.*

35. "A Red Girl's Reasoning" was first published in the Feb. 1893 edition of *Dominion Illustrated* and included in *Moccasin Maker* (1913).

36. Webling, *Peggy,* p. 215.

CHAPTER SIX: WINNIPEG

1. Courtesy of Saskatchewan Archives Board, Regina, Sask.
2. *Winnipeg Tribune,* 26 Dec. 1899.
3. J. Walter McRaye, *Town Hall To-Night* (Toronto: Ryerson Press, n.d.), p. 34.
4. Ibid., p. 27.
5. *Winnipeg Tribune,* 30 Dec. 1897.
6. Peggy Webling, *Peggy: The Story of One Score Years and Ten* (London: Hutchinson and Co., 1924), p. 212.
7. Letter from Evelyn (Eva) Johnson to J. S. Rowe, New York City, 22 April 1924, McMaster University Library, Hamilton, Ont.
8. *Manitoba Morning Free Press,* 14 Jan. 1898.
9. E. Pauline Johnson, "The Happy Hunting Grounds," *Flint and Feather* (Toronto: Hodder and Stoughton, 1969), p. 71.
10. Johnson, "At Crow's Nest Pass," *Flint and Feather,* p. 118.
11. Mrs. W. Garland Foster, *The Mohawk Princess* (Vancouver: Lions' Gate Publishing, 1931), p. 104.
12. Letter from Mrs. W. Garland Foster to Irene Burkholder, 2 Nov. 1969. Property of Irene Burkholder.
13. *Brantford Expositor,* 24 Feb. 1898.
14. E. Pauline Johnson, *The Moccasin Maker* (Toronto: William Briggs, 1913), pp. 95–96.
15. *Brantford Expositor,* 5 March 1898: reprinted from the *Toronto Globe and Mail,* 2 March 1898.

16. *Manitoba Morning Free Press,* 5 Nov. 1898.
17. *Macleod Gazette,* 24 March 1899.
18. Letter from Ernest Thompson Seton to Pauline Johnson, 17 Aug. 1899, Queens University Archives, Toronto, Ont. Until 1901 the writer-artist used the name Seton-Thompson. After a disagreement with his father, whose surname was Thompson, he signed himself Ernest Thompson Seton, honouring his mother's family name.

CHAPTER SEVEN: HALIFAX

1. *Vancouver Province,* 4 April 1899.
2. *Cranbrook Weekly Herald,* 27 April 1899.
3. Mrs. W. Garland Foster, *The Mohawk Princess* (Vancouver: Lions' Gate Publishing, 1931) p. 110.
4. E. Pauline Johnson, "A Prodigal," *Flint and Feather* (Toronto: Hodder and Stoughton, 1969), p. 108.
5. *Winnipeg Tribune,* 23 Dec. 1899.
6. *Globe and Mail,* 10 Jan. 1900.
7. Foster, *Mohawk Princess,* p. 77.
8. Letter from E. Pauline Johnson to A. H. O'Brien, 3 Oct. 1903, Queens University Archives, Toronto, Ont.
9. Sifton Papers, date stamped 30 Jan 1900, Public Archives of Canada, Ottawa, Ont.
10. Letter from E. Pauline Johnson to Clifford Sifton, 9 Feb. 1900, Sifton Papers.
11. Ibid., 15 Feb. 1900.
12. Laurier Papers, Provincial Archives, British Columbia.
13. *Saint John Daily Sun,* 23 Nov. 1900.
14. Gertrude O'Hara papers, Public Archives of Canada, Ottawa, Ont., Copyright, Queens University.
15. Hector Charlesworth, *Candid Chronicles,* vol. 1 (Toronto: Macmillan Co., 1925), p. 96.
16. *McMaster University Monthly,* 14 (1904): 104.
17. From a letter to Frank Lawson included in an article entitled "Some Living Canadian Poets," *London* (Ont.) *News,* 9 May 1900.
18. Gilbert Parker, Introduction to *The Moccasin Maker* (Toronto: William Briggs, 1913), p. 8.

19. Ernest Thompson Seton from Introduction to *The Shagginappi* by E. Pauline Johnson (Toronto: William Briggs, 1913), p. 6.
20. Charles Mair, "An Appreciation," *The Moccasin Maker,* p. 16.
21. E. Pauline Johnson, "A Strong Race Opinion on the Indian Girl in Modern Fiction," *Toronto Sunday Globe,* 22 May 1892.
22. Reprinted in Jean H. Waldie, "Pauline Johnson," *Ontario History,* vol. 40, Ontario Historical Society, 1948, p. 66.
23. Provincial Archives, British Columbia. This document is undated but has been correctly placed here.
24. Laurier Papers, 9 Jan. 1904, Public Archives of Canada.
25. Introduction to *Flint and Feather,* p. xiii.
26. Laurier Papers, letter dated 6 July 1906, London, Provincial Archives, British Columbia.
27. Foster, *Mohawk Princess,* p. 71.
28. Sifton Papers, Public Archives of Canada.
29. Ibid.

CHAPTER EIGHT: REGINA AND POINTS WEST

1. Unsigned review, *Ottawa Citizen,* 7 Nov. 1901.
2. Ibid.
3. Unsigned review, *Vernon News,* 28 Aug. 1902.
4. *Regina Standard,* 25 June 1902, reprinted from the *Globe Democrat,* unspecified date, 1899.
5. *Vancouver Province,* 9 Sept. 1902.
6. Letter from Evelyn (Eva) Johnson, to J. S. Rowe, Esq., Principal, Dufferin School, Brantford, 31 March 1924, Brantford County Museum, Brantford, Ont.
7. Eva Johnson to Rowe, 22 March 1924, Brantford County Museum.
8. Letter from E. Pauline Johnson to A. Harry O'Brien, 6 Oct. 1903, Queens University Archives, Toronto, Ont.
9. Ibid.
10. From a clipping in the Mills Memorial Library, McMaster University, Hamilton Ont.
11. "Pauline Johnson Receives Friends," from a Winnipeg newspaper (neither the *Tribune* nor the *Free Press*), 7 June 1902, McMaster University Library.
12. Kit Coleman, *Mail and Empire,* 31 May 1902.

13. Ibid.
14. "Pauline Johnson Receives Friends," 7 June 1902.
15. Letter from Madame Forget to Pauline Johnson, Regina, 12 June 1902, McMaster University Library.
16. Letter from E. Pauline Johnson to "Bonnie Girl," Brandon, June 1902 (probably about 15 June), Provincial Archives, British Columbia.
17. E. Pauline Johnson, "Among the Blackfoots," *Toronto Globe,* 2 Aug. 1902.
18. Ibid.
19. Ibid.
20. Ibid.
21. Ibid.
22. Unsigned, undated report, *Rossland Miner.*
23. *Sandon Paystreak,* 9 Aug. 1902.
24. *Slocan Drill,* 15 Aug. 1902.
25. *Kamloops Standard,* 12 Sept. 1902, reprinted from *Boundary Creek Times.*
26. J. Walter McRaye, *Town Hall To-Night* (Toronto: Ryerson Press, n.d.), p. 49.
27. *Peterborough Examiner,* March 1900, reprinted from *Washington Star,* McMaster University Library.
28. *Vancouver Province,* 9 Sept. 1902.
29. T. S. H. Shearman, "Pauline's Shy Sister Devoted Life to Her," *Vancouver Sun,* 25 Nov. 1939.
30. Peggy Webling, *Peggy: The Story of One Score Years and Ten* (London: Hutchinson and Co., 1924), p. 139.
31. Letter from E. Pauline Johnson to Frank Lawson, included in an article entitled "Some Living Canadian Poets," *London* (Ont.) *News,* 9 May 1900.
32. Jean Stevenson, "The Real, Lovable, Tender, Fun-loving Pauline Johnson," *Vancouver Province,* 6 March 1932.
33. McRaye, *Town Hall To-Night,* p. 52.
34. Mrs. W. Garland Foster, *The Mohawk Princess* (Vancouver: Lions' Gate Publishing, 1931), p. 75–77.
35. Isabel Ecclestone MacKay, "Pauline Johnson: a Reminiscence," *Canadian Magazine,* July 1913.
36. Letter from E. Pauline Johnson to A. Harry O'Brien, 3 Oct. 1903, Queens University Archives.
37. Unsigned review, *Toronto Globe,* 11 July 1903.

38. Father Athol Murray, "A Black Bass Fry Fit for the Gods," *Maclean's,* 6 July 1957. In 1906 when he was fourteen years old, Murray went on a canoeing and camping expedition with Allen Johnson.

39. E. Pauline Johnson to A. Harry O'Brien, 3 Oct. 1903.

40. Letter from E. Pauline Johnson to Sir Wilfrid Laurier, Brantford, Ont., 9 Jan. 1904, Provincial Archives, British Columbia.

41. This anecdote is courtesy of Mrs. Florence Pratt of North Vancouver. Another version is to be found in the Vancouver City Archives.

42. Pauline Johnson, "Coaching on the Cariboo Trail," *Canadian Magazine,* Feb. 1914.

43. Ibid.

44. McRaye, *Town Hall To-Night,* p. 49.

45. The Barkerville anecdote and the one which follows concerning Lac la Hache are both from Walter McRaye's memoirs, which unfortunately makes them somewhat suspect. However, they are historically accurate as well as characteristic of both Johnson and McRaye.

46. From a note written on Hotel Vancouver stationery in Pauline's handwriting, late 1908.

CHAPTER NINE: LONDON AGAIN

1. Letter from Evelyn (Eva) Johnson to J. S. Rowe, Esq., Principal, Dufferin School, Brantford, 22 April 1924, Brantford County Museum, Brantford, Ont.

2. Recollections by her daughter, Mrs. Florence Pratt of North Vancouver.

3. Box and Cox, "Variety Stage," *Stage and Sport,* 26 May 1906, McMaster University Library, Hamilton, Ont.

4. From *M.A.P.,* reprinted in the *Brantford Courier,* 22 June 1906, McMaster University Library.

5. J. Walter McRaye, *Town Hall To-Night* (Toronto: Ryerson Press, n.d.), p. 53.

6. E. M. Pomeroy, *Sir Charles G. D. Roberts* (Toronto: Ryerson Press, 1943), p. 159.

7. From "Plaint of the Siwash," author unknown, probable source *Vancouver World,* McMaster University Library.
8. L. W. Makovski, "A Mirror of Joe Capilano," *Vancouver Province,* 26 March 1910.
9. "Plaint of the Siwash."
10. "The King and the Red Indian Chiefs," *London* (Eng.) *Weekly News,* 16 Aug. 1906, McMaster University Library.
11. Ibid.
12. Ibid.
13. McRaye, *Town Hall To-Night,* p. 39.
14. Property of McMaster University Library.

CHAPTER TEN: CHAUTAUQUA

1. Letter from Elizabeth Ansley, ed. of *Mother's Magazine* to Pauline Johnson, 4 March 1907, McMaster University Library, Hamilton, Ont."
2. Invoice from *Mother's Magazine* to Pauline Johnson, 8 April 1907, McMaster University Library.
3. Invoices from *Boys' World* to Pauline Johnson, 2 April 1907 and 7 April 1907, McMaster University Library.
4. Manuscript, McMaster University Library.
5. Ibid.
6. J. Walter McRaye, *Town Hall To-Night* (Toronto: Ryerson Press, n.d.), p. 95.
7. Ibid., p. 211.
8. *Boston Herald,* Sept. 1907, McMaster University Library.
9. *Winnipeg Tribune,* 5 Oct. 1907, McMaster University Library.
10. Invoice from *Boys' World* to Pauline Johnson, 4 Nov. 1907, McMaster University Library.
11. Invoice from *Mother's Magazine* to Pauline Johnson, 5 Nov. 1907, McMaster University Library.
12. Letter from the ladies of a church group in Saint John, N.B., April 1907, McMaster University Library.
13. A. Buckley, "The Poetry of Pauline Johnson," *Spectator* (Eng.), reprinted in *News Advertiser* (Vancouver), 16 March 1913.
14. "Poetess of the Indians," *Vancouver World,* 29 June 1908.
15. Recollections by Florence Pratt of North Vancouver, daughter of Rosalind Webling Edwards.

CHAPTER ELEVEN: VANCOUVER

1. Jean Stevenson, "The Real, Lovable, Tender, Fun-loving Pauline Johnson," *Vancouver Province,* 6 March 1932.
2. Ibid.
3. Ibid.
4. Isabel Ecclestone MacKay, "Pauline Johnson: A Reminiscence," *Canadian Magazine,* July 1913.
5. Lionel Makovski, *Vancouver Province,* 10 March 1961.
6. J. N. J. Brown, "Legends of Vancouver," *Vancouver Province,* 18 June 1929.
7. *Vancouver Province,* 10 March 1961.
8. Letter from Jean Stevenson to Frank Yeigh, 21 April 1931, Public Archives of Canada, Ottawa, Ont.
9. Harold Weir, "Great Figures," *Vancouver Sun,* 20 Feb. 1961.
10. Ibid.
11. Recollections by Florence Pratt of North Vancouver, daughter of Rosalind Webling Edwards.
12. Letter from E. Pauline Johnson to Sir Wilfrid Laurier, 1 Aug. 1911, Provincial Archives, British Columbia.
13. Stevenson, "The Real . . . Pauline Johnson."
14. Ibid.
15. Letter from E. Pauline Johnson to Frank Yeigh, 11 June 1912, Public Archives of Canada.
16. Ethel Wilson, "The Princess," *Canadian Literature* 12 (Summer 1961), 60.
17. Letter from Evelyn (Eva) Johnson to F. G. Lees, c. 1935, Provincial Archives, British Columbia.
18. Stevenson to Yeigh, 21 April 1931, Public Archives of Canada.
19. Makovski, *Vancouver Province,* 10 March 1961.
20. Letter from Evelyn (Eva) Johnson to J. S. Rowe, 27 May 1924, Brant County Museum, Brantford, Ont.
21. Mrs. W. Garland Foster, *The Mohawk Princess* (Vancouver: Lions' Gate Publishing, 1931), p. 147.
22. Lionel Makovski, *Vancouver Province,* 10 March 1961.
23. Charles Mair, "An Appreciation," *The Moccasin Maker* (Toronto: William Briggs, 1913), p. 16.
24. Stevenson, "The Real . . . Pauline Johnson."

CHAPTER TWELVE: PURIFICATION BY FIRE

1. Jean Stevenson, "The Real, Lovable, Tender, Fun-loving Pauline Johnson," *Vancouver Province,* 6 March 1932.
2. Recorded telephone conversation, 28 July 1945, Vancouver City Archives.
3. "In Mohawk Church," *Daily Province* (Vancouver), 10 March 1913.
4. "Poetess Given Last Rites," *Vancouver World,* 11 March 1913.
5. Letter from Mrs. Jonathan Rogers to J. S. Matthews, July 1945, Vancouver City Archives.
6. *News Advertiser* (Vancouver), 14 March 1913.
7. Letter from Evelyn (Eva) Johnson to J. S. Rowe, 27 May 1924, Brant County Museum, Brantford, Ont.
8. Letter from Evelyn (Eva) Johnson to W. D. J. Wright, 4 April 1922, McMaster University Library, Hamilton, Ont.
9. T. S. H. Shearman, "Pauline Johnson's Shy Sister Devoted Life to Her," *Daily Province,* 25 Nov. 1939.
10. Evelyn Johnson to Rowe, 27 May 1924.
11. Mrs. W. Garland Foster, *The Mohawk Princess* (Vancouver: Lions' Gate Publishing, 1931), p. 169.
12. Ibid.
13. Ibid.
14. Evelyn Johnson to Rowe, 22 March 1924, Brant County Museum.
15. Evelyn Johnson to Rowe, 22 April 1924, Brant County Museum.
16. Evelyn Johnson to Wright, 4 April 1922, McMaster University Library.
17. Don Stainsby, "Books and Bookmen," *Vancouver Sun,* 4 March 1961.

Selected Bibliography

Banks, J. A. and Banks, Olive. *Feminism and Family Planning in Victorian England.* Liverpool: Liverpool University Press, 1964.

Charlesworth, Hector. *Candid Chronicles.* Vol. 1. Toronto: Macmillan Co. of Canada, 1925.

Forster, J. W. L. *Under Studio Lights.* Toronto: Macmillan Co. of Canada, 1928.

Foster, Mrs. W. Garland. *The Mohawk Princess: Being Some Account of the Life of Teka-hion-wake (E. Pauline Johnson).* Vancouver: Lions' Gate Publishing Company, 1931.

Furniss, Harry. *Paradise in Piccadilly: The Story of Albany.* London: John Lane, the Bodley Head, 1925.

Hale, Horatio, ed. *The Iroquois Book of Rites.* Originally published in Philadelphia by D. G. Brinton in 1883. Facsimile edition, Toronto: Coles Publishing Co., 1972.

Howard, Lady Constance. *Etiquette.* London: F. V. White and Co., 1885.

Howay, Frederic W. and Scholefield, Ethelbert O. S. *British Columbia from the Earliest Times to the Present.* Vancouver: S. J. Clark and Son, 1914.

Johnson, Emily Pauline. "Among the Blackfoots." *Toronto Globe,* 2 August 1902.

———. "The Cariboo Trail." *Toronto Saturday Night,* 13 October 1906.

———. "Coaching on the Cariboo Trail." *Canadian Magazine,* 42, February 1914.

———. *Flint and Feather, the Complete Poems of E. Pauline Johnson (Tekahionwake).* Toronto: Hodder and Stoughton, 1969.

———. "From the Child's Viewpoint." Chapter 1. *Mother's Magazine,* May 1910, pp. 30-31.

———. "From the Child's Viewpoint." Chapter 2. *Mother's Magazine,* June 1910, pp. 60-62.

————. "Iroquois of the Grand River." *Harper's Weekly,* 23 June 1894.

————. *Legends of Vancouver.* 8th ed. Vancouver: Saturday Sunset Press, 1913.

————. *The Moccasin Maker.* With an Introduction by Sir Gilbert Parker and an Appreciation by Charles Mair. Toronto: William Briggs, 1913.

————. "A Strong Race Opinion on the Indian Girl in Modern Fiction." *Toronto Sunday Globe,* 22 May 1892.

Johnson, Emily Pauline, and Smily, Owen. "There and Back." *The* (Toronto) *Globe,* 15 December 1894.

Johnston, Charles M., ed. *The Valley of the Six Nations: A Collection of Documents on the Indian Lands of the Grand River.* With an Introduction by Charles M. Johnston. Toronto: Champlain Society for the Government of Ontario, University of Toronto Press, 1964.

Keen, Dorothy and McKeon, Martha as told to Mollie Gillen. "The Story of Pauline Johnson, Canada's Passionate Poet." *Chatelaine,* Feb. and March 1966.

Klinck, Carl F., ed. *Literary History of Canada.* Toronto: University of Toronto Press, 1965.

London, Ontario. The D. B. Weldon Library, University of Western Ontario, Regional Collections. Johnson Collection: two letters from Pauline Johnson to Charlotte Jones.

Loosley, Elizabeth. "Pauline Johnson." In *The Clear Spirit: Twenty Canadian Women and their Times,* edited by Mary Quayle Innis. Toronto: University of Toronto Press, 1966.

MacBeth, Reverend R. G. *Policing the Plains.* Chapter 11. Toronto: Hodder and Stoughton. n.d.

MacEwan, Grant. *Eye Opener Bob.* Edmonton: Institute of Applied Art, 1957.

MacKay, Isabel Ecclestone. "Pauline Johnson: A Reminiscence." *Canadian Magazine,* July 1913.

————. "A Romance of Yesterday." *Toronto Globe,* 30 November 1912.

McRaye, J. Walter. *Town Hall To-Night.* Toronto: Ryerson Press, n.d.

Mair, Charles. "An Appreciation." *Canadian Magzine,* July 1913.

May, J. Lewis. *John Lane and the Nineties.* London: John Lane, the Bodley Head, 1936.

Morehouse, Ward. *Matinee To-Morrow.* New York: Whittlesey House, McGraw Hill, 1949.

Nelson, James G. *The Early Nineties: A View from the Bodley Head.* Cambridge: Harvard University Press, 1971.

Ottawa. Public Archives of Canada, MG 27, II D 15. Clifford Sifton Papers: letters from Johnson dated 1900–1901.

————. Public Archives of Canada, MG 30, D 58. Frank Yeigh Papers: letters and clippings concerning Johnson, two poems by Johnson, and one letter from Johnson.

————. Public Archives of Canada, MG 22, A 14. Gertrude O'Hara Papers: a letter from Johnson to Frank Yeigh.

Pomeroy, E.M. *Sir Charles G. D. Roberts.* Toronto: Ryerson Press, 1943.

Shearman, T. S. H. "Pauline Johnson's Shy Sister Devoted Life to Her." *Vancouver Province,* 25 November 1939.

Stevenson, Jean. "The Real, Lovable, Tender, Fun-Loving Pauline Johnson." *Vancouver Province,* 6 March 1932.

Victoria. Provincial Archives of British Columbia. Sir Wilfrid Laurier Papers (microfilm of materials stored at the Public Archives of Canada, Ottawa, MG 26 G).

Waldie, Jean H. "Pauline Johnson." Ontario Historical Society. *Ontario History* 40 (1948) 66–75.

Webling, Peggy. *Peggy: The Story of One Score Years and Ten.* London: Hutchinson and Co., 1924.

Welton, Cecilia. *The Promised Land: The Story of the Barr Colonists.* Lloydminster: Lloydminster Times, 1953.

Wilson, Ethel. "The Princess." *Canadian Literature* 12, Summer, 1961.

Index

Titles in bold face are original works by Pauline Johnson.

M